WHEN MAJORITIES FAIL

When Majorities Fail is a study of institutional failure in Russia's first democratic legislature. Inadequate rules and a chaotic party system combined to make it nearly impossible to pass a coherent legislative program, including a new constitution. The peculiar form of internal instability in Russia's parliament is known as cycling, one of the most important theoretical concepts in the formal study of legislatures. There are few recorded cases of cycling in politically important settings: this book documents, with comprehensive case analyses and exhaustive statistical analyses of roll call data, the presence of cyclical majorities in the Russian Parliament, and it demonstrates how the resulting failure to adopt a new constitution led directly to the violent confrontation between parliament and president in the fall of 1993. Earlier theoretical work has shown that the design of a legislative institution is crucial in preventing a breakdown in majority rule. In this study, the author shows how the institutional design of the parliament failed to preventing cycling, underscoring the importance of institutional design in a democratic transition.

Professor Josephine T. Andrews received her Ph.D. from the Department of Government at Harvard University in 1997; her dissertation won the 1997 Sumner Prize from the department. She is Assistant Professor of Political Science at the University of California, Davis, with her primary area of research being democratization in post-Communist countries.

POLITICAL ECONOMY OF INSTITUTIONS AND DECISIONS

Series Editors

Randall Calvert, Washington University, St. Louis
Thrainn Eggertsson, Max Planck Institute, Germany, and University of Iceland

Founding Editors

James E. Alt, Harvard University
Douglass C. North, Washington University, St. Louis

Other Books in the Series

Lee J. Alston, Thrainn Eggertsson, and Douglass C. North, eds., *Empirical Studies in Institutional Change*
Lee J. Alston and Joseph P. Ferrie, *Southern Paternalism and the Rise of the American Welfare State: Economics, Politics, and Institutions, 1865–1965*
James E. Alt and Kenneth Shepsle, eds., *Perspectives on Positive Political Economy*
Jeffrey S. Banks and Eric A. Hanushek, eds., *Modern Political Economy: Old Topics, New Directions*
Yoram Barzel, *Economic Analysis of Property Rights*, 2nd edition
Robert Bates, *Beyond the Miracle of the Market: The Political Economy of Agrarian Development in Kenya*
Peter Cowhey and Mathew McCubbins, eds., *Structure and Policy in Japan and the United States*
Gary W. Cox, *The Efficient Secret: The Cabinet and the Development of Political Parties in Victorian England*
Gary W. Cox, *Making Votes Count: Strategic Coordination in the World's Electoral System*
Jean Ensminger, *Making a Market: The Institutional Transformation of an African Society*
David Epstein and Sharyn O'Halloran, *Delegating Powers: A Transaction Cost Politics Approach to Policy Making under Separate Powers*
Kathryn Firmin-Sellers, *The Transformation of Property Rights in the Gold Coast: An Empirical Analysis Applying Rational Choice Theory*
Clark C. Gibson, *Politics and Poachers: The Political Economy of Wildlife Policy in Africa*
Ron Harris, *The Legal Framework of Business Organization: England, 1720–1844*

Continued on page following index

For Robbie and James

WHEN MAJORITIES FAIL

The Russian Parliament, 1990–1993

JOSEPHINE T. ANDREWS

University of California, Davis

CAMBRIDGE
UNIVERSITY PRESS

PUBLISHED BY THE PRESS SYNDICATE OF THE UNIVERSITY OF CAMBRIDGE
The Pitt Building, Trumpington Street, Cambridge, United Kingdom

CAMBRIDGE UNIVERSITY PRESS
The Edinburgh Building, Cambridge CB2 2RU, UK
40 West 20th Street, New York, NY 10011-4211, USA
477 Williamstown Road, Port Melbourne, VIC 3207, Australia
Ruiz de Alarcón 13, 28014 Madrid, Spain
Dock House, The Waterfront, Cape Town 8001, South Africa

http://www.cambridge.org

First published 2002

Printed in the United Kingdom at the University Press, Cambridge

Typeface Sabon 10/13 pt.   *System* QuarkXPress [BTS]

A catalog record for this book is available from the British Library.

Library of Congress Cataloging in Publication data available

ISBN 0 521 80112 5   hardback

Contents

Acknowledgments

There are many people whose help, advice, and support made this book possible. I would first like to acknowledge the extraordinary contribution of the members of my dissertation committee, Timothy Colton, Gary King, Kenneth Shepsle, and Joel Hellman. I thank Tim Colton for his unceasing support, his many important substantive suggestions, and the unreserved encouragement he gave me to be bold in my study of the Russian transition. I thank Gary King, who, as a teacher, advisor, and friend, fundamentally shaped the way I think about political science and whose intellectual drive has been an unceasing inspiration. I am grateful to Kenneth Shepsle for enthusiastically taking me on as his student and for the many hours that he spent on this project, which he once called "social choice theory goes to Moscow." I owe much of what is clear and precise in my presentation to his incisive comments and criticisms. I would also like to thank Joel Hellman for our many conversations, each of which was of great help to me in shaping this work. I warmly thank several of my fellow graduate students with whom I shared this work in either written or verbal form: Jane Prokop, Randall Stone, Kathryn Stoner-Weiss, and Alexandra Vacroux. They and the intellectual environment that they fostered were one of the reasons that I undertook this project in the first place.

Since beginning my career at UC Davis, I have received strong support for this project, especially from my colleague, friend, and mentor, Robert Jackman. Bob has read the entire manuscript at least once and has provided encouragement and moral support in abundance, without which I cannot conceive of having produced this book. I have also benefited from the comments and support of my colleagues Scott Gartner, Jeannette Money, Gabriella Montinola, and Randy Siverson. I would also like to thank my colleague Miko Nincic, who, as chairman of the department, helped me obtain the time I needed to finish this book manuscript. Without his support, the book could not have been finished in a timely way.

I would also like to thank George Tsebelis, Timothy Frye, Randy Calvert, and Thomas Remington for their detailed, insightful, and extremely helpful comments on my book manuscript. I take full responsibility for all errors in the manuscript, but there is no question that their comments and criticisms greatly strengthened the final product.

Finally, I would like to thank my family for believing in me and supporting me through some pretty difficult times. I want to thank my husband Rob for his support and encouragement and for helping out as much as he could in order to give me the time I needed to write. I especially want to acknowledge my two sons, Robbie and James. Their presence has been a source of constant inspiration and joy. Truly, without the support and love of my family, this book could never have been written.

I

Introduction

In the spring of 1992, in the aftermath of the collapse of the Soviet Union, deputies in the Russian Parliament struggled to create a constitution that would lay the foundations for a new democratic state, the Russian Federation. For the first time in Russia's long history, the country's elected representatives sought to establish a basis for the rule of law, defense of basic human rights, and the means to foster a market economy. Once the deputies had given their initial approval of the draft prepared by the special constitutional commission (which occurred by majority vote on March 19), they began discussion of each of the draft's six chapters. Their goal was to forward a final version of the draft constitution to the Congress of People's Deputies, a superlegislative body that alone had the authority to adopt a new constitution.

Discussion of the draft's six chapters began on March 25. On that day, parliamentary deputies discussed and approved the constitution's first chapter, "Principles of the Constitutional Order," in which the basic provisions of the constitution were outlined. The next day, March 26, the deputies began discussing the draft constitution's second chapter, which concerned "The Basic Rights, Freedoms, and Responsibilities of the Individual Citizen." Over the course of the day's debate, deputies amended the draft chapter nine times. At the end of the day, according to parliamentary procedure, deputies were asked to approve the final version of the draft. An affirmative outcome of the vote ought to have been assured, because a majority of deputies had already voted for each successively amended version of the chapter over the course of the day. However, when the vote was held, a majority of deputies voted *against* the final version of the second chapter of the draft constitution.

The presiding chair, first deputy chairman Filatov, was astonished. "Obviously, something needs to be explained here. Who can explain what happened?" One deputy suggested that the result was a fluke; perhaps too many deputies had been lingering in the halls and failed to vote. Another deputy suggested that the draft failed because several of the articles remained controversial. In reply, Filatov asked, "How is that logical, given that this chapter is based on that which has already been passed and approved by the Supreme Soviet (Parliament)?" In the end, a majority of deputies supported Filatov's proposal that the vote be held again, yet the deputies again failed to approve the draft chapter. After a third attempt to approve the chapter, the presiding chairman gave up, announcing that the chapter would nevertheless be included in the version of the draft constitution to be forwarded to the Congress of People's Deputies. "Let the Congress evaluate the situation. . . ."

While considering Chapter 2 of the draft constitution, Russian deputies demonstrated a peculiar form of collective irrationality, known as *cycling*. Majorities of deputies supported first a over c, then b over a, then c over b, which represented a return to the status quo. At that time, Russia's basic law consisted of a much-amended version of the 1978 Soviet-era constitution; this can be thought of as the status quo, or c. When deputies approved the draft constitution, which included the chapter on the rights of citizens, they were, in effect, voting for an alternative to the status quo, a. A majority of deputies preferred a, the draft constitution, to c, the Soviet-era constitution. In the course of their debate on Chapter 2, deputies amended the chapter nine times, in effect approving b, the constitution containing an amended version of Chapter 2. Finally, deputies were asked to approve the amended version of Chapter 2, in effect voting between an amended draft constitution, b, and the original status quo, c, the old Soviet-era constitution. A majority of deputies rejected the amended Chapter 2 and by implication the amended draft constitution. In short, a majority of deputies preferred c, an outcome rejected one week earlier, to b, which they had approved only minutes before.

Exactly the same thing happened on March 27, when the parliament considered Chapter 3 of the draft constitution. On April 4, the deputies completed their debate. In the end, they approved four of the six chapters of the draft constitution, leaving the unresolved issues in Chapters 2 and 3 for the Congress. But, the Sixth Congress of People's Deputies failed even to consider the draft constitution, returning it to the constitutional commission and to the parliament for further work.

The failure of both the Russian Parliament and the Congress of People's Deputies to make progress on providing Russia with a new constitution led to a significant decline in the authority of the legislative branch of government. This legislative failure provided President Yeltsin with the opportunity to pursue a presidential version of a draft constitution, which gave more powers to the executive than did the parliamentary draft that the Congress had failed to approve.

While the parliamentary chairman frequently and pointedly criticized the president for pursuing an alternative constitution and for eschewing the proper and legal means of adopting a new constitution, the only response the parliament made to the constitutional crisis was to curtail the president's existing powers. The parliament never consistently supported a new constitution, and the Congress never adopted a new constitution, but the confrontation between president and parliament became more and more acute.

In fact, Russia did not acquire a new constitution until the fall of 1993, when President Yeltsin disbanded both the parliament and Congress extraconstitutionally and called for a national referendum on his own version of a new constitution. According to Yeltsin, it was the legislature's failure to act that justified the construction of a new governmental structure in which the powers of the legislature – the major forum for public choice in a democracy – were drastically reduced.[1]

THE CASE OF RUSSIA: A REALITY CHECK FOR THEORIES OF MAJORITY RULE

The problem of cyclical majorities illustrated by the sequence of events just described is of central theoretical importance to formal studies of majority rule institutions. Indeed, as Krehbiel (1991, pp. 28–29) has pointed out, scholars adopting a formal theoretical approach often implicitly assume that legislatures are, in fact, designed to prevent cycling. Despite the centrality of cycling to these theoretical accounts, there are few actual

---

[1] On December 14, 1993, the London newspaper *The Independent* called Yeltsin a "tsar" because the imbalance between the president and Duma hearkened back to tsarist divisions of power. During an hour-long phone-in discussion of the draft constitution, which was aired on Channel 1 on December 10, 1993, Yegor Gaidar admitted that "the powers of the legislative authority have been narrowed more than would be justified if one proceeded from the principle of a rational division of authority." In an interview for Mayak radio on December 2, 1993, Oleg Rumiantsev, former head of the Russian Parliament's Constitutional Commission, made clear his disapproval of the new constitution, which in his view created "an administrative system and the utter tyranny of the bureaucrat," at the expense of parliamentarism.

empirical examples of cycling and its consequences, as Krehbiel and others have noted (Hall 1995). James Enelow (1997, pp. 160–162) puts it this way:

> The question of whether real world majority decision making is stable or not has not been given a rigorous answer. . . . We still do not know the general frequency of cyclical decision making in the real world or, when cycling exists, the general size of the alternative space over which cycling occurs. . . . In the end, we may not be able to answer these questions.

This is a major empirical puzzle. It is one thing to construct an argument that shows how institutional rules prevent the breakdown of majority rule (a substantial part of the new institutionalism in political science[2]). However, as the critics of this work have pointed out, the failure to find empirical evidence of majority cycles undermines claims about the importance of institutional rules for the prevention of cycling.

This study of cycling in the Russian Parliament renders such criticism moot. I show that cycling can and does occur in majority-rule institutions, and when it does occur it has important consequences for the effectiveness of democracy. That we have so few empirical examples of cycling and its consequences reflects the fact that research has been confined to legislatures in stable democracies. This book shows the benefits that accrue from broadening our empirical scope to include poorly institutionalized environments. It reflects my working premise that cycling is more likely to be found in uninstitutionalized settings, such as those found in countries undergoing a transition to democracy, where the institutional mechanisms that prevent cycling are as yet not fully formed.

Furthermore, cycling is consequential. The conditions that led to cycling and the occurrence of the cycles themselves seriously undermined the ability of the Russian legislature to make critical decisions on issues requiring immediate resolution – in particular, on the new Russian constitution. The legislature's inactivity on the constitutional question in turn contributed to the confrontation between president and parliament that was played out in the international media. Thus, cycling is not simply an arcane side issue in social choice theory.

---

[2] For a review of neo-institutionalism in political science, see "Review Article: Institutions and Rationality in Politics – Three Varieties of Neo-Institutionalists," by Junko Kato. 1996. *British Journal of Political Science* 25:553–582. Kato distinguishes between those who adopt a rational actor approach and those who take a sociohistorical approach. When I use the term "neo-institutional," I mean to indicate only that part of the literature that falls within the rational choice paradigm.

At the same time, the analysis of cycling in the Russian legislature does more than simply help us verify the relevance of social choice theory to the study of real world politics. My analysis of the conditions under which cycling did occur and the implications of its occurrence for the consolidation of democracy in post-Soviet Russia also adds to our understanding of the complexities of majority-rule institutions. The Russian Parliament was, after all, a majority-rule institution that did not work. Why not? The answer is both complex and nonobvious. In the ensuing chapters, I analyze the role of committees, parties, and amendment rules, all of which figure as explanatory variables in theoretical expositions on functional legislatures. My study demonstrates, just as social choice theory predicts, that without committees, parties, or amendment rules to prevent it, the goals of a parliamentary leader may supplant those of a parliamentary majority.

One of the most important consequences of cycling is the opportunity it creates for an individual with control over the legislative agenda to obtain his own most-preferred outcome, an implication of his "chaos" result of which McKelvey was immediately aware. In his classic 1976 article, McKelvey (1976, p. 481) showed that if the space of alternatives is multidimensional and all alternatives within the space are in order, "It follows from the above consideration that if any one voter, say the 'Chairman,' has complete control over the agenda (in the sense that he can choose, at each stage of the voting, any proposal . . . to be considered next) that he can construct an agenda which will arrive at any point in space, in particular at his ideal point." This means, in effect, that if outcomes cycle, a person who controls the agenda, the *agenda setter*, can decide in which order issues will come before deputies so as to ensure the passage of his own most-preferred outcome.

In the legislatures of emerging democracies, if cycling occurs and an agenda setter exists, we would expect to see that person or group amass inordinate control over the legislature's decisions. The potential for well-positioned elites to benefit in an institutionally poor environment is well documented for Russia's economic institutions (Aslund 1995, Blasi, Kroumova, and Kruse 1997). However, the potential for well-positioned elites to reap analogous rewards from weak *political* institutions is much less well understood. We ought to suspect, however, that in an institutionally poor environment, individuals with control over key political resources (such as a legislature's agenda) ought to be able to ensure that they benefit from their institutional position.

With this study of a majority-rule representative institution during a time of transition, I address a major gap in the *empirical* study of public choice. Russia's first democratic national legislature in over seventy years, the Russian Parliament, was a legislature in which institutional features that prevent cycling were absent. My primary goal in this study is to discover whether cycling did, in fact, occur in the Russian Parliament, and whether it led to predicted results. Did it create conditions under which the speaker was able to manipulate the agenda in order to obtain his own most-preferred outcomes? In addition, I hope to enlighten the debate on the relative importance of institutional design (committees and rules) and the organization of preferences (political parties) in creating an effective legislature.

This study also bears directly on Russia's democratic transition and on post-Communist transitions more generally. Institutions matter; therefore, the choice of institutions matters. The relative power of institutional actors in post-Communist countries had a profound effect on the institutional arrangements ultimately chosen (Geddes 1996, Elster et al. 1998), no less in Russia. The fact that the Russian Federation inherited from the Gorbachev period a legislature incapable of passing a new constitution meant that the choice of post-Soviet constitutional arrangements was left to the president. The reasons for the Russian Parliament's weakness are therefore of interest to students of Russian democracy and superpresidential systems in general (Colton 1995).

Particulars of Russia's Early Legislative Experience

Russia began its transition to democracy in March 1990, with the election of the Congress of People's Deputies of the Russian Republic. This body had over 1000 members, each of whom was directly elected from single-member districts. Although the Congress of People's Deputies was technically "the highest organ of state power in the Russian Federation,"[3] Russia's legislature was the Supreme Soviet, a much smaller, approximately 250-person body elected by the deputies of the Congress of People's Deputies from among its own membership. The Supreme Soviet was Russia's "permanently active, legislating, managing, and monitoring organ of state power."[4] Throughout this book, I refer to the Supreme Soviet, elected by the Congress of People's Deputies in 1990,

---

[3] See Article 104 of the April 21, 1992 Russian Constitution. After the breakup of the Soviet Union, legal references to the "RSFSR" were changed to the "Russian Federation."

[4] See Article 107 of the April 21, 1992 Russian Constitution.

as the "Russian Parliament." The Russian Parliament functioned as an independent national legislature from its first session in June 1990 until September 1993, when Russia's President disbanded it. Although the legislature was called the Russian Parliament, it was not responsible for electing the Prime Minister and Cabinet. In this respect, the Russian Parliament was similar to a congressional legislature.

For the first one and a half years of its transition, while still a republic of the Soviet Union, Russia made extraordinary progress. During this period, the parliament pushed for economic reform, expansion of human rights, and an end to the privileged rule of the Communist Party of the Soviet Union (CPSU). In its efforts to proceed along a course of political and economic reform despite the hesitation of Gorbachev and the central Soviet government, the parliament successfully created the position of Russian President, a move that frightened Soviet hard-liners and contributed to the coup attempt in August 1991.

During the coup, the power and purposefulness of the parliament was at its height. On August 19, 1991, the first day of the coup, parliament and president united to defeat an attempt by reactionary Soviet leaders intent on preserving the USSR and the central bureaucracies that were the source of their power. President Yeltsin together with parliamentary leaders staged a popular resistance in front of the building that housed the Russian legislature, because it was the seat of Russia's quest to achieve sovereignty and democracy.

In the weeks following the failed coup, when the collapse of the Soviet Union was imminent, deputies in the Russian Parliament along with the Russian President faced the difficult and urgent task of constructing political institutions adequate to govern a newly sovereign nation. They also faced the even more daunting task of creating conditions that would allow a market economy to take seed and grow in the wake of the dismantling of the command economy. At this critical historical moment, six weeks after the president and parliament's triumphant defeat of Soviet extremists, the Russian Parliament abdicated much of its responsibility to deal with the crises facing the country. Deputies in the parent body of the Russian Parliament, the Congress of People's Deputies, voted overwhelmingly to grant the Russian President the power to choose his own Cabinet and to create other executive bodies without parliamentary approval. Furthermore, the legislature placed the problem of reforming the country's economy directly into the hands of the president, granting him the right to carry out economic reform by decree for one year.

7

At the moment of real opportunity to achieve the goals for which it had fought so successfully, a democratic state and market economy, the Russian Parliament lost its ability to act decisively. Throughout the next year, the first year of an independent and sovereign Russia, the Russian Parliament failed to sustain a coherent legislative record on either of the major issue areas of the day: (a) the establishment of guarantees of basic human rights and (b) the establishment of the basic framework for a market economy. On November 28, 1991, the parliament passed the Law on Russian Citizenship, a law that encompassed elements of previously approved amendments to the Soviet-era constitution as well as previously approved laws on related human rights issues. Four months later, the parliament was unable to pass the chapter of the draft constitution dealing with similar issues, even after the presiding chair reminded deputies that they had approved almost all elements of the draft chapter earlier. In late June 1992, the parliament passed the Law on Privatization of State and Municipal Property, a major cornerstone of market reform. Subsequently, however, the parliament was unable to consistently support measures to maintain the stability of the ruble, nor was it able to pass other laws necessary to the creation of a market economy, such as a law authorizing the sale and purchase of land, a law establishing a workable system of bankruptcy, and laws creating an appropriate tax structure. By the end of 1992, political and economic reform had stalled in Russia, and the Russian Parliament had become an ineffective and weak institution.

If the Russian Parliament was capable of pursuing a consistent policy agenda before the dissolution of the Soviet Union, why was it incapable of doing so afterwards? The answer to this question has important implications for countries in transition, because it was at a critical moment that the parliament lost its effectiveness as a legislative institution. According to Adam Przeworski, countries making a transition to democracy and a market economy have only a short window of time in which to do so (Przeworski 1991). Those countries that make changes swiftly and completely stand the best chance of success (Hellman 1998). At such a critical juncture, a country in which the national legislature cannot act effectively – or worse yet, one in which the legislature's aimlessness becomes an impediment to government action – cannot enact and carry through on a program of rapid reform. Certainly, this was Russia's situation. Also, Russia's current economic and political difficulties are directly related to problems that surfaced in the first year after the collapse of the Soviet Union.

Introduction

From the point of view of Russia's citizens, the legislature's ineffectiveness was disastrous. Robert Sharlet, an expert on Soviet and post-Soviet constitutionalism, states (Sharlet 1993, p. 319), "The underlying political crisis in Russia, which was expressed in constitutional terms [in the confrontation between president and parliament], was the primary source of the ongoing, profound economic crisis." According to Anders Aslund (1995), Yeltsin had a unique window of opportunity after the collapse of the Soviet Union; and, while he credits Yeltsin for using this opportunity to push through important economic reforms, he blames Yeltsin for ignoring the importance of establishing workable democratic institutions. Aslund believes that if after the collapse of the Soviet Union Yeltsin had immediately called for competitive parliamentary elections (for December 1991 *instead* of December 1993) and for the adoption of a new constitution in which the powers of legislature and president were clearly demarcated, economic reform would not have been stalled and almost derailed in 1993. Sharlet, a political scientist, and Aslund, a noted economist and advisor to the Russian government, clearly believe that the design of Russia's legislature had a profoundly debilitating affect on the process of economic reform in Russia.

The Nonobvious Implications of an Underinstitutionalized Legislature

Clearly, something about the parliament changed when the Soviet Union broke down; features of the parliament that had prevented cycling before the collapse no longer did so afterwards. As I report in Chapters 6 and 7, evidence from the roll call votes of deputies supports the contention that the problem of cyclical majorities existed throughout 1992. As I suggest above and discuss fully in Chapter 4, the institutional design of the Russian Parliament was never sufficient to prevent outcomes from cycling. This design, as expressed in the rules and regulations of the parliament, remained essentially unchanged throughout the three years of the parliament's existence, yet cycling did not occur during the first year and a half of the parliament's existence. It was not a change in rules that led to cycling. What changed was the array and complexity of political issues: (a) the dimensionality of the issue space and (b) the array and complexity of deputy preferences.

Up until the events of fall 1991, the Russian Parliament focused on one and only one overriding issue, Russian sovereignty. Within the parliament, deputies formed two coalitions, one in support of sovereignty

9

(the democratic reformers) and one opposed (the communist conservatives); and within these two coalitions, the preferences of deputies were homogeneous.

However, after the failed coup and the collapse of the Soviet Union, deputies were faced with many new issues having to do with economic reform, human rights, and the federal structure of a now independent Russia. In the language of social choice theory, the policy space became multidimensional. Throughout 1992, deputies debated laws on property rights, privatization, tax and banking systems, bankruptcy, land reform, and many other building blocks of a market economy. They also discussed laws and treaties bearing on the federal structure of Russia and on the rights and responsibilities of Russia's constituent units. In addition, deputies were faced with the task of creating a judicial system that could defend individual and property rights. Added to this, deputies debated a new Russian constitution, a document that incorporated all of these important political dimensions simultaneously.

Because of the dramatic change in relevant issues that occurred after the collapse of the Soviet Union, deputy preferences, which had been relatively homogeneous beforehand (deputies were either for Russian sovereignty or for the status quo), became heterogeneous afterwards. As democratic deputies experienced economic reform, their preferences regarding the best way to bring it about began to diverge. Similarly, when faced with the fait accompli of a sovereign Russia, communists and nationalist conservatives began to differ in their ideas about the rights of citizens of the new country. Thus, with the proliferation of issues after the political and economic institutions of the Soviet Union collapsed, it became impossible to define deputies in terms of democrat and conservative, and as a result the two coalitions broke into many factions.[5] No stable majority existed in the parliament. A multidimensional policy space coupled with the absence of adequate institutional design created the potential for cycling.

Obviously, cycling undermines the legislature's ability to make decisions, but in a legislature in which one person has the ability to control

---

[5] Even in those countries where the communist party heavily influenced the first elections, as in Russia in 1990 and in Poland in 1989 (Geddes 1996), so that the number of parties was at first limited, reform-oriented groups such as Solidarity in Poland and Democratic Russia in Russia quickly fragmented as soon as they were faced with the many issues of the transition. In both countries, as soon as the legislature began to grapple with economic reform and human rights, the legislature had, in effect, many political parties.

the agenda, its effects are even more devastating. The speaker of the Russian Parliament had unusually extensive powers to influence the legislative agenda. As chairman of the parliament, he was also chairman of a superior organizing body, called the Presidium. The Presidium, a holdover from the Soviet past, was responsible for preparing the legislative agenda, assigning legislation to committees, and distributing deputy input to the relevant committees. Most important of all, the Presidium controlled the legislature's budget. Thus, the head of the Presidium could use these prerogatives to influence the final content of legislation as well as the order in which legislation was brought before the deputies for a vote. In other words, the chairman of the Presidium was an agenda setter; and in a legislature with no stable majority, he could manipulate the agenda and so use the legislature to achieve his own most-preferred outcome, just as McKelvey described.

During its three-year existence, the Russian Parliament had two chairmen: Boris Yeltsin, who served until his election as Russia's first President in June 1991, and his successor, Ruslan Khasbulatov, who served until the parliament's dissolution in the fall of 1993. The difference in the structure of deputies' preferences before and after the collapse of the Soviet Union determined the extent to which these two chairmen could influence parliamentary decision making.

While Yeltsin was chairman, he was the head of a majority coalition of democratic deputies that was opposed by a near-majority coalition of communist conservatives.[6] Although Yeltsin used his position as head

---

[6] Lacking political parties and the disciplining effect of party organizations, deputies in the Russian Parliament formed loose associations based on their preferences alone. Because of this, it is always difficult to count the number of members of any deputy group. In the first few weeks after the March 1990 elections, spokesmen for the umbrella organization Democratic Russia reported that slightly over half of the deputies considered themselves to be democratic reformers. The fact that Boris Yeltsin was elected chairman of the parliament supports this assertion. Experts disagree on the exact number of democrats in the parliament during the entire first year and a half, but Alexander Sobyanin (1994) believed that growth in the number of undecided centrists meant that neither the democrats nor the communists had a majority. However, if one examines the voting record, it is clear that the democrats were much more successful in passing their agenda than were the conservatives. Thus, when deputies were forced to vote, the only reliable indication of many deputies' political preferences, a majority tended to vote consistently for political and economic reforms. Therefore, I believe that a democratic coalition based solely on deputy preferences maintained a slight majority throughout 1990 and 1991. In Chapters 3 and 4, I discuss in detail the nature of this majority and its dissolution after the collapse of the Soviet Union.

of the Presidium to influence the legislature's agenda (most of the major issues on the agenda were central to the democratic coalition), as head of the democratic coalition, Yeltsin was subject to constant reassessment by that coalition. Just as the reformers depended on Yeltsin to spearhead their initiatives, Yeltsin depended on the coalition for support. So long as his own goals and those of the democratic coalition were similar, Yeltsin could accomplish much of what he wanted. Because the size of the two coalitions was so close, Yeltsin spent much of his energy rallying centrist deputies to support democratic initiatives. It is a testament to his skill as a politician that on so many issues important to his agenda he was able to hold together his slight majority.

Khasbulatov, on the other hand, was the leader of no group in the parliament. After the collapse of the Soviet Union, while he was chairman, the two-party dynamic in the parliament broke down in reaction to the total collapse of Soviet institutions and the emergence of a bewildering array of problems facing the deputies and the country. As chairman, Khasbulatov could not rely on a stable majority coalition to support his initiatives – there was no such coalition for him to ally with or lead. Because the role of majority leader was not an option for him, using his powers as chairman of the Presidium to control the agenda, Khasbulatov was able to manipulate the shifting majorities of deputies to support his goals. Thus, Khasbulatov's power did not emanate from his position as head of a majority coalition; instead it emanated from the institutional rules that made him chairman of the Presidium. It is a testament to Khasbulatov's consummate skill as a back-room strategist that he was able to use the Presidium to achieve his agenda without the consistent backing of any faction in the legislature.[7]

The difference in institutional context affected the political machinations and strategies of the two chairmen as well as their perceived personal style. As the leader of the democratic coalition, Yeltsin promoted a consistent political agenda, the goal of which was to promote democratic and market reform in the Russian Republic and to increase Russia's sovereignty from the Soviet Union. Throughout his term as chairman, Yeltsin never wavered in his support for an end to communist domination in Russia, for the competitive politics and basic human rights

---

[7] Not only did no particular faction back him, but also factions of different political orientations tried at different times to remove him from office. The Democratic Russia faction did so in September 1992, and the Russia faction did so in January 1993. A similar attempt was made by a group of centrist deputies in May 1993.

that are the foundation of a democratic system, and for a rapid transition to a market economy.

Khasbulatov, on the other hand, espoused many contradictory and shifting policy positions. He always claimed to be a strong supporter of market reform,[8] yet he began to criticize President Yeltsin's economic reform program almost the instant it was launched. Throughout the spring of 1992, Khasbulatov savagely criticized every aspect of the government's program for economic reform; he started calling for the government's resignation in January 1992.[9] Yet, in June 1992, Khasbulatov came out in favor of the government's plan to privatize most of Russia's state-owned industries and businesses. Khasbulatov always claimed to be a democrat[10] who supported, among other things, freedom of the press, but starting in September 1992 he increasingly tried to silence the newspaper *Izvestia*, probably the most vocal critic of the parliament and of Khasbulatov himself. In the fall of 1992, Khasbulatov's chameleon-like behavior was especially pronounced as he repeatedly shifted from calling for the resignation of Yeltsin's government to announcing his reconciliation and support of Yeltsin's government.[11]

Because Khasbulatov was the leader of no majority, nor even of one of the factions, he could achieve his goals only by manipulating unstable majority coalitions first one way, then another, until he had shifted debate to the topic central to his own political goals, the relative power of president and parliament. Khasbulatov's record throughout 1992 reflects this strategy. Indeed, as the parliament declined in effectiveness, his power and influence increased.

During its third year, the parliament concerned itself almost exclusively with issues designed to eliminate Khasbulatov's critics both inside and outside the parliament. Deputies discussed strikingly fewer issues than they had the year before. For example, fewer roll call votes were held (only 33 roll call votes were held in 1993, as compared to 388 in 1992). Among the issues they did discuss were

---

[8] He made this claim in interviews with the press in 1991 and 1992, and he made this claim forcefully in my interview with him in June 1996.

[9] Remarks reported in *Izvestia*, January 14, 1992, pp. 1–2.

[10] For example, this is how he described himself in an interview with me in June 1996.

[11] The many changes in the relationship between Khasbulatov and Yeltsin during the period of debate over the Law on the Government are well-reported in the Russian press at that time, especially by the newspaper *Izvestia*.

attacks on three parliamentary committees: the Committee on the Media and the Committee on Human Rights, which in 1993 were two of the main sources of criticism of the parliamentary leadership emanating from within the parliament, and the Legislation Committee, which had refused to acquiesce in the chairman's attack on the activity and autonomy of parliamentary committees.[12] In addition, the parliament gave serious discussion to taking control of the newspaper *Izvestia* and limiting freedom of the press in a more general sense, an issue that was blatantly the result of the chairman's anger at criticism of himself and the parliament for their poor performance.[13] In an interview in the June 26, 1993 edition of *Izvestia* (p. 2), deputy speaker Nikolai Riabov, commenting on the disbandment of the parliamentary legislation committee, stated that Ruslan Khasbulatov "has finally cast aside the democratic mask he used to wear, and entered upon the path of establishing his autocratic dictatorship" in Parliament.

Four Russian scholars, editors of a book on the confrontation between president and parliament (Dobrokhotov et al. 1994, p. 4), summarize the conflict in their introduction:

Given our historical tradition, the politics of which is characterized by personal factors and explanations, especially on the contemporary stage, with its unformed or weakly developed political parties and movements, the sharp rivalry between legislative and executive branches of power found its personal expression in the confrontation between Yeltsin and Khasbulatov.

In interviews with me in June 1996, two parliamentary leaders representing very different political views, Lev Ponomarev of the Democratic Russia faction and Sergei Baburin of the nationalist faction Russia, characterized the confrontation as a personal conflict between Yeltsin

---

[12] Both Bragin and Ponomarev (chairman and member, respectively, of the Committee on Media) said in interviews with me that Khasbulatov attacked their committee because it was critical of his leadership.

[13] After the results of the April 25, 1993 referendum made it clear that efforts by the parliament and its chairman to reduce Yeltsin's power and effectiveness were clearly not supported by the population at large, Khasbulatov lashed out at the media for its coverage of the referendum and its results. The newspaper *Izvestia* was especially critical of Khasbulatov's statements against the media, accusing him of attempting to introduce censorship. (See, in particular, the April 28, 1993 issue of *Izvestia*.) In reaction to *Izvestia*'s harsh criticisms of himself as well as *Izvestia*'s pro-democracy coverage of the referendum, Khasbulatov organized a parliamentary attempt to gain control over *Izvestia* by subordinating the newspaper to the parliament. The resolution passed, but members of Yeltsin's executive branch prevented the resolution from being put into practice.

and Khasbulatov. Both Ponomarev and Baburin insisted that the conflict had little to do with debate or divisions within the parliament; they both asserted that Khasbulatov did not act on behalf of a group of deputies, he acted on his own behalf.

In the 1993 referendum on President Yeltsin, the legislature (in this case the Congress of People's Deputies), and Yeltsin's program of economic reform, over 50% of those participating (and over half the eligible voters did participate) said that they supported Yeltsin and his economic reform program. Thus, in contradiction to his public statements that he was acting on behalf of the Russian people, Khasbulatov was clearly acting against the wishes of a majority of Russians in attempting to reduce the power of Yeltsin's government and to halt economic reform.

By ignoring the country's need for decisive action on economic problems and, throughout 1993, focusing mainly on a confrontation between the president and parliament, which was certainly not supported by the population at large, the parliament placed the Russian economy and polity in grave danger and eroded the public's respect for their representative institution. Throughout the confrontation with Yeltsin, popular support for the parliament declined, reaching the low point registered in the referendum of April 1993.[14] In many respects, the behavior of the deputies seems singularly self-destructive.

The conflict between legislature and executive was resolved when President Yeltsin disbanded the parliament on September 21, 1993. Many deputies refused to acknowledge the validity of Presidential Degree 1400 – indeed, it was not an act supported by the Russian constitution. Led by the parliament's chairman, these deputies barricaded themselves in the parliament building and elected Alexander Rutskoi, Yeltsin's vice-president, as the new president. After twelve tense days, violence erupted on October 3 when in response to a speech by Rutskoi, an angry mob attacked the office of Moscow's mayor. The crisis ended the next day when troops loyal to Yeltsin fired on the White House, forcing the chairman of the parliament and his supporters to surrender, leaving the seat of Russian democracy in flames as they walked into the custody of

---

[14] At the insistence of the Congress of People's Deputies and its chairman, a referendum on President Yeltsin and his economic reform program was held across the nation on April 25, 1993. Sixty-five percent of Russia's citizens turned out to vote; of these, 60% indicated that they supported President Yeltsin, and 55% supported Yeltsin's economic policies, a result surprising to everyone, including Yeltsin. In addition, 45% supported early parliamentary elections, demonstrating dissatisfaction with the parliament.

Yeltsin's waiting troops. Weakened as it was by a year and a half of indecision and costly confrontation with the executive, the legislature could not withstand the president's attack.

OTHER INTERPRETATIONS OF THE CAUSES OF RUSSIA'S LEGISLATIVE FAILURE

Some scholars have argued that Khasbulatov's power as head of the parliament was based on a conservative majority that crystallized in the parliament soon after the collapse of the Soviet Union. In an influential article, Remington et al. (1994) argue that with the loss of democratic members of parliament to Yeltsin's administration, the balance between conservatives and democrats changed after Yeltsin became president. However, although certain democratic leaders, such as Sergei Shakhrai, did leave the Parliament to join Yeltsin's administration, other well-known democratic leaders, such as Lev Ponomarev, Viacheslav Bragin, Oleg Rumiantsev, Victor Sheinis, Gleb Iakunin, and Sergei Kovalev, remained in the parliament and continued to play prominent roles until well into the last year of the parliament's existence.

Russian scholar Alexander Sobyanin (1994) argues that deputies became more conservative as time went on. Because analysts agree[15] that a communist or conservative majority did not exist prior to the collapse of the Soviet Union, in order to sustain the argument that a conservative majority appeared in the parliament after the collapse of the Soviet Union, one must show that deputies changed their minds. According to Remington et al. (1994), who base their conclusions on a careful analysis of the roll call votes of members of the Congress of People's Deputies (the parent body of the parliament, or Supreme Soviet), over 200 deputies changed their position from the democratic wing to the conservative wing after the collapse of the Soviet Union. If one-fifth of the deputies in the Congress of People's Deputies changed their political positions, then some percentage of deputies in the parliament (whose membership is a subset of the Congress) must have changed their positions as well. Although neither Remington et al. nor Sobyanin analyze roll call votes from the parliament, Sobyanin (1994, p. 203) implies that most of

---

[15] In his interview with me, Lev Ponomarev said that a very slight democratic majority existed during the summer of 1990, which was enough to elect Boris Yeltsin as the parliament's first chairman. Although Sobyanin is skeptical that the democratic majority existed throughout the period before the collapse of the Soviet Union, he agrees that a conservative majority certainly did not exist at that time (1991).

Table 1.1. *Median Sobyanin Index for All Deputies in Sessions 2–6*

Session 2	Session 3	Session 4	Session 5	Session 6
0	5	39	36	32

the deputies who switched position were members of the parliament; therefore, by implication, the percentage of members who changed from democrat to conservative would have been greater in the parliament than in the Congress.

If one uses an index measuring commitment to democracy devised by Sobyanin before the collapse of the Soviet Union, the number of so-called democrats *increased* after the collapse of the Soviet Union (Sobyanin and Yur'ev 1991). The index ranges from +100, which corresponds to a committed, Westernizing democrat, to –100, which corresponds to a committed, Soviet-style communist; a value of 0 corresponds to a neutral deputy. Thus, a positive value indicates some degree of support for democracy, and a negative value indicates some degree of opposition to democracy. In Table 1.1, I present the median Sobyanin index for deputies in Sessions 2–6. Sessions 2 and 3 correspond to the period before the collapse of the Soviet Union, while Yeltsin was chairman, and Sessions 4, 5, and 6 correspond to the period after the collapse of the Soviet Union, while Khasbulatov was chairman. In all sessions, the number of democrats exceeded the number of communists, and the number of democrats was actually greater in Sessions 4 through 6 than in Sessions 2 and 3.

If more than half of the deputies after the collapse of the Soviet Union were democrats, what then is meant by a conservative? For the most part, analysts have ignored the crucial first half of 1992, when the confrontation between Khasbulatov and President Yeltsin was not yet apparent[16] and when there was clearly no consistent opposition to reform. Even in 1993, when the parliament appeared reactionary to many, one can imagine many deputies voting with Khasbulatov and in opposition to Yeltsin only because the range of issues on which they were asked to vote was limited. An inspection of the actual content of deputy voting shows that very few laws of any kind were passed in 1993. The parliament considered legislation pertaining to political and

---

[16] Dobrokhov et al. (1994) refer to this period as a period of compromise, which ended in December 1992.

economic reform only during the first six months of 1992. The fall 1992 session of parliament was dominated by the attempt to reduce the power of the executive branch, and all of 1993 was dominated by attacks on President Yeltsin and his allies inside and outside the parliament.

Finally, whatever the explanation for the distribution of deputy preferences from session to session, to argue that the presence of a conservative majority explains the confrontation between president and parliament, one must argue that it was in the interest of this majority to pursue the confrontation. This argument is hard to sustain. Why in 1993 did a majority of deputies pursue a set of policies that was, in the words of deputy Alexander Kopeika, "a process of self-destruction"?[17] After the April 1993 referendum, it was clear to the whole country that Khasbulatov was one of the least popular men in Russia and that his personal ambition was destroying the prestige and popularity of the parliament as well. Had a conservative majority existed in parliament, why did it not at some point replace Khasbulatov with the much more respected, charismatic, and *conservative* nationalist Sergei Baburin or *conservative* communist Ivan Rybkin, each of whom was a highly visible critic of Boris Yeltsin?

In contrast to an interpretation based solely on changes in deputy preferences, my explanation takes into account institutional features as well as the implications of changes in the number of issues facing deputies after the collapse of the Soviet Union. An extensive analysis of the deputies' voting record before and after the collapse strongly supports my theoretical contentions. My account provides a consistent and comprehensive explanation of some of the strange inconsistencies of Russia's first three years as a democracy. I explain why the parliament was effective before the collapse and why it was so ineffective afterwards. I also explain why for many months after the collapse of the Soviet Union, the parliament waffled in its support and opposition to political and economic reform. My explanation helps us understand why the parliament appeared so obedient to Khasbulatov in 1993, why so few roll call votes were held, and why so many important votes in the last year of the parliament's existence concerned attacks on Khasbulatov's opponents within the parliament and in the press. I also explain why the parliament became wholly engaged in a fruitless struggle with President Yeltsin. By spring

---

[17] ITAR-TASS, April 30, 1993, parliamentary correspondent Liudmila Yermakova.

of 1993 one could no longer speak of parliament's goals, because the goals of the parliament reflected those of its chairman. Thus, while it could not have been in the interest of the majority of parliamentary deputies to risk their jobs and political future in opposing an extremely popular and powerful president, it was, conceivably, in the interest of an ambitious individual to try and increase his own power vis-à-vis the president, using the parliament as a platform from which to do so.

CONCLUSIONS

Many scholars interested in the former Soviet Union are trying to understand the processes by which stable, democratic institutions evolve. One approach is to study how exogenous factors, such as popular support for democratic values (Gibson et al. 1992, Duch 1993, Hahn 1993, Bahry and Way 1994, Hough 1994, Andrews and Stoner-Weiss 1995, Whitefield and Evans 1998, Colton 2000), the electoral system (Colton 1990, Helf and Hahn 1992, Moser 1993, Remington and Smith 1995, 1997), political culture (Stoner-Weiss 1997), and political parties (Fish 1995a,b, Urban 1997, McFaul 2001) shape evolving democratic institutions. Another approach is to study the effects of endogenous institutional mechanisms, such as rules and incentive structures, on institutional stability and success (Prokop 1996, Solnick 1998, Smith and Remington 2001). In this book, I have chosen the latter approach. This is a study of how inadequate institutional design coupled with poorly developed political parties created the conditions for instability in the Russian national legislature.

For the past 15 years, scholars taking a neo-institutional approach to the study of democratic national legislatures have made great progress in determining the institutional features that lead to legislative stability. However, theorists have rarely applied the formal study of institutional design to legislatures other than the United States Congress.[18] By testing arguments derived from social choice theory in a setting other than Congress, one in which neither committees nor parties are as strong as in Congress, I hope to provide an important addition to legislative scholarship in the neo-institutional tradition.

One of my goals in studying an institutionally poor, transitional legislature such as the Russian Parliament is to ascertain the relative impor-

---

[18] Some notable exceptions: Cox (1987a), Myagkov and Kiewiet (1996), and Remington and Smith (1995, 1997).

tance of those features identified by Congressional scholars that structure the institution (committees) and those features that structure deputies' preferences (political parties) in determining the effectiveness of a legislature. The effectiveness of the Russian Parliament changed over time, from a period of relative effectiveness before the collapse of the Soviet Union to one of extraordinary ineffectiveness after the collapse of the Soviet Union. Furthermore, while the nature of political coalitions changed from one period to the other, the structure of the institution did not change. This "natural experiment" provides an opportunity to isolate the effect of one determinant of stability, political parties, while holding constant another determinant, legislative design.

The implications of work that formally derives and precisely states the conditions under which equilibria in legislatures can exist seem especially important to students of emerging democracies. To my knowledge, there are few studies of actual cases of cycling, and there are no cases that are so clearly politically important.[19] Thus, my study shows that this theoretical construct exists empirically and occurs exactly under those circumstances where one would expect it, in an institutionally poor, multidimensional environment. Furthermore, I show that the consequences of legislative instability are quite serious indeed, especially if it occurs in times of transition, when democratic institutions first begin to function. Only when we understand the determinants of stability within individual institutions, or within classes of institutions, can we understand why transitions to democracy succeed or fail.

PLAN OF THE BOOK

I begin in Chapter 2 with a description of the most important example of cycling that occurred in the Russian Parliament, the March 1992 parliamentary debate on the draft Russian constitution. It is this debate that I describe in the book's opening paragraphs. Not only do I describe the immediate consequences of cycling and the deputies' reaction to a breakdown in majority rule, but I also consider the long-term implications for Russia's constitutional debate. Cycling disrupted the debate on

---

[19] The most well known example is the story of the flying club reported by William Riker in *The Art of Political Manipulation*. Evidently, Riker searched for years to find an important example of cycling, and eventually he had to settle for this somewhat trivial example. I am indebted to Timothy Frye for this observation.

the constitution, preventing the legislature from adopting a new constitution at that time. But, it also enabled the parliament's chairman, using his power to control the agenda, to structure the subsequent constitutional debate in such a way that deputies focused solely on reducing the president's power by amending the existing constitution. Because a new constitution would have put an end to the Presidium and thereby ended the source of Khasbulatov's power, the chairman aggressively resisted Yeltsin's efforts to pass a new constitution, using his power over the parliament's agenda to keep the deputies from entertaining the president's option. Russia's drawn-out struggle to pass a new constitution demonstrates the empirical significance of cycling, and it shows nicely how the chaotic environment of a democratic transition can foster, and thus be affected by, this seemingly esoteric problem of majority rule.

After a detailed discussion of this important case, I move to Chapter 3, in which I lay out the theoretical framework used in the book. In Chapter 3, I describe in formal but accessible language the theoretical concepts that I use in my book. I discuss differences in majority decision making in one-dimensional and higher-dimensional cases, and I show how cycling occurs in multidimensional settings. I present a detailed discussion of cycling and agenda control in the presence of cycling. I conclude the chapter with a discussion of the implications of cyclical majorities in legislative settings and the institutional mechanisms that prevent cycling.

In Chapter 4, I describe the institutional structure of the Russian Parliament, including the committee system and the rules of procedure governing the passage of legislation. Because of its importance to the agenda-setting powers of the parliamentary chairman, I describe in some detail the organizing body known as the Presidium, and I discuss the powers accruing to the chairman through his dominance of the Presidium.

In Chapter 5, I discuss the political groups that existed in the parliament both before and after the collapse of the Soviet Union, including descriptions of the groups' political platforms and characteristics of their members. Partisanship in the Russian Parliament was complicated, and it changed after the collapse of the Soviet Union. Before the collapse of the Soviet Union, two loosely organized coalitions – the communist conservatives and the democratic reformers – existed in the parliament. After the collapse of the Soviet Union, these two grand coalitions fell apart, and deputies organized themselves into three blocs.

My goal in Chapter 6 is to support empirically the hypothesis that the policy space was one-dimensional before the collapse of the Soviet Union and multidimensional afterwards. Toward this end, I present the results of a principal components analysis of roll call votes that suggest that one dimension dominated debate before the breakup of the Soviet Union, and that more than two issue dimensions were present afterwards. Using the estimates of deputy ideal points, I map the positions of members of the deputy groups before and after the collapse of the Soviet Union, showing that the preferences of deputies were relatively homogeneous before the collapse of the Soviet Union and relatively heterogeneous afterwards.

In Chapter 7, I operationalize Norman Schofield's concept of a cycle set. Because the issue space was not multidimensional before the collapse of the Soviet Union (and because only two relevant deputy groups existed at that time), I look for cycle sets after the collapse. I find that cycle sets existed in Sessions 4 and 5. Furthermore, I provide tabular and graphical evidence that only in the session immediately after the collapse of the Soviet Union (Session 4) were the votes distributed in such a way that outcomes would have fallen within the cycle set (that is, within the area bounded by three minimal winning coalitions in the parliament). Finally, I present three concrete examples of cycling that occurred in the session immediately following the collapse of the Soviet Union. I could find no concrete examples of cycling in any other period before or after the collapse of the Soviet Union.

In Chapter 8, I compare the power of an agenda setter in a one- versus a two-dimensional setting. I present graphical evidence that Chairman Yeltsin's powers were constrained in the way predicted by Romer and Rosenthal's setter model (Romer and Rosenthal 1978). In contrast, Chairman Khasbulatov was able to obtain his most-preferred outcome as predicted by McKelvey (1976). Finally, I support the hypothesis that it was Chairman Khasbulatov's ability to dominate legislative outcomes that led to the parliament's self-destructive confrontation with President Yeltsin.

In Chapter 9, the concluding chapter, I discuss the relative importance of committees and parties in structuring a congressional legislature. When parties are weak, it is particularly important that a legislature does not also have weak committees, or an otherwise weak institutional design. Furthermore, if cycling occurs in an institutionally weak legislature, the danger exists that a person or group with the power to set the legislative agenda will be able to dominate the legislature.

I discuss the importance of cycling as a phenomenon that may exist in weakly structured legislatures during times of political and economic transitions. For example, cycling on the issue of the government budget occurred in the first year of the Polish Parliament. The institutional rules governing the Polish Sejm prevented an outcome like that which occurred in Russia. Instead, the government fell, and ultimately new elections were held, which eliminated the potential for cycling.

Until now, cycling has been treated as an interesting but empirically esoteric concept. With this study I show not only that cycling is an empirical reality, but also that it has just those serious consequences for majority rule that have concerned some of social science's most creative theorists.

2

Cycling in Action: Russia's Constitutional Crisis

Recent history has shown that it is not easy for a new democracy to adopt its first constitution. Many post-communist countries struggled to pass new constitutions, limping along for years under amended versions of communist-era documents. Russia was no exception. Until Russia's President in the fall of 1993 used his powers of decree to disband the existing legislative institutions and call for a national referendum on a new constitution, Russia was mired in a constitutional impasse. Russia's constitutional crisis lasted almost two years (1992–1993), not long among post-communist transitions. Yet, unlike most other post-communist cases, its resolution was not the result of negotiation and compromise but of violence and armed confrontation.

Yeltsin's draconian solution to the constitutional crisis was a pivotal moment in the brief history of Russian democracy. Few of Yeltsin's supporters and none of his opponents would forget the haunting image of presidential troops firing on deputies holed up in the parliament building. Many lamented the harm that Yeltsin's precipitous and unconstitutional actions did to democratic reform. Even members of Yeltsin's closest circle of advisors criticized the strong presidential republic that Yeltsin's constitution created.[1]

---

[1] Obviously, the chairman of the parliament, Ruslan Khasbulatov, along with many hostile members of the legislature immediately claimed that Yeltsin's actions were a violation of the constitution. But, surprisingly, reformers both inside and outside the legislature criticized Yeltsin's actions. Many local political leaders as well as well-known national proponents of reform such as Grigory Yavlinsky called Yeltsin's decree illegal and unconstitutional (see *Sevodnya*, September 23, p. 1). In the weeks following the dissolution of the legislature, many newspapers that had championed democratic reform, such as *Nezavisimaya gazeta* and *Komsomolskaya pravda*, were highly critical of Yeltsin's "undemocratic" and "unconstitutional" actions. Western scholars were also harsh, and Yeltsin's Decree #1400 has come to be known as a "presidential coup."

The constitutional crisis began with the collapse of the Soviet Union at the end of 1991. At that time, according to Russia's existing constitution, only the legislative branch of government had the authority to adopt a new constitution. Russia's two-tiered legislative structure included the large and ceremonial Congress of People's Deputies and the much smaller functional parliament (the Supreme Soviet). The responsibilities of the two legislative bodies differed. While the parliament was responsible for day-to-day lawmaking, there were a handful of issues about which the Congress had the final say, the most important of which was the constitution. While it was the parliament's responsibility to prepare a new constitution, only the Congress of People's Deputies' could adopt it. Thus, according to the existing constitution, it was up to the legislature to take the initiative for constitutional reform, and, at first, it rose to the challenge. But, at the crucial moment, in the spring of 1992, the legislature faltered.

Although the parliament did succeed in forwarding a draft constitution to the Sixth Congress, it was a draft that had been only partially supported by the deputies. Repeating patterns of inconsistent voting – in other words, cycling – disrupted debate on two of the six chapters. First deputies supported the chapters, and then they rejected them outright. Parliamentary leaders decided to include the two rejected chapters in the draft constitution anyway, not knowing what to make of a legislature that could support each chapter of the constitution, reaffirming their support with many specific amendments, then reject two of the chapters in a matter of days. Furthermore, the parliament failed to resolve one of the most important and controversial points: the number of seats that each of Russia's eighty-nine regions would have in the Federal Assembly, the new upper house created in the draft constitution. Not wanting a repeat of the fiasco that had disrupted passage of Chapters 2 and 3, Chairman Khasbulatov simply decided to vote on the fifth chapter *excluding* the key article. Thus, the parliament failed in its mission to prepare a solid and uncontroversial draft for the Congress. Yet, members of parliament voted to forward the draft to the Congress anyway. It came as no surprise when the large and unwieldy Congress sent the draft back to the parliament for further work.

Yeltsin expressed his disappointment in the Congress in a speech on the final day of meetings. "A number of extremely important questions were not resolved." The fact that the parliament and Congress had failed to adopt a new constitution was propelling the country into a constitutional crisis (*Rossiiskaya gazeta*, April 23, 1992, p. 3).

A constitution provides the legal framework for all other laws. Whereas most laws address a particular issue, such as bankruptcy, land reform, or minority rights, a constitution sets baseline rules and principles that affect all subjects of legislation. While individual statutes may encompass more than one issue, a constitution *always* does. Because cycling can occur only when deputies are asked to vote on more than one issue at a time, it should not be surprising that if cycling did surface in the Russian parliament, it would do so during constitutional debate.

It is my contention that a systematic breakdown in majority rule played an instrumental role in the legislature's inability to pass a new constitution. Shifting majorities in the parliament prevented it from consistently supporting and promoting its draft constitution. Furthermore, as McKelvey's original work predicts, the presence of majority cycles provided the parliament's powerful chairman, Ruslan Khasbulatov, with the ability to manipulate the agenda for his own purposes.

From the time of the Sixth Congress and throughout the fall of 1992, the parliament became focused on reducing the president's powers, a result obviously commensurate with the ambitious chairman's own quest for increased power. The path by which the parliament reached this point was the result of a combination of external circumstances and Khasbulatov's manipulation of the legislative agenda. During the following year, Khasbulatov used his control of the agenda to maintain the parliament's focus on this issue.

Khasbulatov's interest in increasing the power of the legislature and his dominance of the legislative agenda contributed to the constitutional crisis. Once Khasbulatov recognized that he could alter the balance of power between president and parliament by amending the existing constitution, he began to oppose adoption of a new constitution and to exacerbate the constitutional crisis. Throughout 1993, he kept the issue of a new constitution off the legislative agenda. When Yeltsin offered an alternative means to pass a new constitution (a national referendum followed by a Constitutional Assembly), Khasbulatov successfully framed his suggestion as an attempt to destroy the power of the legislative branch. Although eventually Yeltsin succeeded in calling the Assembly, Khasbulatov kept the issue of parliamentary participation in the Assembly off the agenda. Deputies were given the opportunity to vote only on whether or not to send Khasbulatov, as the parliamentary representative, to the Assembly. Also, it was Khasbulatov who would not allow the parliament to consider calling a Congress to deal with the issue. When members of the parliamentary leadership questioned his behavior, rightfully pointing out that it was in the country's and their own interest to pass a new constitution, Khasbulatov orchestrated their dismissal from positions of power, going so far as to disband the Committee on Legislation. He used his control over the agenda to prevent the parliament from participating in the Constitutional Assembly, and it was the lack of parliamentary participation that ultimately undermined this final attempt to resolve the constitutional crisis.

Other interpretations of this period are possible. Perhaps it was not Khasbulatov that spearheaded the attacks on presidential power and the resistance to constitutional reform; instead, a conservative majority in both the parliament and Congress pursued these policies. There are two problems with this interpretation. In the first place, not only did the democratic faction attempt to oust Khasbulatov in September 1992, in January 1993 one of the most reactionary factions did so as well. Each attempt failed. Certainly by the fall of 1992, the democrats did not have a majority in the parliament, but neither did the conservatives. If a conservative majority was responsible for the legislature's strategy, why was it unsuccessful in ousting Khasbulatov and replacing him with one of its own?

In the second place, although the legislature's attacks on the president and his policies were consistent with the self-interested behavior of a conservative majority, this was true only until it became clear that such a strategy was profoundly damaging the legitimacy of the legislative branch. By the spring of 1993, even Yeltsin's opponents began to speak of the need to rid the country of the Congress of People's Deputies, and Yeltsin began seriously to entertain the option of dissolving the legislature and calling for new elections. At this point, powerful members of the parliament, such as first deputy chairman Nikolai Riabov and chairman of the Chamber of Nationalities, Ramazon Abdulatipov, spoke out against Khasbulatov and attempted to compromise with the president. For several weeks, support for their position grew within the parliament. However, we do not know what the ultimate result of their rebellion would have been, because Khasbulatov moved quickly and efficiently to destroy all sources of opposition within the parliament. In his interview with me, Ponamarev suggested that the vote to disband the Committee on Legislation was orchestrated from above and was suspect.

Although there has been much theoretical work on the problem of cycling and its consequences, there has been relatively little written on real-world manifestations of cycling. Outside the stylized constraints of a formal model, political scientists do not really know what a "cycle" looks like in a legislative setting. Even more to the point, we do not know if cycling actually has empirical consequences and, if so, what they are. If cycling occurs, are deputies aware that something has gone wrong? Does it lead to problems in legislative decision making? The inability of deputies to pass a new Russian constitution contributed directly to the constitutional crisis of 1993. If cycling prevented deputies from passing a new constitution, and if it enabled a powerful chairman to dominate the agenda, using the unresolved debate on a new constitution to justify a dangerous confrontation with the Russian President, the real-world consequences of cycling were serious indeed.

In this chapter, I focus on the most important example of cycling that occurred in the Russian Parliament, the debate on a new constitution in the spring of 1992, just three months after the Russian Federation had officially been born. I discuss the debate and the votes that made up the cycles. In addition, I describe both the immediate and long-term consequences of the breakdown in majority rule, especially the ways in which Khasbulatov took advantage of the multidimensional nature of the constitutional question to promote changes to the existing constitution that increased legislative power at the expense of executive power. However, before I begin discussing the details of cycling and its consequences, I provide some background information on the progress of constitutional reform before the collapse of the Soviet Union, including a brief discussion of the changes in the structure of deputy preferences that made cycling possible.

THE BEGINNINGS OF CONSTITUTIONAL CRISIS

The debate about Russia's new constitution began in May 1990 at the first meeting of the superlegislature, the Russian Congress of People's Deputies. At that time, Russia was still a republic in the Soviet Union. Like all republics of the USSR at that time, Russia had its own constitution, which was modeled after that of the Soviet Union and which was subordinate to that at the Union level.[2] Members of the democratic coali-

---

[2] Russia's existing constitution had originally been written in 1978, one year after the Brezhnev-era Union-level constitution was adopted, but had been significantly amended as part of Gorbachev's democratic reforms. The important constitutional changes that Gorbachev made to the Union-level constitution were mimicked throughout the Soviet Republics, and Russia was no exception. Russia's two-tiered legislative structure, which included the large and ceremonial Congress of People's Deputies and the much smaller functional parliament (the Supreme Soviet), was

tion supported the idea of a new constitution because it would help Russia to move faster than the center (and Gorbachev) on economic reform and on establishing the necessary human rights for a democratic order. Yeltsin, the democrats' nominee for chairman, spoke in support of a new Russian constitution during the inaugural meeting of the Congress of People's Deputies, making it a key element of the political platform on which he ran for the post of Chairman of the Supreme Soviet (parliament) and Congress. Once he was elected chairman, he, along with his democratic majority, created a Constitutional Commission to draft a new Russian Basic Law.[3] Although Yeltsin continued to support the idea of a new constitution, for the next year and a half he gave the issue only limited attention.

In the first place, Russia was not an independent nation. As a part of democratic reforms adopted during Mikhail Gorbachev's perestroika (1988–1990), the existing constitution granted Russia's newly elected legislative institutions much more independence and legitimacy than the republican institutions had enjoyed in the past. Russian law was nevertheless subordinate to Soviet law; therefore, the status of a Russian constitution was ambiguous at this time. When the commission presented its hastily prepared first draft[4] to the parliament in October 1990, it was quickly rejected by a large majority on precisely this point.

modeled on Gorbachev's Union-level innovations. See Remington 2001 for an authoritative discussion of Gorbachev's institutional reforms.

[3] The constitutional commission included about 100 members, all of whom were elected at the first meeting of the Congress of People's Deputies. Boris Yeltsin, newly elected chairman of the parliament, served as the commission's nominal chair, but the real leader of the commission was its secretary, Oleg Rumiantsev, an intellectual, liberal reformer, who had also been elected a member of the parliament. Rumiantsev supervised the day-to-day working of the commission, and his name was closely associated with the draft constitution that the commission produced. Reflecting the balance of power in both the Congress and parliament, membership on the commission was politically balanced, with almost equal numbers of members from the communist and democratic coalitions, the relevant partisan groups before the collapse of the Soviet Union. However, the democrats had a slight advantage. This slight majority enabled them to ensure that liberal reformers such as Rumiantsev occupied the key positions on the Constitutional Commission – in particular, membership in the Working Group, a much smaller group responsible for most of the commission's work. Thus, the earliest version of the draft constitution, which was prepared while the Soviet Union existed and which formed the basis for all future versions, reflected the goals of the more reformist wing of the democratic coalition.

[4] The first draft constitution, as well as a list of members of the Constitutional Commission, was published in *Konstitutsionnyi Vestnik*, No. 1, December 1990, pp. 55–120.

In the second place, Yeltsin and his democratic majority were able to achieve most of their objectives through legislation and amendments to the existing constitution. Even though the parliament rejected the commission's first draft, in succeeding months the democratic majority passed many pieces of legislation that were essentially reproductions of sections or parts of sections of the draft constitution. For example, the parliament passed legislation to allow the Russian Republic to develop a market economy, many aspects of which were reflected in the draft constitution's sections on individual rights and civil society. The parliament endorsed the Universal Declaration of Human Rights, which formed the basis for most of the constitution's section on human rights. Also, the parliament created the office of a popularly elected Russian president, an institution defined and described in the draft constitution.

Finally, the confrontation between Russia's newly elected leaders and the communist party officials that still dominated the Soviet Union became increasingly serious starting in the fall of 1990. For several months, the standoff was tense, and Russians spoke openly about the possibility of civil war. The issue of a new constitution drifted into the background until the crisis within the Soviet leadership was resolved.

Once the coup attempt by disgruntled Soviet bureaucrats failed, it was clear to Russia's leaders, both democrats and communists, that Russia's status as a "republic" of the Soviet Union was bound to change. An extraordinary session of the Fifth Congress of Peoples Deputies was held for just four days, October 28 to November 2, to consider several critical issues facing the emerging new democracy. One of the most important of these issues was Russia's need for a new constitution. As Yeltsin stated in a speech to the Fifth Congress, "Constitutional reform on a grand scale is long overdue . . . [The existing] constitution has become a brake on our political course. It is an obstacle in the way of radical reforms that are today vitally necessary for Russia and its inhabitants."[5] The problem was that Russia's status was still ambiguous. On its way to full independence, but not yet there, it was difficult to create an outline for Russia's future. Therefore, for the time being, deputies put the issue of a new constitution aside and instructed the Constitutional Commission to revise its draft for adoption by the Sixth Congress.

Two months later, the Soviet Union had ceased to exist.[6] At that point, Russia was officially an independent state, and support for the rapid

[5] FBIS-SOV-91-213. November 4, 1991, p. 56.
[6] The Soviet Union was formally dissolved on December 25, 1991.

adoption of a new constitution built steadily over the next three months.[7] The Constitutional Commission, parliamentary leaders, and members of the executive branch worked furiously to create a passable draft for the Sixth Congress, scheduled for April 1992.

From comments made by deputies in discussions of earlier drafts, the biggest impediment to passage of a new constitution seemed to be disagreement over the rights and responsibilities of the national and territorial units in the new Russian Federation. Working outside the commission (mostly through the parliament's Presidium), Khasbulatov spearheaded efforts to gain passage of a Federal Treaty before the Sixth Congress was scheduled to begin.

The Federal Treaty was written as an agreement between the "federal bodies of state authority" and the "bodies of authority of the republics within the Russian Federation." It was, in effect, a document designed to mollify the concerns of Russia's ethnic republics and gain their representatives' support for the constitution that was being presented to parliament at approximately the same time.

Both Yeltsin and Khasbulatov believed that if the draft constitution was to be adopted by the upcoming Congress, it was essential to gain support for the Federal Treaty before it began its meetings. Thus, both the executive branch and parliamentary leaders worked very actively to get the Federal Treaty signed before the Sixth Congress. As it happened, leaders (analogous to governors) in eighteen of the twenty key ethnic regions signed the Treaty on March 31, right in the middle of the parliamentary debate.

Because the chapter of the constitution that dealt with the federative structure duplicated the Federal Treaty, Rumiantzev and others believed that once the ethnic regions had approved the Federal Treaty, the representatives of those regions (and other national-territorial regions) would support that section and, by implication, the constitution as a whole.

The parliament's legislative record supported the conclusion that a democratic majority supported most aspects of the draft constitution. After all, the parliament had succeeded in passing legislation to establish a presidential republic, individual rights, and market reform. In fact, much of the draft constitution directly reflected work of that majority.

---

[7] One of the most important supporters was Valery Zorkin, Chairman of the Constitutional Court, who was strongly in favor of the speedy adoption of a new constitution. He viewed it as Russia's "last chance" to prevent the disintegration of the Russian Federation. See interview in *Pravda*, February 21, 1992, p. 2.

The chapter of the constitution dealing with human rights followed closely the language of the Universal Declaration of Human Rights, which the parliament had endorsed in November 1990. The chapter on executive/legislative relations outlined a presidential republic that, in many ways, resembled the American model of a presidential system. The executive and legislative spheres were distinct, and the president and legislature were independent of each other; that is, the president could not dissolve the legislature, and the legislature could impeach the president only with great difficulty. This was very similar to the executive/legislative structure that had resulted when the office of president was tacked onto the remnants of the Soviet legislatures. The new constitution clarified the relative powers of the two branches, but it did not significantly change the balance of power between them. Furthermore, the parts of the constitution dealing with a market economy were supported either by existing law or by laws under preparation.

Therefore, most observers assumed that once the federal question was properly addressed – that is, once a majority could be convinced to support Section 4 of the draft constitution – the constitution would be passed easily.

THE EMERGENCE OF INSTABILITY

Rumiantzev and others tackled the problem of passing the constitution by addressing deputies' concerns issue by issue, never realizing that even if they did obtain majority support for each chapter of the constitution, this would not ensure majority support for the constitution as a whole. The problem was that to adopt a constitution, all issues had to be decided at once, and there were at least four key issues covered in the new constitution: (1) the definition of individual rights, (2) the balance of power between executive and legislature, (3) economic reform, and (4) the distribution of rights in a federation. When members of a majority-rule institution vote on more than one issue at a time, the potential for cycling is created. So long as a two-party dynamic continued, cycling was impossible. However, at the same time that the momentum for the new constitution was building, the parliament's two-party alliance was breaking down. When the constitution came up for debate in March 1992, the partisan structure of the deputy corps had changed, and the herculean effort to resolve the federative question was to no avail.

One of the first to comment on the reorganization of deputy preferences was the first deputy chairman of the parliament, Sergei Filatov, in an interview with a *Nezavisimaya Gazeta* reporter in March 1992. According to Filatov, "a definite regrouping of forces" was under way. The democrats were "losing some of [their] old allies, but gaining new ones."[8]

By the time that the parliament began its debate on the third draft of the constitution, deputies were highly fragmented. The two grand coalitions were gone, and taking their place were the many small factions that until then had been associated with one of the two coalitions. These changes profoundly altered political debate in the parliament and had an effect on the constitutional debate as well. Different groups of deputies (e.g., different majorities) supported different sections of the draft constitution.

While some of the deputies who had been associated with the democratic coalition supported a strong president, others, especially members of a faction called the Radical Democrats, supported a parliamentary form of government. Members of the communist faction, who also supported a strong legislature, and thus opposed Chapter 5 of the draft, joined the Radical Democrats. Opinions on the issue of Russia's federative structure also did not follow the earlier divisions in the legislature. Representatives from the national-territorial units almost uniformly supported granting more powers and special status to Russia's ethnic regions, and these representatives supported the Federal Treaty and Chapter 4 of the draft constitution. They were joined by members of the communist and nationalist factions, but also by members of some of the democratic factions. Many of the staunchest democrats, however, opposed anything but equal representation for all members of the federation. Following the launching of President Yeltsin's economic reform program, differences among deputies in the two original coalitions on the dimension of economic reform emerged. While members of the communist faction always opposed market reform, members of the democratic, nationalist, and centrist factions were divided. Some "conservative" members supported Yeltsin's program, whereas other "democratic" members opposed it. Although no chapter of the constitution was devoted exclusively to economic reform, the necessary rights to allow individuals to engage in market activity (owning property and making profits) were part of the two chapters on individual rights. Thus, in debating Chapters 2 and 3, deputies considered two issues at once, creating the conditions for cycling.

[8] English translation of the interview is reported in FBIS-SOV-92-049, pp. 49–51.

Before the collapse of the Soviet Union, alliances among factions were constant: About half the deputies belonged to factions that were permanently in the communist/conservative camp, and about half belonged to factions that were permanently in the democratic reformist camp. But, after the collapse, alliances among factions were temporary and depended on the particular issue under consideration. Such a changing alliance structure might have little impact on passage of a particular piece of legislation, so long as the legislation represented only one policy dimension. But, such changing alliances would prove fatal to passage of a constitution, a complex law in which many dimensions must be decided at once.

AT THE CRUCIAL MOMENT A BREAKDOWN IN MAJORITY RULE: RUSSIA'S FIRST AND LAST CHANCE FOR PEACEFUL CONSTITUTIONAL REFORM

While work to gain approval of the Federal Treaty continued across Russia's regions, the Russian Parliament began its work on the Constitutional Commission's third draft.[9] Although responsibility for crafting the draft constitution lay with the Constitutional Commission, the par-

---

[9] This draft consisted of a Preamble, six substantive chapters, and a final "seventh" section dealing with issues of transition once the new constitution had been adopted. The Preamble laid out the general principles of the constitution, most important of which were individual rights and the rule of law. Chapter 1, "Principles of the Constitutional Order," Chapter 2, "The Basic Rights, Freedoms, and Obligations of Man and Citizen," and Chapter 3, "Citizen's Society," were concerned mostly with fleshing out the details and extent of individual and human rights guaranteed under the constitution. These chapters were considered uncontroversial and received little attention prior to the parliamentary debate. Chapter 4 described the federal structure and laid out the rights of Russia's constituent units. The commission had reworked much of this chapter in response to earlier criticism. Chapter 5 described the institutional arrangement of government. A strong president was balanced by a bicameral legislature. Chapter 6, the concluding chapter, was uncontroversial. The seventh section included a plan for the implementation of the new constitution, including a schedule for new elections both to the legislature and presidency. It stipulated that new elections would not be held until the current People's Deputies had fulfilled their terms in office, and that in the meantime, People's Deputies would fill the new legislative institutions. The number of legislative seats in the new institutions was lower than in the current two-tiered structure; still this was a highly favorable clause from the standpoint of the deputies. Not only would many of them not lose their jobs as a result of constitutional reform, the current deputies would choose those that would occupy posts in the new legislatures. Those deputies chosen to be members of the new institutions would be in an excellent position to contest the first competitive elections.

liament's role was an important one. Parliamentary leaders understood that it was the parliament's job to work with the constitutional commission to ensure that the constitution prepared by the commission was a document that could, in fact, be supported by the two-thirds majority of Congressional deputies needed for adoption of a new constitution.[10] It was in the process of parliamentary discussion and debate that divisive issues were to be ironed out. In the debate leading up to the Sixth Congress, Khasbulatov said that it was the parliament's responsibility to do a "good" job and give the draft "broad" support so that the Congress would be able to pass the constitution without getting bogged down in further debate.[11] Furthermore, it was up to the parliament to decide whether or not the draft constitution would be forwarded to the Congress for possible adoption. Not only did the parliament have the final word on the content of the draft constitution, they had to decide whether or not to place the constitution on the agenda of an upcoming Congress in the first place. Thus, parliamentary approval of a draft constitution was the first step in constitutional reform. Without the parliament's approval, there was no chance that the Congress could adopt a new constitution.

Although ultimately a majority of deputies approved the draft constitution, inconsistent voting made it impossible to tell whether deputies did or did not support the draft constitution. Deputies did not approve Chapters 2 or 3, yet the constitution was forwarded including these chapters. Deputies did not resolve the question of how many representatives each federative unit would send to the new upper house. When deputies approved the final version of the draft, this critical clause was not encompassed by their vote – it had simply been set aside. The deputies did not send a "good" draft to the Congress, and they did not demonstrate their "broad" support for the draft. The result of votes to forward the draft to the Congress showed that a majority of deputies in the parliament supported the need for a new constitution and the general principles of

---

[10] In deciding how to proceed on drafting a new constitution for Russia, deputies looked to the existing constitution. According to the existing constitution, only the Congress of People's Deputies could adopt a new constitution. Recall that the parliament, a legislature of 250 deputies, was chosen from among the membership of the Congress, a body of 1060 deputies. Thus, members of parliament, having dual membership in the Congress as well, would also vote on whatever constitution the parliament might forward to the Congress.

[11] See Khasbulatov's address to the parliament as recorded in Bulletin No. 45, pp. 3–5 of the stenographic report of Russia's Supreme Soviet – the full Russian citation appears in the following footnote.

the current draft. However, cycling within the debates on particular chapters of the constitution demonstrated that there was no stable majority in support of the specific details of all chapters of the constitution.

Before describing the particular votes in detail, let me summarize the votes of parliamentary majorities over the course of the debate. On February 14 a majority of deputies voted their general approval of the draft constitution by agreeing to put it on the agenda of the upcoming Congress. On March 19, a majority of deputies again voiced their general approval of the draft when they voted to consider the draft chapter by chapter. I do not argue that those deputies who voted in favor of placing this constitution on the agenda of the Congress did so as a result of overall support of the draft in its entirety. After all, they knew when they voted on March 19 that they would have a chance to amend the constitution during parliamentary debate. What I do assert is that in supporting this draft, a majority of deputies went on record as supporting some alternative constitution, one with many of the features of the parliamentary draft, over the Brezhnev era, status quo constitution. I believe that the vote indicated that a majority of deputies did, indeed, support the adoption of a new constitution.

On March 25 a majority of deputies first rejected the Preamble and Chapter 1 of the draft, which implied a rejection of some of the general features of the constitution as a whole, but later they reversed themselves and voted for the drafts without amendments. On March 26, deputies amended Chapter 2 nine times and then rejected the section, including their amendments, completely. On March 27, the deputies amended Chapter 3 five times and then rejected the chapter, including their amendments, completely. On April 3, deputies approved Chapter 4. On April 4, deputies approved Chapters 5 and 6 and the final appendices. They also approved the draft and agreed to forward it to the Congress.

It seems unlikely that the majority that supported the constitution as a whole on February 14 and March 19 was the same majority that rejected Chapter 2 on March 26 or the majority that rejected Chapter 3 on March 27. Likewise, the majorities that supported amendments to Chapters 2 and 3 were not the majorities that ultimately rejected these chapters!

Unfortunately, not all votes on the constitution were roll call votes. Therefore, I cannot compare the deputies who voted for the constitution on February 14 and March 19 with the deputies who voted against Chapter 2 on March 26 and against Chapter 3 on March 27. However, the votes on Chapters 2 and 3 were roll call votes; therefore, I can compare the deputies who voted for amendments on Chapter 2 with deputies who voted against Chapter 2 and likewise for Chapter 3.

In the case of Chapter 2, only 47 deputies voted for all nine successful amendments, showing that a different majority supported each of the nine amendments. If we take the most serious amendment to Chapter 2, which was a challenge to property rights, and compare those who voted for this amendment and those who voted against the entire chapter, again the overlap is only 69 deputies. In the case of Chapter 3, only 76 deputies voted for all five successful amendments, and only 59 deputies voted for the most divisive amendment, an effort to eliminate the term "class hatred" from Article 67, and against the entire chapter. At least in the case of these two chapters, we see clearly the existence and effect of many different majorities.

In the next few pages, I describe the debate surrounding the key votes on the constitution. Part of the goal of this chapter is to investigate the reactions of legislators when cycling has occurred. Do they recognize that something has gone wrong? How do they respond to the inconsistency of their actions? Obviously, the answers to these questions will vary from one legislative body to another, but because there are so few reported cases of actual cycles in legislative voting, it is worthwhile to investigate any interesting cases that we do have.

I now discuss specific votes in order of occurrence.

Vote to Place the New Constitution onto the Agenda of the Sixth Congress[12]

The first step in adopting a new constitution was to get a majority of parliamentary deputies to support putting the draft constitution onto the agenda of the forthcoming Sixth Congress. The debate on this question

---

[12] My primary source of information about the debate on the draft constitution, which occurred in March and April 1992, is *Sessiia Verkhovnogo soveta, biulleten . . . sovmestnogo zasedaniia Soveta Respubliki i Soveta Natsionalnostei*. Moscow: Supreme Soviet of the Russian Federation. This document is the verbatim stenographic report of the full Supreme Soviet or "parliament." For most of the period, it is organized into numbered Bulletins, each of which corresponds to a particular day's debate. Certain debates are not organized by numbered Bulletin, but simply by the date of the debate. Throughout this and subsequent chapters, I refer to this source as "the stenographic report of the Russian Parliament" or simply "the stenographic report." I indicate Bulletin number or date, as appropriate.

For the particular discussion of the vote to place the new constitution onto the agenda of the Sixth Congress, I rely on the debate reported in Bulletin No. 35 of the stenographic report.

Figure 2.1. Vote to place the new constitution onto the agenda of the Sixth Congress. This image represents the parliament's movement from Q, the status quo old constitution, to A, a new alternative (i.e., the draft constitution) by majority vote on February 14, 1992.

occurred on February 14, 1992. At the end of the debate, a bare majority of deputies supported the motion. For the first time, a majority of deputies chose an alternative (new constitution) to the status quo (existing constitution), a result that was widely interpreted as a show of parliamentary support for the draft constitution (Figure 2.1). After all, never before had a majority of deputies voted to place the draft constitution on the agenda of the Congress.

Khasbulatov, the parliament's new chairman,[13] presided over the debate, and his forceful voice in support of the draft constitution may have helped persuade many to support the new constitution.[14] In a brief speech at the end of the discussion, he urged deputies to support placing the item on the agenda of the upcoming Congress.[15] He dismissed the major arguments against the draft one by one, and he scoffed at those who urged further delay. When one deputy suggested that they vote on changing the agenda item from a consideration "of the new constitution" to a consideration "of the concept of constitutional reform," Khasbulatov

---

[13] Khasbulatov had been elected to succeed Yeltsin as Chairman of the parliament on October 28, 1991, at the Fifth Congress of People's Deputies.

[14] In Khasbulatov's view, the main obstacle to parliamentary approval had been the lack of support in Russia's regions, but even as the debate in the parliament began, Khasbulatov and others were working behind the scenes to obtain the necessary signatures on the Federal Treaty. Also, because the prospect for signing looked good, Khasbulatov felt that the time was finally ripe for parliament and Congress to support the new constitution. Although he did not expect the Sixth Congress to adopt the constitution in final form, he was hoping that the Congress would adopt the draft as a basis, and he thought that strong approval by the parliament would make this likely. If the Congress were to adopt the constitution as a basis, the process of actual and legitimate ratification could begin, and most certainly this process would have included some sort of national referendum. In any case, the possibility of finally getting out of the constitutional impasse was at this point in time very real.

[15] Remarks reported in stenographic report, Bulletin no. 35, p. 26.

remarked, "How interesting, after two years of discussion we now begin to talk about concepts."[16] From his tone and offhand remarks, it is clear that Khasbulatov was annoyed by the opposition but even more so by the ambivalence of those who preferred to sit on the fence.[17]

Once the parliament had decided to move forward with passing the draft constitution, established procedure dictated that the Constitutional Commission had only two more weeks to put the finishing touches on its draft. On March 2, the commission submitted the draft to the parliament's standing committees and other interested deputy groups. The committees were in turn given about two weeks in which to consider the draft and submit suggested changes to the commission. In a final round of revisions, the commission had just a few days to consider the committees' suggestions.[18] Their final draft was distributed to the full parliament on March 18.

Vote to Approve General Draft of the New Constitution[19]

On March 19, the parliament reaffirmed its approval of the draft constitution. The purpose of the March 19 debate was to decide at what

---

[16] Remark reported in stenographic report, Bulletin no. 35, p. 27.

[17] Much of the opposition came from representatives of the autonomous republics, most of whom were members of the Chamber of Nationalities. As one such deputy said, "we deputies from national territories have repeatedly spoken against the draft constitution." Deputies from ethnic regions preferred to continue amending the old constitution; they felt this was the best way to maintain their historical identity and rights within greater Russia. Other deputies, such as Vladimir Isakov (see pp. 10–11 of Bulletin no. 35), Nikolai Pavlov (a coordinator of the faction Russia), and Viacheslav Polosin (a coordinator of the faction Change-New Policy), spoke against the new constitution for different reasons. These deputies argued that the time was not ripe for a new constitution, that it is historically impossible to pass a new constitution in a time of transition, and that it would be better to continue amending the old constitution rather than risk trying to adopt a new one.

[18] The Constitutional Commission had a great deal of discretion in making their final revisions. In general, they adopted as many of the amendments as possible, but they rejected amendments that changed the intent of the draft. In this particular iteration, the commission worked closely with two deputy factions, Sovereignty and Equality and Change-New Policy. Sovereignty and Equality was the faction of representatives from the Russian republics. Because of the controversy surrounding Chapter 4, the section outlining Russia's federative structure, the commission needed the support of these deputies. In addition, the committee paid special attention to changes suggested by the centrist faction, Change-New Policy, which had spent considerable effort on changes to the governmental arrangements outlined in Chapter 5.

[19] In discussing this debate, I draw upon the stenographic report of the Supreme Soviet, Bulletin No. 45.

Figure 2.2. Vote to approve general draft of the new constitution. On March 19, 1992, the parliament reaffirmed their support for the draft constitution (A) over the old constitution (Q); hence, the arrow is bolder than in Figure 2.1.

level of detail the parliament would consider the constitution (Figure 2.2). Supporters of the new constitution wanted to avoid a detailed discussion. Opponents of the constitution wanted the opposite. From arguments that each side made, it is clear that both supporters and opponents realized that the more detailed the discussion, the more likely it would be that disagreements would arise. Supporters hoped that deputies would only be asked to vote on the draft as a whole; opponents hoped to open up the debate and thereby uncover inconsistencies in support of particular aspects of the constitution.

Chairman Khasbulatov opened the discussion. Hoping to avoid prolonged debate, he urged the deputies to support a procedure that would limit debate. Using the technical terminology of parliamentary procedure, he asked deputies to agree to move rapidly to a vote to pass the draft constitution as a basis. Although a few deputies from the Constitutional Commission's working group agreed with Khasbulatov, many more deputies spoke against a procedure that would deny the parliament the right to discuss the draft. These deputies demanded an opportunity to review the constitution article by article, the smallest complete units contained in the constitution.[20] Many deputies advocated a compromise position: Allow the parliament to discuss the constitution chapter by chapter.[21] The constitution included six chapters, each of which encompassed a major topic, such as Chapter 4 on Russia's federative structure.

---

[20] Some of those who wished to review the draft article by article were deputies such as Sergei Polozkov of the centrist faction Change-New Policy or Sergei Baburin of the nationalist faction Russia who had stated many times their opposition to a new constitution.

[21] Supporting this position were Nikolai Riabov, the chairman of the Chamber of the Republic, and Sergei Kovalev, a leading human rights activist.

At the end of the debate and after some controversy, the parliament's first deputy chairman, Filatov, asked the deputies to vote on a resolution stating that the parliament would consider the draft constitution chapter by chapter in anticipation of forwarding it to the Congress. A majority of deputies supported this resolution. As on February 14, a majority of deputies again voted for the alternative (a possible new constitution) over the status quo (the existing constitution). The fact that they agreed to debate the constitution chapter by chapter is relevant for two reasons. By rejecting the proposal to discuss the draft article by article, deputies rejected a procedure that would make it more difficult to give strong and unequivocal support to the draft constitution. However, as we will see shortly, deputies reversed themselves several days later.

A Vote Against the Preamble and Chapter 1[22]

On March 25, the parliament began its detailed debate of the draft constitution, beginning with the Preamble and Chapter 1. As one deputy noted, these two parts of the constitution contained the basic outline of the entire document, implying that a vote against or in support of these parts was a vote against or in support of the entire draft constitution.

Deputies had agreed on March 19 to proceed with the discussion chapter by chapter. Commission secretary Rumiantzev intended to make a presentation on the commission's decisions to either adopt or reject suggested amendments. He anticipated that at the end of his presentation, the parliament would vote to approve both the Preamble and Chapter 1.

Perhaps because he wanted the debate to proceed quickly, Chairman Khasbulatov suggested that they first vote on the Preamble and Chapter 1 as a basis, because this was the "tradition" of legislative work they normally followed.[23] (Throughout the debate on the constitution, Khasbulatov constantly urged deputies to "hurry up!") However, when Khasbulatov called for the vote "as a basis," the Preamble and Chapter 1 did not pass, an outcome that directly contradicted the vote on March 19 (Figure 2.3). This is the first of several votes that are inconsistent with

---

[22] In discussing this debate, I draw upon the stenographic report of the Supreme Soviet, Bulletin No. 47.

[23] Generally, deputies were first asked to vote for a draft law "as a basis." They then amended the draft, voting on each amendment in turn. Finally, they voted for the draft law "as a whole." After this, the new law was implemented. I discuss the procedural rules of the parliament in Chapter 4.

Figure 2.3. Vote against the Preamble and Chapter 1. On March 25, the parliament voted to reject the Preamble and first chapter of the draft constitution. Because the Preamble and Chapter 1 laid out the basic outlines of the draft as a whole, this vote implied a rejection of the draft constitution (A) and a return to the status quo (Q); hence, the arrow shows movement from A to Q.

parliamentary decisions passed just days (or, as we will see, even hours) earlier. Deputies' reactions to this apparent inconsistency depended on how they felt about the draft constitution. Supporters tried to ignore the anomalous vote; opponents used it to justify halting the debate.

Vladimir Isakov, a communist and member of the reactionary Agrarian Union faction, argued that the parliament's failure to approve the Preamble and Chapter 1 meant that the parliament did not support the draft constitution and that the discussion should be discontinued. He interpreted the vote as a vote against the new constitution.

Surprisingly, Rumiantzev agreed, but for different reasons. He believed that it was the Constitutional Commission's sole responsibility to prepare and submit the draft constitution to the Congress and that the parliamentary debate was an intrusion on the authority of the commission. Shocked at Rumiantzev's agreement with Isakov, Khasbulatov exclaimed, "Have you lost your head, Oleg Germanovich?"[24] As a supporter of the new constitution, Khasbulatov knew that strong parliamentary approval of the draft was essential for smooth passage in the Congress. Presumably, he believed that it was up to the parliament to make certain that all controversies were resolved before the Congress. But, by pushing the debate forward, Khasbulatov papered over the controversy, leaving it unresolved.

A Vote for the Preamble and Chapter 1

In the end, Khasbulatov imposed his will on the parliament. He ignored the vote against the Preamble and Chapter 1 and asked

[24] Comment by Khasbulatov, Bulletin No. 47, p. 11.

Figure 2.4. Vote for the Preamble and Chapter 1. Later in the day on March 25, the parliament reversed itself and voted to approve both the Preamble and Chapter 1 of the draft constitution.

Rumiantzev to begin his presentation, avoiding a vote on this procedural question.

During Rumiantzev's presentation, many deputies challenged the commission's decisions regarding their amendments, and Rumiantzev had to field quite a few hostile inquiries; however, deputies did not vote on any of the rejected amendments. Thus, in this first debate, the parliament played only an advisory role. This did not go unnoticed by the deputies.[25]

After about two more hours of discussion, Khasbulatov pushed for closure. He asked deputies to vote to approve the Preamble and Chapter 1 as a basis; this time a majority approved them both (Figure 2.4). This is the second example of inconsistent voting. A majority of deputies had voted for the same two sections of the constitution that a majority rejected only two hours earlier. Although the result of the second vote reaffirmed the parliament's approval of the draft constitution, the fact that deputies had already flip-flopped twice over the course of one week, the last reversal occurring over a span of two hours, was evidence that there did not exist a *stable* majority to support the draft constitution.

---

[25] At one point, an unidentified deputy remarked that if the parliament was going to discuss amendments rejected by the Constitutional Commission, then they ought to do so in the manner that such amendments were discussed during normal debate on draft laws. In other words, he suggested that the parliament ought to vote on these amendments. In making this suggestion, the deputy was only the first among a number of deputies who began to question the manner of procedure. At this juncture, the chairman ignored the suggestion and reminded deputies that they had already discussed this issue. (He was referring to the debate on March 19.) In his view the parliamentary discussion was intended to generate support from the deputies, not to make further changes to the draft. Several other deputies – Sergei Polozkov of Change-New Policy, Vladimir Isakov of the Agrarian faction, and Viacheslav Liubimov of Russia – all of whom were opponents of the new constitution – continued to raise this issue throughout the day's debate.

Different majorities existed and asserted themselves depending on the particular section or version of the draft under consideration. Despite these irregularities, debate continued.

Votes in Favor of Nine Amendments to Chapter 2 and a Final Vote Against the Chapter[26]

On March 26, the parliament began discussing Chapter 2 on "The Basic Rights, Freedoms and Obligations of Man and Citizen." Chapter 2 was considered one of the two uncontroversial sections of the draft constitution (the other was Chapter 3), because most of Chapter 2 was taken directly from the Universal Declaration of Human Rights that the parliament had approved one year earlier. In addition, as commission spokesman Sergei Kovalev pointed out, other parts of Chapter 2 were adopted from laws that had already been passed or from changes that had been made to the existing constitution. It was his belief, therefore, that debate on Chapter 2 would proceed smoothly.[27]

Despite the fact that the chapter was devoted mostly to the issue of individual rights, some of these rights had a direct bearing on another issue, economic reform of the command economy. Individual rights to hold and use private property were a necessary condition for market reform to succeed. Therefore, in supporting this chapter, deputies were being asked to decide on two major issues simultaneously, and it is certainly possible that some deputies were in favor of expanding individual rights, but against a fully market-driven economy. We can therefore imagine one majority of deputies supporting an expansion of individual rights compatible with the Universal Declaration of Human Rights. We can also imagine a different majority rejecting a highly privatized market economy, thereby rejecting the rights to private property necessary for such an economy. This explains how deputies voted twice in support of the constitution (which of course included Chapter 2) and how

---

[26] In discussing this debate, I draw upon the stenographic report of the Supreme Soviet, Bulletin No. 48.

[27] Sergei Kovalev was a well-known human rights advocate, member of the faction Democratic Russia, and chairman of the parliamentary Committee on Human Rights. He was well-respected and admired, and at the start of the day's debate many deputies noted his appearance, rather than Rumiantzev's, with approval. Although Rumiantzev was also respected, his manner was arrogant and overbearing, and he had made so many remarks disparaging the work of his fellow deputies that he was neither liked nor trusted by many of his colleagues.

they supported nine amendments to Chapter 2, but in the end rejected Chapter 2. It is precisely when deputies are asked to vote on two issues simultaneously that cycling can occur.

Kovalev began the discussion of Chapter 2 with a monologue justifying the decisions of the Constitutional Commission. He was almost immediately interrupted by a procedural challenge to the legitimacy of the day's debate. Conservative deputy Sergei Polozkov and several others insisted that the parliament vote on every amendment, a time-consuming procedure that a majority of deputies had already rejected on March 19, one week earlier.[28]

Bowing to pressure and with an overwhelming need to keep the discussion on track, Filatov decided that they should continue the debate in a manner more in accord with standard procedure; that is, they should discuss the draft constitution article by article, voting on each amendment in turn. When Filatov asked the deputies to vote on this suggestion, a majority passed it; thus, the day's debate began with deputies reversing an earlier decision.

The detailed debate on specific articles highlighted the two issues subsumed in Chapter 2, individual rights and property rights. In addition, the fact that deputies began voting on particular amendments opened up the potential for cycling.

Following the resolution of the procedural issues, the parliament spent the next several hours discussing the amendments that the committees had submitted to the Constitutional Commission, but which the commission had rejected. They proceeded in the order of the articles affected. The parliament passed nine of the thirty-five amendments it considered, holding a roll call vote on each one. Most of these nine amendments made only trivial changes to Chapter 2. The only significant successful amendment had to do with an individual's right to property, and therefore it was an amendment that bore directly on the issue of economic reform.

The leader of a faction called Fatherland, a nationalist group that regretted the dissolution of the Soviet Union and opposed market reform, offered the amendment. The purpose of the amendment was to alter Article 34 and thus provide a basis for potentially restricting individual property rights, especially the right to own land. The draft version of the

---

[28] The deputies responsible for asking that procedure be modified were Sergei Polozkov and Andrei Golovin of Change-New Policy and Viacheslav Liubimov of Russia.

article stated that every individual had "the right to acquire, own, use and manage any objects of property." Fatherland's amendment changed the wording to simply "the right to property."[29]

Kovalev argued against the amendment to Article 34, saying that it would change the conception of the draft constitution both on the issue of property rights and on the issue of individual rights. Fatherland's spokesman, Boris Tarasov, admitted that the amendment got at the heart of a source of divisions in the parliament. Leonid Volkov, a specialist on property law, justified the original wording with the following statement. "The fact of the matter is that in the existing Constitution, as you all know, for decades we had established strong limits on the right of the citizen to acquire private property and the tools and means of production. Today we are implementing privatization, and we have already all agreed on this. Therefore . . . it is necessary for the Constitution to strengthen the right of the citizen to acquire property instruments and the means of production."[30]

Nevertheless, a majority supported Fatherland's amendment to Article 34, and in so doing made an important change to the draft constitution. The deputies rejected another Fatherland amendment, which would have imposed even stronger restrictions on the right to private property.[31] Deputies' decision on the amendment to Article 34 did not mean that a majority of deputies opposed privatization. In fact, a majority of deputies would vote to support the government's privatization plan on June 5 and 21, 1992. What the vote signified was that deputies' views on economic reform and private property were complex, with different groups (sometime majorities) of deputies favoring different combinations of property rights, individual rights, and economic reform.

---

[29] The wording of Article 34 was as follows: In the Russian Federation the economic freedom of every individual is realized in the right to acquire, own, use, and manage any objects of property, the right to free enterprise, and the right to free work. Tarasov wanted to change Article 34 to read: In the Russian Federation the economic freedom of every individual is realized in the right to property, the right to free enterprise, and the right to free work.

[30] See page 32 of Bulletin no. 48.

[31] The wording of Article 35 was: (1) The right to property is a necessary condition for the realization of the rights and freedoms of the individual and citizen. The exercise of this right *shall not infringe on the public good.* (2) The right of inheritance is guaranteed. Tarasov wanted to change Article 35 to read: The right to property is realized in accordance with the law and may not infringe on the public good or on social justice. Tarasov's proposed change to Article 35 was an even stronger check on private ownership, because it would allow the state to restrict ownership if it violated either the public good or social justice.

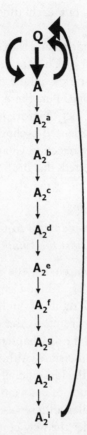

Figure 2.5. Votes in favor of nine amendments to Chapter 2 and a final vote against the section. On March 26, the parliament voted to amend Chapter 2 nine times. In the image, A_2 is the general notation for amendments to Chapter 2, and each successful amendment is notated with a different superscript letter, a through i. At the end of the debate, deputies voted to reject Chapter 2, placing in doubt the meaning of prior votes to accept the draft constitution as well as the Preamble and Chapter 1 in favor of the old constitution.

After considering every outstanding amendment, the presiding chair asked deputies to approve the final version of Chapter 2 as a basis, just as they had approved the Preamble and Chapter 1 after the previous day's debate (Figure 2.5). He assumed that the chapter would pass easily, because deputies had, by implication, already approved the chapter on March 19, and they had again approved the chapter nine times, by implication, when they passed the nine amendments that very day. Therefore, Filatov was shocked when the vote failed. The vote was held two more times, but each time it was rejected by a slim majority.

By Filatov's shocked statements and the considerable confusion caused by the parliament's rejection of Chapter 2, we know that deputies did, indeed, take notice of this stark example of inconsistent voting. Something had gone terribly wrong. But, there is no evidence that deputies understood the problem. In fact, Filatov did exactly what Khasbulatov had done when he had experienced cycling: He ignored it! Later, when deputies pointed out that by rejecting Chapter 2 (and then 3), the parliament had, in effect, rejected the draft constitution, parliamentary leaders ignored this as well.

Votes in Favor of Five Amendments to Chapter 3 and a Final Vote Against the Chapter[32]

Continuing its debate on March 27, the parliament began discussing Chapter 3 on "Citizen's Society." Like Chapter 2, Chapter 3 concerned human rights, in this case the rights of public associations, and was considered uncontroversial. According to the commission's representative, deputy Tzann-Kai-Si, the intent of Chapter 3 was to delineate a sphere of public life separate from the state. Although there did not appear to be any serious opposition to the idea of civil society, several factions took exception to the different kinds of associations that would be protected under the chapter. In particular, differences arose over the future status of the Communist Party under the new constitution and over the status of professional associations (as opposed to trade unions, which are associations of workers). Again, the deputies' views on economic reform affected their position on the question of professional associations. In addition, we see the effect of another, relatively minor issue, the status of the Communist Party. The debate on Chapter 3 was complicated by at least two dimensions in addition to that of human rights.

As on the day before, deputies voted by roll call on each amendment that the Constitutional Commission had rejected. Deputies passed five of twenty-five amendments.

The most important amendment concerned Article 67, which banned groups that promoted hatred on the basis of race, nationality, religion, and social or class hatred. The last two categories of "hatred" proved contro-

---

[32] In discussing this debate, I draw upon the stenographic report of the Supreme Soviet, Bulletin No. 49.

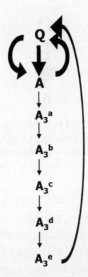

Figure 2.6. Votes in favor of five amendments to Chapter 3 and a final vote against the chapter. On March 27, the parliament voted to amend Chapter 3 five times. In the image, A_3 is the general notation for amendments to Chapter 3, and each successful amendment is notated with a different superscript letter, a through e. As they did with Chapter 2, at the end of the debate, deputies voted to reject Chapter 3, again placing in doubt the meaning of prior votes to accept the draft constitution, not to mention the votes to amend Chapter 3.

versial. As written, the article might have provided a basis for banning communist parties, which had traditionally discussed class conflict. In the end, deputies voted to remove the word "class" from the article.

Finally, after amending Chapter 3 five times, Filatov asked deputies to approve the chapter as a basis. Just as had occurred the day before, a majority of deputies failed to approve Chapter 3 (Figure 2.6). This time, there was no outcry. Filatov proceeded with business as usual, accepting as commonplace the complete reversal of votes on February 14 and March 26 and the invalidation of the day's work.

The result of the first week's debate on the constitution was ambiguous. Inconsistent voting made it impossible to tell whether deputies did or did not support the draft constitution.

FINAL WEEK OF DEBATE ON DRAFT CONSTITUTION

After the parliament's inconclusive work during the first week of debate, the deputies took a brief respite from the process. Khasbulatov did not want to begin discussion of Chapter 4, the next chapter in line for dis-

Figure 2.7. Vote to approve Chapter 4. On April 3, deputies voted to approve Chapter 4 without amendments. Because they had rejected Chapters 2 and 3, the vote on April 3 represented a straightforward acceptance of the draft constitution (A) over the old constitution (Q). In a sense, the deputies were back where they started.

cussion, until after the Federal Treaty was signed. Representatives of the republics had given verbal approval of the treaty on March 13; therefore, he believed that deputies would have the signed treaty in short order. In fact, the Federal Treaty was signed on March 31, but deputies did not have copies of the official version until April 2. Finally, on April 3, with the signed Federal Treaty in their hands, the deputies began discussing Chapter 4.

Vote to Approve Chapter 4[33]

The discussion of Chapter 4 proceeded smoothly. Deputies considered only five amendments, each of which was defeated. After the short debate, presiding chair Khasbulatov asked deputies to approve Chapter 4 as a basis, and it passed easily (Figure 2.7). Even though deputies had rejected Chapters 2 and 3 of the draft, their support for Chapter 4 implied that there still existed a majority in favor of an alternative to the status quo.

Deputies moved immediately to the discussion of Chapter 5. At that point, deputies had only two days remaining to finish their work on the constitution. The Sixth Congress was scheduled to begin on April 6, and Khasbulatov was in a frenzy to get the thing passed.

Votes in Favor of Six Amendments to Chapter 5 and Final Vote to Approve the Chapter

Of all the discussions over chapters of the draft constitution, the discussion over Chapter 5 was the most protracted and serious. The primary

---

[33] In discussing the debate over Chapters 4, 5, and 6 of the draft constitution, I rely on the stenographic report of the Supreme Soviet for April 3 and 4, 1992.

issue in Chapter 5 was the balance of power between the executive and legislative branches of government. Of the six successful amendments, five reduced the president's power significantly.[34] One eliminated the president's power to hold a referendum. Another eliminated the president's right to head a Security Council and to create consultative and subsidiary organs attached to the presidency. Another curtailed slightly the president's power of executive decree. Also, one amendment prevented any institution from eliminating another governmental institution by referendum. All of these amendments passed easily. *It was clear that there was a stable majority in favor of reducing the president's powers.*

Along with the debate over the specific powers of the president, deputies also discussed the number of seats that each republic, *krai*, and *oblast* would have in the Federal Assembly, the new upper house. This highly contentious debate concerned the issue of Russia's federative structure. Representatives to the Federal Assembly were to be elected from each federal unit (republic, *krai*, *okrug*, or *oblast*), regardless of population size. In the draft under discussion, each unit received two representatives, an arrangement similar to that in the United State Senate.[35] Although the number of representatives each region should have in the upper house seems a simple characteristic of the legislature, in fact, it is one of the most critical issues in the design of Russia's federation. Deputies from the autonomous republics believed that their regions ought to have more representatives than other units. Deputies from nonethnic regions strongly disagreed.

The debate on Chapter 5 encompassed at least two of the key issues in the constitution – the balance of power between president and parliament and Russia's federative structure. The debate was highly contentious, and any solution would have displeased a sizable proportion of the deputies. If, as had happened in the debate over Chapters 2 and 3, Chapter 5 failed in the final vote, the whole constitutional process would have been derailed. In the interest of showing "unity" to the Congress, Khasbulatov decided unilaterally not to hold a vote on any of the amendments having to do with this question.[36]

---

[34] The only other successful amendment to Chapter 5 dealt with procedural issues concerning the Constitutional Court's duty to decide on the constitutionality of laws.

[35] The exact number of representatives from each federal unit changed from draft to draft. The main problem in the debate on Chapter 5 was not the number of representatives but whether or not the autonomous republics ought to have more representatives than other units of the federation.

[36] April 3 debate, page 35.

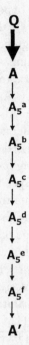

Figure 2.8. Votes in favor of six amendments to Chapter 5 and final vote to approve the chapter. On April 4, the deputies approved Chapter 5 after amending the chapter six times. At the end of this debate, deputies had chosen an amended version of the draft constitution, notated as A', over the status quo, Q.

When deputies were asked finally to vote to approve Chapter 5 as a basis, *they did not vote on the federative question.* When Khasbulatov asked the deputies to vote to approve Chapter 5 as a basis, a majority did so (Figure 2.8). But, Khasbulatov achieved this victory by ensuring that the final vote was on one issue alone, presidential power. By restricting the final vote in this way, Khasbulatov may have ensured that the votes on Chapter 5 did not cycle. The problem with this solution was that in putting the issue aside, the parliament left unresolved one of the most controversial constitutional issues facing the deputies. If the main purpose of parliamentary debate was to resolve controversy before the Congress, this decision, taken in conjunction with the rejection of Chapters 2 and 3, ensured that the parliament failed in doing its job.

Vote to Approve Chapter 6

After approving Chapter 5 on April 4, deputies moved immediately to a discussion of Chapter 6. The debate was short, deputies passed no amendments, and the chapter passed easily (Figure 2.9). By approving Chapter 6, deputies were again voting to approve the amended version of the draft that they affirmed when they approved Chapter 5.

Immediately afterwards, deputies began discussing the final section concerning the transitional period that would begin once the old constitution was supplanted but the new constitution was not yet completely realized. For the deputies, one of the most important issues in this section was how the seats of the new legislature were to be filled. The section stipulated that until the deputies' current five-year term was served out, no new elections were to be held. Current deputies were to fill the seats in the new legislature. From a purely self-serving perspective, this was the only time that deputies had the opportunity to preserve their jobs in this way. The section also put an end to the president's extraordinary powers. Not surprisingly, this section passed without controversy.

Finally, on April 4, after voting in favor of Chapters 5 and 6 and the transitional appendices, Khasbulatov asked the deputies to approve the entire draft constitution as a basis. One of the leaders of the faction Change-New Policy, Andrei Golovin, pointed out that it was procedurally impossible to approve the draft constitution given that the deputies had rejected two of its chapters. Khasbulatov dismissed this suggestion, and with little further ado, a majority of deputies voted to approve their amended version of the draft constitution and to forward it to the Sixth Congress.

Figure 2.9. Vote to approve Chapter 6. At the end of the day on April 4, deputies voted to approve Chapter 6 without amendments. By so voting, deputies were again voting for an amended version of the draft constitution, A', over the old constitution; thus, the arrow from A to A' has been darkened.

Table 2.1. *Possible Votes by a Five-Person Legislature Consisting of Members A, B, C, D, E*

Members Voting "For"	Amendments
A, B, C	Strong individual rights
A	Strong property rights
B, C, D, E	Modest property rights
Members Voting "Against"	Final Vote on Amended Document
A, D, E	Strong individual and modest property rights

Although the deputies finally did support the draft constitution, they presented neither a "good" draft nor a "unified" stand to the Congress. The draft that the Sixth Congress received had not been consistently supported by the deputies, and it was weakened by issues left unresolved. The only consistent signal sent by the parliament was support for a reduction in the powers of the executive branch – in particular, the president.

Because a constitution is a multidimensional document, it is possible that different majorities may support different outcomes on distinct issues. To see this, consider a legislature with only five members, A, B, C, D, and E. I illustrate this example in Table 2.1. In a five-person legislature, it takes three or more members to constitute a majority. The majority that supports strong *individual* rights (say, members A, B, C) may not be the same majority that supports modest *property* rights (say, B, C, D, E). (The majority that supported Fatherland's amendment to Article 34 of Chapter 2 was voting in support of modest, rather than strong, property rights.) Only two of the members, B and C, voted for both the amendment on strong individual rights and the amendment on modest property rights; thus, only members B and C support the final result, namely, strong individual rights and modest property rights. Therefore, a majority rejects the final result. Recall that in the series of amendments to Chapter 2, different majorities supported different amendments, but there was no majority to support the particular combination of strong individual rights and modest property rights that resulted from the voting on amendments.

In the end, a large majority of parliamentary deputies supported the draft constitution that they had spent two weeks debating. But, that same majority had not supported Chapters 2 and 3, and very likely would not have supported any resolution to the controversial issue of seat allocation in the Federal Assembly. A majority of deputies supported the need for a new constitution, and a majority wanted the procedure to continue, but cycling within the debate on the new constitution demonstrates that there was not a stable majority to support the specific formulation of the draft constitution.

Vote on New Constitution at Sixth Congress

At the Sixth Congress, debate on the draft constitution was brief and dismissive (Figure 2.10). The deputies did not adopt the draft constitution; they did not even accept the draft as a basis. Instead, they returned the draft to the parliament and Constitutional Commission for further work. Neither the parliament nor the Congress ever again considered adopting a new constitution.

Cycling in the parliament was only one factor in the Congress's decision to reject the draft constitution. Resistance to constitutional change was stronger in the Congress than in the parliament, and the two-thirds majority necessary to adopt a new constitution was prohibitive. Nevertheless, if the parliament had given strong and consistent support to a new constitution, it would have been very difficult for the Congress to dismiss the draft so easily.

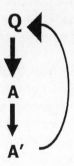

Figure 2.10. Vote on new constitution at Sixth Congress. When the amended version of the draft constitution, which the parliament forwarded to the Congress, came up for vote, deputies at the Congress rejected it. After months of preparation and prolonged debate in the parliament, the final position that the Russian legislature took on the issue of a new constitution was to return to the status quo, exactly where they had started!

AGENDA CONTROL AND CONSTITUTIONAL REFORM

In the short term, cycling disrupted debate on the draft constitution at a crucial historical moment. Never again would the legislature come so close to resolving the constitutional crisis. The long-term effects were equally grave. Not only did cycling inhibit the legislature's ability to adopt a new constitution, it also enabled the parliament's powerful chairman to dominate the legislature and use the constitutional question to set an agenda that worked to his own advantage at the expense of the legislature's legitimacy.

Khasbulatov's dominance was the result of a combination of two institutional factors: (1) the agenda-setting powers granted to the parliament's chairman in its rules of procedure and (2) the absence of a stable majority coalition (which led to cycling).[37] In the following sections, I discuss both these factors in turn, beginning with a brief discussion of the source of the chairman's agenda-setting powers.

Khasbulatov as Agenda Setter

Using his position as head of the parliament's Presidium, the organizing body responsible for day-to-day running of the parliament, Khasbulatov had considerable latitude to determine the parliament's day-to-day and long-term agenda. The Chairman's budgetary power was the cornerstone of his power. Khasbulatov used the parliamentary budget, which was under the control of the Presidium, to reward key parliamentary leaders (especially committee chairmen) with such perquisites as apartments in Moscow, oversees travel, and even vacation homes in prime spots.

There is evidence to suggest that Khasbulatov began to use his budgetary clout as early as the summer of 1992, when he attacked the power of the committees. As Lev Ponomarev explains, Khasbulatov began to impede the work of those committees that took a public position that differed from his own; that is, he withheld funds from the committees, he withheld the means to copy and distribute committee reports, and he prevented committee members from taking the floor during sessions of the parliament.[38]

---

[37] See Chapter 4 for a full discussion of the parliament's rules of procedure and the chairman's agenda-setting powers.
[38] Personal interview with author in June 1996.

An important moment occurred in September 1992, when the head of the Committee on Mass Media, Viacheslav Bragin,[39] attempted to organize the democratic committee heads to press for an investigation into the unconstitutional actions of the Chairman of the Presidium. According to his former colleague, Ponomarev, Bragin met privately with key democrats such as Sergei Stepashin, chairman of the Committee on Defense and Security, and obtained their support. However, when the moment came to push forward the complaint in the Presidium, Stepashin and others simply sat silent. According to Ponomarev, Stepashin and other democratically minded deputies were "afraid" to speak. If they had accepted favors from Khasbulatov, then they certainly knew that Khasbulatov had the power to take such perquisites away. Bragin's attempt was a failed effort from within the Presidium to confront Khasbulatov and reduce his dictatorial power over the parliament. By that time, Khasbulatov, in Ponomarev's words, "had put down all opposition within the Presidium."

By controlling committee chairmen, Khasbulatov could influence significantly the content of legislation. In addition, his position as Chairman of the Presidium, the organization responsible for disseminating amendments to the appropriate committees, gave him almost complete power to veto amendments that he opposed.

In January 1993, a reporter from the newspaper *Rossiia* interviewed Sergei Filatov, shortly before he was replaced as the parliament's first deputy chairman. In the interview, Filatov described Khasbulatov as nothing short of a parliamentary dictator.[40]

There is a Supreme Soviet, but there is also an administrative superstructure in the form of the Chairman and his deputies. This is indeed a monster that could concentrate uncontrolled power in its hands, all the laws and regulations notwithstanding. The Deputies on one committee or another may draft a law, which can always be blocked if it doesn't suit the leadership. As you know, the joint and standing committees are supervised by the Supreme Soviet's Chairman or Vice-Chairmen, who can create commissions working in parallel and come up with the decisions they want. This has already happened. While we are looking all around to see where a dictatorship might come from, one is springing up right here, since the concentration of authority in the Supreme Soviet is a concentration of power, some of it in the hands of the Chairman. . . . We must create a basis so that under no circumstances can the Chairman say, as he does now: "Two people answer for the situation in the country – the President and I." No, it's the President and the parliament!

---

[39] Personal interview with author in June 1996.   [40] *Rossiia*, Jan. 13–19, pp. 1, 3.

The chairman also influenced the agenda of the Congress. The decision to call a Congress was first taken by the parliament's Presidium; and the Congress's agenda, which the parliament had to approve, was first drafted by the Presidium. Therefore, by controlling the parliament's agenda, Khabulatov was able to influence when the Congresses would meet and what they would discuss. And of course, as chairman, Khasbulatov presided over the highly publicized meetings of the Congress.

Implications of Agenda Setter

For a majority rule, democratic institution, cycling in the presence of an agenda setter is a potentially fatal combination. By determining the order in which particular issues are debated and by determining the alternatives against which particular issues are paired, *so long as there is no stable majority coalition* the agenda setter can lead the parliament to support any point within the set of acceptable alternatives. (The formal theory behind this is explained fully in Chapter 3.) It follows that such an agenda setter, if he is aware of his power, will construct an agenda that results in parliamentary support for his own ideal outcome. Only a stable majority opposition could prevent the chairman from abusing his position in this way.

Let us assume that Khasbulatov's primary goal was to increase his political power. To accomplish this, he would first and foremost take advantage of the powers bequeathed to the chairman of the parliament and its Presidium. All evidence supports the conclusion that he used these powers very aggressively. In addition, if possible, he would seek an increase in the legislature's power and responsibility. In this he was also successful.

In the following section, I describe the crisis that began almost immediately after the Sixth Congress failed to adopt the new constitution, and I make the case that Khasbulatov used his dominance of the parliament to reduce the president's power, undermine his legitimacy, and prevent consideration of a new constitution. I provide evidence to support my contention that Khasbulatov did, in fact, manipulate the parliament's agenda to achieve these ends.

Khasbulatov's Strategic Control of the Legislative Agenda

In my view, Khasbulatov's manipulation of the legislative agenda began with the March/April 1992 debate on the draft constitution. Recall that during the last day of debate on the new constitution, the parliament passed five amendments reducing the president's power. In the final vote on Chapter 5, deputies reaffirmed their support for these amendments. Therefore, the cyclical debate on the constitution finished with votes to reduce the president's powers and increase legislative control of the government. Although it seems unlikely that Khasbulatov orchestrated this result, he cannot have failed to notice that a majority consistently supported reducing the president's powers.

Khasbulatov's behavior at the Sixth Congress is also suggestive. Although he was on record as supporting the new constitution, and he worked hard to pass the Federal Treaty, he did not push to pass the new constitution at the Sixth Congress. Instead, most of his efforts at the Congress went toward (a) gaining ratification of the Federal Treaty (which he did) and (b) beginning an uphill battle to restore some of the legislature's rights to influence the appointment of government ministers. Despite the position of Yeltsin's supporters, the legislature's attempt to retrieve some role in the government's policy making was reasonable and responsible. However, I think it significant that Khasbulatov used the highly publicized meetings of the Sixth Congress to criticize the government and the president quite harshly.[41]

After all of his work with the parliament on the draft constitution, it is remarkable that Khasbulatov spent almost no time on this issue at the Congress. Perhaps even more significant is the fact that after the Sixth Congress, neither the parliament nor the Congress ever again made a serious attempt to pass the draft constitution prepared by their own Constitutional Commission. I contend that once the constitutional debate became focused on reducing executive power, Khasbulatov used his control of the agenda to keep it there. Indeed, following the Sixth Congress, the parliament's agenda (and the agendas of the Seventh, Eighth, and Ninth Congresses) was dominated by efforts to reduce the president's power while increasing the powers of the legislative branch.

---

[41] At the Sixth Congress, criticism of the government's economic reform program was harsh. In the middle of the Congress, on April 12, the Cabinet resigned in protest. On April 13, in an address to the Congress, Khasbulatov made the following inflammatory remarks. "Our esteemed friends from the government have clashed with the Congress for the first time and lost their heads.... No one should try blackmailing us. We aren't afraid of anyone or anything. Excuse me, but let's speak frankly now: I can't tell you how much ingenuity I've shown in order to save this government from being torn to pieces." Later in the address, Khasbulatov referred to the Cabinet ministers as "boys."

In the aftermath of the August coup, the Fifth Congress of People's Deputies had granted the president extraordinary powers to constitute his Cabinet without parliamentary approval; these powers were set to expire at the end of November 1992. The approaching end to the president's extraordinary powers prompted debate on a new law to delineate the powers of the executive branch and to clarify the role of the legislature in appointing key members of the government. The purpose of the so-called Law on the Government was to clarify responsibility for final approval of the Prime Minister and other Cabinet ministers.

The parliament worked on the law throughout the fall of 1992. Because the approaching end of Yeltsin's extraordinary powers mandated the Law on the Government, I do not argue that Khasbulatov placed this item on the parliament's agenda. However, evidence does suggest that during the course of the debate, Khasbulatov used his powers as chairman to affect the final draft through the amendment process. (I present a systematic investigation of this proposition in Chapter 8.) The original draft of the Law on the Government was submitted to the parliament by the government. The parliament's role was to modify the draft to ensure passage by the Seventh Congress. Thus, the parliamentary contribution consisted mainly in amendments to the original draft. According to leaders both of Democratic Russia and the nationalist faction Russia, Khasbulatov began to be especially solicitous of the leaders of one faction, Change-New Policy, forming a close working relationship with this faction at that time.[42] Oddly enough, Change-New Policy put forward almost all successful amendments to the Law on the Government, and almost all of these amendments restricted the president's powers in some way. (Change-New Policy had also been especially active in restricting presidential power in the parliament's debate on Chapter 5 of the draft constitution.)

Most laws passed by the parliament did not need the approval of Congress. But because the Law on the Government was a constitutional issue, Congress had the final say. Debate on this law at the Seventh Congress was tense, and the implicit confrontation between legislature and executive was palpable. After all, the legislature was proposing to limit the

---

[42] Khasbulatov himself, in an interview with me, singles out the members of Change-New Policy for praise. In interviews with me, Lev Ponomarev accused the leaders of Change-New Policy of accepting substantial favors from Khasbulatov, such as vacation homes and apartments in Moscow, and Sergei Baburin concurred.

president's extraordinary powers, and the president and his supporters were not pleased. In the end, the Congress passed a version of the Law on the Government that restored to the parliament the right to approve the president's appointee for Prime Minister, a reasonable modification of the status quo. There are few presidential democracies, including our own, in which the legislature does *not* have the right to approve the president's cabinet appointees.

Nonetheless, I believe that it was the debate over the Law on the Government, both in the parliament and at the Seventh Congress, that demonstrated to Khasbulatov the legislature's power and ability to reduce the president's powers. Just as the Fifth Congress increased Yeltsin's powers, the Seventh Congress took some of those powers away. It is significant that at this juncture the parliament did *not* work to resolve its disagreement with the executive branch by promoting a new constitution, such as the one prepared by its own Constitutional Commission, in which the powers of executive and legislature were balanced, more balanced than in the existing status quo, even after passage of the Law on the Government. Furthermore, after the Seventh Congress successfully reduced the president's powers, Khasbulatov abandoned all efforts to pass a new constitution, concentrating instead on modifying the old one. A few weeks after the Seventh Congress, Khasbulatov began to speak out against the need for a new constitution.[43]

Beginning in January 1993, Khasbulatov's manipulation of the parliament's agenda was apparent even outside the Presidium and parliamentary sessions. Throughout 1993, the parliament considered very few issues other than those that directly affected the power of the president or Khasbulatov's control over the parliament. In fact, the lawmaking activity of the parliament in general decreased significantly in 1993.

President Yeltsin was frustrated with the results of the Seventh Congress. He came to believe that the best way to recover or even strengthen the powers of the executive branch was to pass a new constitution, one written not by the parliament but by his own advisors. Thus, at this juncture Yeltsin became the chief supporter of constitutional

---

[43] In addition, by the end of January, he was on record as saying that the country no longer needed a new constitution and that the amendments to the existing constitution, which had been drafted by the parliament and ratified by the Congress, were sufficient. *Komsomolskaya Pravda*, January 30, p. 1.

reform, and Khasbulatov became its staunchest opponent. Yeltsin's strategy was to hold a national referendum on the basic principles of constitutional reform. The referendum would be followed by a Constitutional Assembly, during which representatives of Russia's national and territorial regions and representatives of the major branches of government, including a parliamentary delegation, would write the actual document. The exact method for ratification was unclear.

Khasbulatov responded to Yeltsin's initiative by calling an Eighth Congress. The Eighth Congress began on March 10. Both the chairman and new vice-chairman, Riabov, were highly critical of the president's plan. Obviously, Yeltsin's suggestion was threatening to the legislature, because, according to the existing constitution, only the legislature had the right to adopt a new constitution. But, the Congress did not respond by moving immediately to adopt the highly favorable draft constitution, which was, after all, written by members of the parliamentary Constitutional Commission. Indeed, such an option was never proposed. Instead, at the Eighth Congress, deputies took no initiative on constitutional reform, choosing only to reject the idea of a referendum.

Khasbulatov was the referendum's loudest critic.[44] He argued that Yeltsin's plan was an attack on the legislative branch. In the meeting of the parliament at which the Eighth Congress had been called (March 5), Khasbulatov asked that parliament's committees with jurisdiction over the militia and other security forces take measures to ensure the Congress's security, implying by his request that the Congress was under siege and threatened with violence.[45] The implication that the threat came from the president was very clear.

Khasbulatov's behavior and the actions of the parliament and especially the Eighth Congress began to take their toll on the reputation of the legislature. After the Eighth Congress there were few voices to praise the work of the People's Deputies. Even Valery Zorkin, the Chairman of the Constitutional Court, who had sided with the legislature and against the president on most questions of constitutionality, urged the deputies to support the president's proposal for a national referendum followed by a Constitutional Assembly. He further urged the deputies to

---

[44] On January 10, *Rossiiskaya gazeta* published a lengthy interview with Khasbulatov in which he criticized the referendum as a method of passing a new constitution.

[45] *Izvestia*, March 6, p. 1.

adopt a law to "do away with the Congress as an independent legislative body and to hold elections to a bicameral parliament."[46]

A few days after the Eighth Congress ended, Yeltsin issued a presidential decree calling for a national referendum on his own popularity, a new draft constitution, and a law to set the date for new parliamentary elections. He justified his actions in the following way:[47]

Over the past several months, there has been an excruciating search for a compromise that would enable the country and the legislative and executive branches to operate normally. In the past few months, one option after another has been proposed, but none of them has been adopted. This road came to a dead end at the Eighth Congress. The crisis could have been resolved with the help of a referendum. But the referendum was shelved, too. . . . [T]he principal method of resolving the constitutional crisis remains the same – the adoption of a new Constitution.

Furious with Yeltsin's decree, Khasbulatov immediately called for another extraordinary Congress to respond to the proposed referendum. At the Ninth Congress, which began on March 26, just two weeks after the Eighth Congress ended, deputies considered a list of questions prepared by the parliament's Presidium. The four questions were as follows:

1. Do you have confidence in B. N. Yeltsin, President of the Russian Federation?
2. Do you approve of the social and economic policy that has been conducted by the Russian Federation president and the Russian Federation government since 1992?
3. Do you consider it necessary to hold an early election for President of the Russian Federation?
4. Do you consider it necessary to hold early elections for Russian Federation People's Deputies?

The questions followed the general guidelines outlined in Yeltsin's decree; that is, they queried the public on support for the president and they raised the issue of early elections. However, the most important question, that of the draft constitution, had been removed. Thus, the Ninth Congress altered the purpose of the referendum. Instead of a first step in constitutional reform, the referendum became simply a measure of Yeltsin's popular support. Khasbulatov had managed to turn a

---

[46] Zorkin's speech to Ninth Congress, reported in *Rossiiskaya gazeta*, March 27, pp. 1–2.

[47] Yeltsin's speech to Ninth Congress, reported in *Rossiiskaya gazeta*, March 27, p. 1–2.

constitutional question into a means of undermining the president. He was not alone in assuming that a majority of voters no longer had confidence in Yeltsin or in his reform policies; thus, he and presumably most of the deputies assumed that Yeltsin would "lose" the referendum. What the chairman's plans were under such a scenario we will never know, because to everyone's surprise a clear majority of voters supported both Yeltsin and his reform program.

The referendum was held on April 25. Well over 50% of the voters (turnout was over 60%) supported both Yeltsin and his economic policies. There was no majority support for new elections to either the presidency or the legislature.[48]

Khasbulatov reacted angrily to the referendum and attempted to discredit the results. According to Khasbulatov, the referendum created a "split in society." Other than that, it had "no results." He accused the news media of using "information terror" to discredit him and the legislature.[49]

Yeltsin interpreted the referendum as a show of support for his plan to pass a new constitution. He immediately began preparing for a Constitutional Assembly, to be held in the summer. Representatives of each of Russia's regions as well as representatives of the president, government, parliament, and Constitutional Commission were to attend.[50] In addition to the parliamentary draft constitution, which the Constitutional Commission was still working on, Yeltsin introduced a "presidential" draft, which had been prepared by his own advisors. It created a presidential republic in which the powers of the president were considerably more than in the parliamentary draft. He began circulating his draft constitution to the heads of Russia's regions, asking for amendments by early June.

The parliament's failure to pass its own draft constitution, along with its poor showing in the April referendum, had paved the way for Yeltsin to introduce a draft far less favorable to the legislature. Still, parliament had every opportunity to participate in the Assembly and at a minimum to work with other delegates on a compromise draft, one that blended features from the presidential and parliamentary versions.

---

[48] By the final tally, 58.7% approved of Yeltsin, 53% approved of the government's social and economic policies, 31.7% wanted early presidential elections, and 43.1% wanted early legislative elections.

[49] *Sovetskaya Rossia*, April 27, p. 1.

[50] Filatov outlined the proposed participants in the Constitutional Assembly. *Izvestia*, May 19.

In an obvious and ultimately disastrous misuse of his power as parliamentary chairman, Khasbulatov rejected Yeltsin's call for a Constitutional Assembly and began a campaign to discredit any attempt to pass a new constitution outside the rules of the existing constitution. No longer asserting that the existing constitution was adequate, he became a strong supporter of the Congress's sole right to pass a new constitution.

For a time, parliament supported Khasbulatov's negative interpretation of Yeltin's plan, seeing the Constitutional Assembly as a way to deprive the legislature of its constitutional powers. However, once Yeltsin invited parliament to participate, and once his advisors began working closely with Rumiantzev, the chief architect of the parliamentary draft, an increasing number of deputies began to question Khasbulatov's motives in keeping parliamentary deputies from participating in the Assembly.

At a meeting of the Presidium in May, Khasbulatov's vice-chairman Riabov, an outspoken opponent of the President, and Ramazan Abdulatipov, the conservative head of the Chamber of Nationalities, supported parliamentary participation in the Assembly. According to Riabov, the referendum showed that the people were strongly opposed to the confrontation between legislature and executive. Furthermore, he believed that a constitutional assembly was an excellent way to resolve the crisis. "This is a question of the future of the country and the parliament."[51] Khasbulatov again asserted that the Constitutional Assembly was a way to pass a new constitution unconstitutionally. Riabov and Abdulatipov agreed, but they argued that the only way for the parliament to be involved in passing a new constitution was to participate in the Constitutional Assembly.[52] On May 20, a majority of parliamentary deputies voted to approve the Constitutional Commission's draft constitution as a basis, a repeat of their April 4 vote, one year earlier. This vote was one indication that a parliamentary majority in favor of adopting a new constitution still existed. It can also be interpreted as an effort to lend the parliamentary draft added legitimacy in anticipation of its review at the Constitutional Assembly.

Khasbulatov reacted violently to the defection of Riabov and Abdulatipov. He began actions to disband the Legislation Committee, the equivalent of a committee on rules and procedures. He excluded Riabov from meetings of the Presidium. Also, he kept the matter of

[51] *Nezavisimaya gazeta*, May 15, p. 1, 3.   [52] *Sevodnya*, May 18, p. 1.

parliamentary participation in the Constitutional Assembly off the agenda of the parliament. According to Riabov, by removing his opponents from the Presidium and avoiding a parliamentary vote, Khasbulatov "torpedoed participation in [the Constitutional Assembly] by both the Supreme Soviet and the corps of deputies." Khasbulatov then instructed the Presidium to designate him as the parliament's sole delegate to the Assembly. Again according to Riabov, "this was done in order to derail the process [of adopting a new constitution]."[53]

As the parliament's delegate to the Constitutional Assembly, Khasbulatov's behavior was disruptive. On the first day, after the opening address by Yeltsin, he interrupted the proceedings by demanding that he be given the opportunity to speak next. Given that Khasbulatov had until that moment shunned the Assembly, he was not on the scheduled list of speakers. When he was denied the opportunity to speak then and there, he left the hall and held a conference outside, calling Yeltsin a dictator.[54] He used his exclusion from the podium as a reason to try and discredit the entire proceedings. When he was asked to speak several days later, he was found to be ill and could not attend.

Without the participation of a parliamentary delegation, the Constitutional Assembly fizzled out, and the confrontation between the two branches increased over the summer. Finally, in September, Yeltsin issued a decree disbanding the country's legislative institutions and calling for both (a) a national referendum on his own draft constitution and (b) elections to a new legislative institution. Yeltsin's decree was unconstitutional, and while it ended the two-year long, crippling confrontation between executive and legislature, it began the new institutional order most unsatisfactorily.

CONCLUSIONS

The constitutional crisis that engulfed Russia after the breakup of the Soviet Union was the result of a bizarre and ultimately violent confrontation between the two major branches of government. The crisis was facilitated by the existence of a constitution that was philosophically and logistically inadequate for an emerging democracy. The language specifying the powers of executive and legislature were vague, but the legislature had the clear right to modify the existing constitution. Technically, therefore, the legislature had the advantage over the

[53] *Izvestia*, June 4, pp. 1–2.   [54] Event discussed in *Izvestia*, June 5, 1993, p. 102.

executive. In reality, however, President Yeltsin had a popular mandate to lead the new democracy. In some ways it is a testament to the strength of that new democracy that popular will triumphed over the technocratic misuse of a communist-era document. By way of summary, consider the strategic implications of this confrontation for the actors that participated in it.

From Khasbulatov's perspective, the existing constitution allowed the legislature to alter at will the balance of power between executive and legislature. So long as he could control the parliament's agenda, he kept deputies focused on the issue of executive power and led them in amending the existing constitution to undermine the president's power and authority. He also very effectively kept the issue of a new constitution off the agenda. Khasbulatov's strategy exacerbated the confrontation between executive and legislature and led to a dramatic increase in his power and influence in government. Even though Khasbulatov ultimately lost his gamble, he was, for a time, clearly the only winner in the constitutional crisis. The crisis propelled him into the public eye, and his own confrontational actions kept him there. He even vied with Yeltsin for control over foreign policy. Also, Khasbulatov might not have lost his gamble. For a brief moment, Khasbulatov and his close ally, Vice-President Rutskoi, were the self-proclaimed leaders of the Russian Federation. At least one American expert predicted that Yeltsin would be removed from office and replaced by his vice-president.

From Yeltsin's perspective, the constitutional crisis became a problem when the confrontation between executive and legislature began to impede his own policy program. Although he had floated the idea of a national referendum and Constitutional Assembly before the Seventh Congress, it wasn't until the deputies had forced him to replace his Prime Minister that he began to pursue alternative means to adopt a new constitution. Clearly, Yeltsin would have liked to see a constitution that was favorable to executive power. However, based on his strong support for the parliamentary version of the constitution in March 1992 and his willingness to compromise with the parliament prior to the Constitutional Assembly, I conclude that his highest priority was to ensure that the constitution was passed in a legitimate manner. His decision to disband the legislature in September 1993 was for him a worst-case scenario.

Throughout the crisis, the goal of the People's Deputies was to retain or strengthen the power and prestige of the legislative branch and to retain their jobs as long as possible. Their first and best opportunity to accomplish both these goals was to pass the draft constitution that they debated in March and April 1992. If they had passed that constitution, they would have strengthened the power and prestige of the legislature, and they would have retained the jobs of many of the deputies, including most of the members of the parliament. As I described, the deputies failed to take advantage of this opportunity. The Law on the Government represented a second opportunity to strengthen the legislature, and in this the deputies were successful. However, the Law on the Government did not address the constitutional question. The results were swept away when the Yeltsin constitution was approved by popular referendum in the fall of 1993.

Once Yeltsin began agitating for an alternative means for adopting a constitution, the deputies had a third opportunity to strengthen the legislature. In the first three months of 1993, the entire country was waiting for the deputies to adopt a new constitution, yet at no time during this period did the deputies consider adopting a new constitution, choosing instead to focus all of their energy on preventing the president from finding an alternative means to do so. I have argued that the deputies made these choices because of the chairman's careful manipulation of the alternatives presented to them. There is no question that the parliament's resistance to constitutional reform undermined its legitimacy and credibility. If the majority of deputies did not understand this, many of the parliament's leaders did – including some like Riabov and Abdulatipov, who consistently supported initiatives to undermine the president, but who rebelled against their chairman when they saw the damage it was doing to the legitimacy of the legislature.

Finally, the deputies had a fourth opportunity to strengthen the legislature and perhaps salvage their jobs. The parliament had the opportunity to send a delegation to the Constitutional Assembly, instructing its deputies to push for a balanced system and some contingency for serving out their terms under the new system. Under such a constitution, the legislature would have fared better than it did under the constitution eventually written by Yeltsin and his advisors. Even more important, the constitution would have been *better* in an absolute sense than the one eventually passed. By failing to participate in the Constitutional Assembly, the deputies failed not only themselves but their country as well.

For a time, the deputies' efforts to decrease the power of the executive branch were, in and of themselves, reasonable. In fact, an excessively powerful presidency is not good for democracy. Despite his inflammatory rhetoric, Khasbulatov's protests and initiatives made a lot of sense, up until the winter of 1993. Also, Yeltsin's notion of democracy, as embodied in the presidential draft constitution, was heavily dependent on a strong president. Thus, we return to the problem of cycling. The ultimate tragedy in the constitutional crisis was the deputies' failure to pass its own draft constitution in March 1992. Doing so would have served their own interests and their country's interests and would have avoided a costly institutional battle.

In the final analysis, there were no winners in the confrontation. The People's Deputies lost their jobs. Khasbulatov lost his gamble, and after a brief stint in prison, he retired into obscurity. Yeltsin remained president, but the image of his military forces storming the building in which the legislature met, and the fact that many deputies were killed, permanently damaged his reputation as a democratic reformer (Brown 1993). The long-term consequences for Russia were even graver. Either the parliamentary draft of 1992 or the compromise draft left unfinished by the Constitutional Assembly would have created a more balanced republic than the "Yeltsin" constitution passed by referendum in December 1993.

In this chapter I have presented the details of an interesting and important example of cycling. I have described what cycling looks like and how deputies involved in approving the cyclical outcome perceived it. In addition, I have investigated the empirical consequences of cycling for the consolidation of Russian democracy. In the next chapter I begin the presentation of a more formal framework in which to understand cycling and its consequences.

3

Cycling and Its Consequences:
A Theoretical Framework

To understand how majority cycles undermine legislative decision making, it is necessary to understand the theoretical concept of cycling. Therefore, I begin this chapter with an exposition of a precise definition of cycling and its consequences. Following this, I discuss the most important solutions to cycling that have been developed by formal scholars of legislatures. The earliest studies, beginning with Kenneth Shepsle's pathbreaking article (Shepsle 1979), focus on how institutional design in the form of committees and rules can prevent cycling. More recent studies – in particular, Gary Cox and Mathew McCubbins' influential book – analyze how political parties, in conjunction with committees and rules, prevent cycling (Cox and McCubbins 1993). Following Cox and McCubbins, John Aldrich shows formally how, in a two-party setting, institutional design and the organization of preferences work together to prevent cycling (Aldrich 1995a). In a multiparty setting, work by Schofield (Schofield 1993) shows how the ideological location of parties, even highly organized parties, cannot prevent cycling if the issue space is multidimensional and parties can be differentiated along more than one of the dimensions. Therefore, in multiparty settings, committees and rules are critical to preventing a breakdown in majority rule.

CYCLING: DEFINITION AND DISCUSSION

Kenneth Arrow first showed that it is generally impossible to amalgamate individual preferences in a "fair" manner such that a consistent and stable social preference is established (Arrow 1963). McKelvey (1976) and others (Plott 1967, Schofield 1978) have shown that given a majority-rule decision-making body and an unconstrained, multidimensional space of alternatives, a stable outcome, an "equilibrium," almost never exists.[1] In such a voting body, for any alternative supported by a majority there is always at least one other alternative supported by a different majority. As different majorities form in support of different outcomes, legislative decisions wander or "cycle" through the alternative space.[2] Hence, the phenomenon is called "cycling."

Imagine a group with three members, M_1, M_2, and M_3, that is faced with a set of at least three alternatives, in this case a, b, and c. Let us further assume that each of the three members is *rational* in the following sense. If M_1 prefers b to a and c to b, then M_1 prefers c to a. Thus, we say that M_1's preferences are *transitive*. No individual member can prefer b to a, c to b, and a to c. By assuming that preferences are transitive, we assume that choices of any individual member cannot form a cycle. However, even when individual members behave rationally, the group as a whole may prefer b to a, c to b, and a to c; this is referred to as the *paradox of voting*.[3] The paradox of voting is typically represented in the following way.

Let members 1, 2, and 3 (M_1, M_2, and M_3) have the preference relations as shown in Figure 3.1.[4]

If we ask these three members to vote on each pair of alternatives $(a\,b)$, $(b\,c)$, and $(a\,c)$, we find that no alternative wins unequivocally. When faced with the choice between a and b, M_1 and M_3 choose a and M_2 chooses b. Thus, a defeats b in a pairwise comparison. When faced with the choice between b and c, M_1 and M_2 choose b and M_3 chooses c. Thus, b defeats c in a pairwise comparison. And, finally, when faced with the choice between c and a, M_2 and M_3 choose c and M_1 chooses a. Thus, c defeats a in a pairwise comparison. We find that this group of individually rational voters has chosen first c over a, then b over c,

---

[1] McKelvey's complex proof assumes that choices are made in a multidimensional spatial setting. Each dimension represents some issue or policy about which voters have an opinion and on which they might be called to vote.

[2] The concept of an alternative space is based on the spatial theory of voting, which was popularized by Anthony Downs in his classic work, *An Economic Theory of Democracy*, 1957, and by Duncan Black in *The Theory of Committees and Elections*, 1958. For more recent explanations of the spatial theory of voting, see Enelow and Hinich (1984) and Krehbiel (1988).

[3] The French mathematician, the Marquis de Condorcet, first discovered the problem in 1785. A translation of an essay by Condorcet in which he describes the paradox can be found in McLean and Urken (1995, Chapter 7).

[4] For the sake of simplicity, I use the notation $a\,b\,c$ to mean that a group member prefers a to b to c. I avoid the more complex notation in which strict preference (P), indifference (I), and the combination of strict preference and indifference (R) are specified.

$$M_1: \quad a\,b\,c$$
$$M_2: \quad b\,c\,a$$
$$M_3: \quad c\,a\,b$$

Figure 3.1. Preferences of three voters over alternatives a, b, and c. Each voter, M_1, M_2, and M_3, has a distinct preference ordering over the three alternatives.

and finally a over b. Furthermore, if c were again put to vote against a, c would be the winner, and so on. Hence, a cycle is often represented as *cabc*.

It is important to note that a cycle can exist only when there are at least three alternatives. If there are only two choices, then no matter what the preference relations of the group members, one of the two choices will receive a majority and win. Conversely, just because there are more than two choices does not mean that a cycle exists. The configuration of the preferences of the group members determines whether or not a cycle exists; however, as the number of alternatives and voters increases, the probability that cycles will exist also increases (Riker 1982, p. 122).

If one represents graphically the cyclical preferences depicted in Figure 3.1, one obtains a picture like that shown in Figure 3.2. This simple graph shows how a group member ranks each of the three alternatives, a, b, and c. If a member ranks a higher than b, then the line that corresponds to M_1 is higher over alternative a than over alternative b. No matter how the alternatives are arranged along the horizontal axis, whether $a\,b\,c$, as shown in the figure, or $c\,a\,b$, the graphical representation of the preference relation of one of the voters will be oriented in a different direction than that of the other two.

The implication of the paradox of voting is that a group of rational voters may not be able to make a stable choice.[5] In the above example, if the group settles on alternative c, what is to prevent M_1 from again proposing alternative a? And, subsequently, what is to prevent M_2 from proposing alternative b? Given the arrangement of preferences presented in Figure 3.1, it is possible to say that the group M_1, M_2, and M_3 cannot make a choice. In such a situation, when there is no Condorcet winner, the choice of these three members is vulnerable to manipulation. If one of the three members, say M_1, has the power to decide the order in

---

[5] In this context, a stable choice is one that is not subject to defeat by an alternative majority.

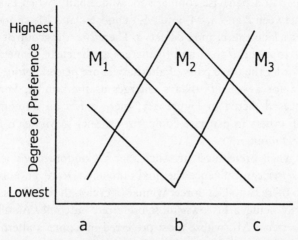

Figure 3.2. Graphical representation of the paradox of voting. In this diagram, the preference orderings of voters M_1, M_2, and M_3 are each represented by a line that is at its lowest point for each voters' least preferred outcome and at its highest point for each voter's most preferred outcome.

$$M_1: \quad a\,b\,c$$
$$M_2: \quad b\,c\,a$$
$$M_3{}^*: \quad c\,b\,a$$

Figure 3.3. Noncyclical preferences for a three-member group. In this preference ordering, the preferences of voters M_1 and M_2 remain the same; only the preference ordering of voter M_3 (now $M_3{}^*$) has changed.

which the amendments will be considered, he can ensure that his own most preferred outcome, in this case outcome a, is the group choice. To do so, M_1 first sets c against b, then b against a. In this case, b defeats c and a defeats b. If M_1 had wanted alternative b to win, he would have first set a against c, then b against c, in which case c defeats a and b defeats c.

Now let members 1, 2, and 3 have the preference relations as shown in Figure 3.3. Given the preferences depicted in Figure 3.3, if we ask these three members to vote on each pair of alternatives, a clear winner emerges. When faced with the choice between a and b, M_2 and $M_3{}^*$ choose b and M_1 chooses a. Thus, b defeats a in a pairwise comparison. When faced with the choice between b and c, M_1 and M_2 choose b and M_3 chooses c. Thus, *b* defeats *c* in a pairwise comparison. And, finally, when faced with the choice between *c* and *a*, M_2 and M_3* choose *c* and M_1 chooses *a*. Thus, *b* defeats *a*, *b* defeats *c*, and *c* defeats *a*. Therefore, the group of three voters prefers *c* to *a* and *b* to *c*, and *b* emerges as the clear winner. No matter in what order the three pairs of alternatives are placed before members 1, 2, and 3 for a vote, *b* always emerges as the winner. For the set of preferences depicted in Figure 3.3, there exists an outcome that can defeat all others in pairwise comparisons. Such a winner is known as a *Condorcet winner*.

Even when preferences are such that a Condorcet winner exists, an agenda setter can influence the final outcome. However, unlike the case in which there is no Condorcet winner (a cycle), the agenda setter cannot necessarily achieve his own most-preferred outcome. Assume that the agenda setter is M_1, whose most-preferred outcome is alternative *a*. No matter in which order he presents the pairwise comparisons among alternatives, *a* can never defeat either *b* or *c*. If *a* is set against *b*, then *b* wins; if *a* is set against *c*, then *c* wins. Thus, the agenda setter can prevent the Condorcet winner, in this case *b*, from winning, but, unless he is a dictator, he can do nothing to ensure that his own first choice will win.

In Figure 3.4, I depict graphically the preference relations presented in Figure 3.3, in which a Condorcet winner exists. The original preferences of M_3 are depicted by a dashed line; the new preferences of M_3 and M_3* are depicted by a solid line. Notice that preference relations M_1, M_2, and M_3* all slope continuously upward or downward or are upwardly peaked. Preferences with this quality are said to be *single-peaked*. As Duncan Black (1958) first showed, a set of preferences with a Condorcet winner always has the quality of being *single-peaked*.

Single-peaked preferences are such that a given voter's preference for other alternatives monotonically decreases on either side of his ideal point. The single-peaked curve is symmetric, so that the farther away an alternative is from a voter's ideal point, the less the voter prefers that alternative. Note that the curve describing the original preference relation of M_3 (indicated by a dashed line) is not monotonically decreasing, so that it is not possible to assume that the farther away an alternative is from M_3's ideal point, the less M_3 prefers that point. On the contrary, *a* is farther from *c* than *b*, but M_3 prefers *a* to *b*. The original preferences of M_3 are therefore not single-peaked. However, M_3's alternate preferences, M_3*, are single-peaked, because M_3* prefers *b* to *a*, and *b* is closer to *c* than is *a*.

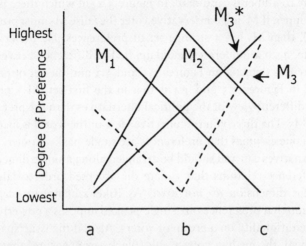

Figure 3.4. Graphical representation of noncyclical preferences. The preferences for voters M_1 and M_2 remain the same. M_3's new preference ordering (labeled M_3^*) is shown by a solid line, and the old preference ordering is shown by a dashed line. When preferences are not cyclical, this means that visually they are "single peaked"; that is, each voter's preference ordering is a single-peaked function of the same underlying continuum. In this case, that continuum ranges from a to c.

In an interesting passage, Riker (1982, pp. 126, 128) discusses the implications of the assumption that preferences are single-peaked:

Single-peakedness is important because it has an obvious political interpretation. Assuming a single political dimension, the fact that a profile [a set of orderings of alternatives by a set of voters] is single-peaked means the voters have a common view of the political situation, although they may differ widely on their judgments. Person i may choose $D_i = x \, y \, z$, and person j may choose $D_j = z \, y \, x$; yet they agree that x is at one end of the scale, z at the other, and y in the middle, which means they agree entirely on how the political spectrum is arranged. This kind of agreement is precisely what is lacking in a cycle, where voters disagree not only about the merits of alternatives but even about where alternatives are on the political dimension.

To see what Riker means, assume that in Figures 3.2 and 3.4, a stands for Liberal, b stands for Moderate, and c stands for Conservative. Implicit in such an arrangement is the assumption that a liberal voter prefers a moderate candidate to a conservative candidate because the views of a moderate candidate are closer to his ideal point than those of a conserva-tive candidate. By the same logic, a conservative voter prefers a moderate candidate to a liberal candidate. In Figure 3.2, in which there is no Condorcet winner, if M_3 is a conservative voter (because M_3 most prefers alternative c), then M_3 has a strange set of preferences. He prefers a liberal candidate, a, to a moderate candidate, b. The difference between the set of preferences depicted in Figures 3.1 and 3.2 and the set of preferences depicted in Figures 3.3 and 3.4 is that in the first set, M_3's preferences reflect a different view of the political alternatives than the preferences of M_1 and M_2. The three voters' collective view of the world is inconsistent.

When one assumes that preferences are single-peaked, one is assuming that alternatives can and should be arranged along a single dimension and that preference relations that violate the accepted order of alternatives along that dimension *do not exist*. As Riker's comment suggests, the assumption that preferences are single-peaked imposes a powerful form of collective rationality on a group of voters. Also, if the issue space is one-dimensional, the median voter result (Black 1958) ensures that if preferences are single-peaked, a stable outcome both exists and corresponds to the position of the median voter. Unfortunately, the median voter result does not hold if the number of political dimensions is greater than one, even if we continue to assume that preferences are single-peaked.[6] Imagine a legislature in which the policy space has two dimensions. Let the three deputies, M_1, M_2, and M_3, have ideal points x_1, x_2, and x_3. As illustrated in Figure 3.5, each ideal point is a coordinate in two-dimensional space, where each of the elements corresponds to the deputy's ideal along one of the two dimensions. The first deputy prefers economic policy d_1 and social policy d_2. Therefore, her ideal point is x_1. Ideal points for the second and third deputies are determined in the same manner.

Recall that each deputy's utility function decreases monotonically from his or her ideal point; this means that the further an option is from the deputy's ideal point, the less the deputy prefers that option. In two dimensions, such a preference relation is represented by either a circle or an ellipse. Circular preference relations are called simple Euclidean preferences, and ellipsoid preference relations are called weighted Euclidean preferences. Throughout this book, I assume that preferences are circular. Circular preferences imply that a voter prefers one alternative to another based on the simple Euclidean distance of each alternative to the voter's ideal point. As in a one-dimensional world, a voter prefers alter-

---

[6] Duncan Black discovered the median voter result in 1942, but his results were ignored for over a decade. Duncan Black's contributions to social choice theory and his great difficulty in getting his English colleagues to recognize the significance of his work are discussed in Coase (1994) and McLean and Urken (1995).

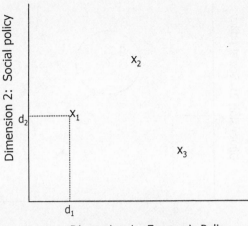

Figure 3.5. Graphical illustration of three ideal points in a two-dimensional policy space. The points x_1, x_2, and x_3 represent the preferred policy positions of three voters along both an economic and social policy dimension. Voter x_1's most preferred economic policy position is d_1, and her most preferred social policy position is d_2. In two dimensions, these preferences can be shown by one point, x_1.

native a to other alternatives if and only if a is closer to his ideal point than all other alternatives.

In general, for any given vote, deputies are offered a choice between two alternatives. A deputy chooses among alternatives based on the proximity of each alternative to his ideal point. He prefers the status quo, q, to some alternative, a, if and only if $\|q - x_2\| < \|a - x_2\|$.

In Figure 3.6 the second deputy must choose between the status quo, q, and an alternative to the status quo, a. Clearly, q is closer to x_2, the second deputy's ideal point, than is a; therefore, deputy 2 votes against a. However, a is closer to both x_1 and x_3 than is q; therefore, in this example, deputies 1 and 3 would vote for a, and that alternative would become the new status quo.

To show how outcomes may cycle in two dimensions (even when preferences are single-peaked; that is, all deputies have monotonically decreasing preferences), let us consider our original three-person legislature when faced with more than two alternatives (Figure 3.7). By inspection (if units are provided, the distances can be determined precisely) we can see that although $|x_1 - a| > |x_1 - q|$ both $|x_2 - a| < |x_2 - q|$ and $|x_3 - a| < |x_3 - q|$; therefore, a defeats the status quo, q. By drawing each member's indifference curves through the status quo, we can see visually

77

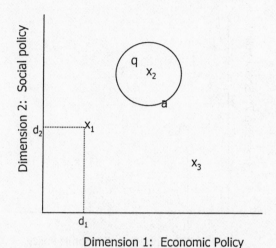

Dimension 1: Economic Policy

Figure 3.6. Spatial representation of x_2's preference for q versus a. Just as in a one-dimensional policy space, we assume that when choosing between alternatives, a voter always prefers the point that is closer to her ideal point. In this diagram, a circle with x_2's ideal point at its center has been drawn so as to pass through alternative a. We see clearly that the status quo, q, is closer to x_2 than is a.

that alternative a is closer to the ideal points of members M_2 and M_3 than is q. The regions where the indifference curves overlap represent the set of alternatives that can defeat q. All points within this petal-shaped region are preferred by a legislative majority to the status quo, q. This region is called the *winset* of q. The winset of a can be easily located by drawing the members' indifference curves through a. Although these curves are not shown in Figure 3.7, alternative b is located within the winset of a; therefore, b defeats a. We can find another point c that defeats b, a point d that defeats c, and a point e that defeats d. Each succeeding alternative is located within the winset of the preceding majority choice.

As in the one-dimensional example of a cycle discussed above, this exercise can be repeated endlessly, because no outcome is preferred to all other outcomes by a majority of group members. Thus, the phenomenon is called "cycling," referring to the fact that outcomes cycle throughout the issue space.[7]

---

[7] Plott (1967) has shown that there does exist a particular configuration of ideal points such that a solution analogous to the median voter result obtains. However, the rigid spatial requirements for a dominant point to exist are such that a dominant point would almost never exist in reality.

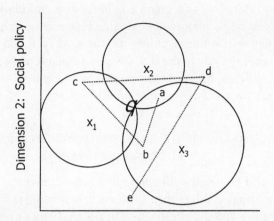

Dimension 1: Economic Policy

Figure 3.7. Cycling in two dimensions. Beginning with the status quo, q, we see from the preference curves drawn around points x_1, x_2, and x_3 that there is a majority made up of voters x_2 and x_3 that prefers alternative a to the status quo. Thus, a defeats q. If we draw preference curves through a, we will find that there is a point, b, preferred by a majority, x_1 and x_3, to a. Thus, b defeats a. Continuing in this manner, we find that c defeats b, d defeats c, and finally e defeats d.

As McKelvey (1976) has shown, it is a straightforward extension of the above example to see that if one of the three members, M_1, M_2, or M_3, has the ability to choose the order in which each pair of alternatives will be voted on, then that member can obtain his own most preferred outcome. Let us assume that M_1 has the necessary power to control the agenda and that his ideal point is located at e. Then, M_1 would first set q against a, then a against b, then b against c, then c against d, and finally d against e, ultimately achieving an outcome that corresponds to his ideal point. If M_1 had immediately started by setting q against e, then q would have been the winner, because q is closer to the ideal points of both M_1 and M_3 (x_1 and x_3, respectively) than is e. However, by strategically choosing the order in which pairs of alternatives come up to vote, M_1 can achieve an outcome that is best for him.

The implications of McKelvey's theoretical discussion of the general lack of equilibria in majority-rule legislatures were immediately appreciated. William Riker was inspired to refer to political science (rather than economics) as the "dismal science," referring to the general lack of equilibria (Riker 1980). It must have seemed unlikely that a complex array of political issues could ever be aligned along a single dimension;

79

and given McKelvey's theorem, equilibria in a multidimensional setting would seem to be almost nonexistent. However, as scholars examined the legislative institution closest to them, they found that outcomes seemed never to cycle in the U.S. Congress (Shepsle 1986, Tullock 1981). The contradiction between theory and practice spurred succeeding scholars to look for mechanisms that prevent cycling.

THE ROLE OF INSTITUTIONAL DESIGN IN INDUCING EQUILIBRIA

Scholars and politicians alike have long known that the rules governing how legislatures conduct their business help determine the power of legislative actors and the effectiveness of the legislature itself (Polsby 1968, Cox 2000). That the institutional design of a legislature can prevent cycling was not apparent until 1979 when Kenneth Shepsle published his path-breaking article, "Institutional Arrangements and Equilibrium in Multidimensional Voting Models" (Shepsle 1979).

In this paper, Shepsle showed how procedural rules enable legislatures to avoid the problem of cyclical majorities. In his words (p. 29), "institutional structure – in the form of rules of jurisdiction and amendment control – has an important independent impact on the existence of equilibrium and, together with the distribution of preferences, co-determines the characteristics of the equilibrium state(s) of collective choice processes." In his model, institutional structure in the form of a stylized committee system induces an equilibrium that he calls a structure-induced equilibrium (SIE). As defined by Shepsle, an SIE is any allowable point in the issue space for which there is no alternative that is preferred by a majority of legislators. Although the location of the SIE depends on the preferences of the committee members, the existence of an equilibrium does not. Thus, a structure-induced equilibrium can exist when a preference-induced equilibrium does not.

There are three basic conditions, enforced by the rules of the institution, which make an SIE possible: (1) Each committee is responsible for a single jurisdiction, which means that all proposed legislation must pass through a specific committee before it reaches the floor for a final vote; (2) once a proposal reaches the floor, nongermane amendments are not allowed; and (3) preferences are single-peaked.

According to Keith Krehbiel (Krehbiel 1988, p. 269), "The keys to Shepsle's SIE are formal rules that divide labor and responsibility. In particular, Shepsle posits a committee system as a set of committees, each of which consists of a subset of the legislature. Just as the committee system divides labor by assigning different legislators to different committees, a jurisdictional system divides responsibilities by assigning different dimensions, x_j, of the m-dimensional policy space to different committees." Thus, there is a "one-to-one-to-one relationship between committees, jurisdictions and single dimensions within the policy space." Furthermore, by assuming that committee decisions are made within one-dimensional jurisdictions, Shepsle's model (Krehbiel 1988, p. 270) "provides the potential for theoretically reverting to [Duncan] Black's world of majority voting in a one-dimensional choice space when legislators have single-peaked preferences." Therefore the final committee proposal will correspond to the position of the median member of the committee. The germaneness rule serves to enforce the jurisdictional monopoly of the committees.

Shepsle's legislative model, although highly stylized, demonstrated the practical importance of institutional design. Yet, although the predictions of the model were borne out in Congress (no cycling), legislative practice was not nearly so clean as the model implied. Since 1979, formal legislative scholars in scores of publications have fleshed out the model of committees and rules, incorporating new institutional elements to bring the model more in line with empirical reality (Shepsle and Weingast 1984a, 1987; Weingast and Marshall 1988; Bach and Smith 1988; Weingast 1989; Krehbiel 1991; Snyder 1992; Londregan and Snyder 1994; Sinclair 1995; Schickler and Rich 1997; Cox 2000). In most of these studies, the goal is to better understand how institutions structure social choices. Although Shepsle (1979) wrote that rules merely "co-determine" (along with preferences) the location of equilibria, for a decade afterwards, succeeding scholars paid little attention to the role of preferences in organizing legislatures. When scholars began again to examine seriously the role of preferences in legislative choices, they did so in the context of the political party and its organization (Rhode 1991, Kiewiet and McCubbins 1991).

In their book *Legislative Leviathan*, Cox and McCubbins (1993, p. 270) characterize political parties as "legislative cartels," with the majority party acting at any given time as the cartel. The majority party asserts its power by means of its control over the appointment of committee chairmen. The committee chairs have the ability to affect the legislative agenda in two ways: They can veto the legislative initiatives of the minority party as well as push their own party's legislative initiatives onto the floor. Committee chairs follow the dictates of the party leadership to the extent that the party has the power to remove them as committee chairs.

The attention to the role of parties in Congress can be seen as a renewed effort to understand the role of preferences in determining social choices. Cox and McCubbins' "cartel model" of Congress suggested an additional institutional corrective to the original McKelvey "chaos" model. Where Shepsle's model showed how institutional organization (in particular, the committees) affects legislative decision making, Cox and McCubbins reminded us that the preferences of key actors within the organization (in this case, committee chairmen) determine the kinds of policy initiatives that the legislature considers. Political parties control committee assignments and the crucial decision of who will chair the committees; therefore, they play an important *structural* role in Congress: Political parties determine the location of the SIE. Thus, it is through political parties that preferences influence Congress.

In his paper entitled "A Model of a Legislature with Two Parties and a Committee System," John Aldrich provides an elegant formalization of the relationship between committees and parties in the institutional organization of a two-party legislature. In Aldrich's model, the legislature is organized *by* parties *into* committees, and the relative importance of committees versus parties in ensuring legislative stability depends on the preferences of the representatives in each party. By showing formally how "the two-party structure can induce equilibrium through agenda control," Aldrich (1995a, p. 182) reaches the important insight that either a pure committee model (such as the SIE model) or a party model in which parties control the legislative agenda, can, in principle, solve the collective choice or chaos problem.

In his model, legislatures have either strong parties or strong committees. Strong parties are those in which members have homogeneous preferences, and weak parties are those in which members have heterogeneous preferences. Thus, parties are strengthened when party member preferences are homogeneous, and committees are strengthened when party member preferences are heterogeneous. By extension, when committees are too weak to contribute to legislative stability, the role of parties, and hence the importance of homogeneous preferences, becomes crucial in determining whether or not a legislature can make lasting decisions.

To illustrate the relationship between deputy preferences and party versus committee strength, he describes two extreme sets of conditions. When the preferences of the parties' members are homogeneous, implying that the members of one party hold quite different preferences than the members of the other party but hold similar preferences to each other, there are clear policy distinctions between the parties. In this situation, parties are strengthened. When the preferences of the parties' members are heterogeneous, implying that the members of one party are almost indistinguishable from the members of the other party, the policy goals of the parties are indistinguishable. In this situation, committees are strengthened. As in the Cox and McCubbins model, in Aldrich's model the parties are more or less powerful depending on their ability to control committees. When the policy preferences of parties diverge, party leaders control the legislation proposed by committees, using the threat of replacement of committee chairmen. However, when the policy preferences of parties are similar, "there is no effective partisan constraint on committee chairs ... and the action shifts to the committees" (Cox and McCubbins 1993, p. 193).

Although others, such as Rhode (1991, 1995) and Cooper and Brady (1981), have observed that the relative importance of parties and committees is not historically constant, Aldrich's contribution is to show how this relationship can be formalized and to provide a precise statement of the structural role of *preferences* in a legislature.

While other recent work on political parties investigates the role of the party *organization* in a legislature, Aldrich's model provides a framework in which it is possible to discuss preferences – in particular, the organization (or structure) of preferences – as an institutional feature. This is important for my study, because political parties as organizations did not yet exist in the Russian Parliament. Partisan groups existed (I discuss these groups in detail in Chapter 5), but as organizations they were very weak, having almost no capacity to punish or reward their members. In this very young democratic legislature, partisanship was based solely on preferences, but nevertheless it impacted legislative decision making. When deputies were organized into two partisan groups with relatively homogeneous preferences, cycling did not occur despite the fact that the committee system alone could not prevent cycling and despite the fact that these partisan groups had no real organization. The Aldrich model provides the necessary theoretical framework to understand why cycling did not occur before the collapse of the Soviet Union.

The two institutional means of preventing cycling that I have reviewed above speak directly to McKelvey's original proof. So long as preferences are single-peaked, cycling cannot occur in a one-dimensional policy space. Thus, Shepsle's solution – the structure-induced equilibrium – is to show how institutions can break down a multidimensional world into one-dimensional choices. Even if there are more than two decision makers, cycling will not occur. Aldrich's model shows how a two-party system, when preferences within parties are homogeneous, reduces the effective number of legislators to two, even if the policy space is multidimensional. Even if the committee system cannot prevent cycling, majority rule will be well-behaved so long as the members of each party vote together and one party has a majority.

In the U.S. Congress, the institution that inspired both Shepsle and Aldrich, there exist at least two mechanisms to prevent cycling: the committee system and a two-party system. Let us call this feature of the highly institutionalized U.S. Congress *institutional redundancy*. Institutional redundancy implies that when one feature of a legislature can no longer prevent instability, another feature is present to do so. In the Russian Parliament, which lacked institutional redundancy, when the two-party dynamic broke down, the inability of the institutional rules to prevent cycling became apparent.

In the multiparty (or, more accurately, the multipartisan group) world of post-Soviet Russia, conditions in the Russian Parliament closely resembled McKelvey's unstructured majority rule institution. Deputies were organized into several partisan groups, and the issue space was multidimensional. Formal work on the problems of decision making in multiparty legislatures has tended to take the multiparty European parliaments as examples (Laver and Schofield 1990, Huber 1996, Baron 1998, Heller 2001). As with Congressional scholars, experts on parliamentary systems have tended to find more stability than McKelvey's analysis would have suggested, although some European parliaments appear to be subject to instability, at least in the formation and sustenance of cabinets (King et al. 1990, Laver and Shepsle 1996).

Researchers analyzing the multiparty world have tried to discover the extent to which cycles can exist (McKelvey and Schofield 1986, 1987). In McKelvey's original proof, cycling can encompass the entire issue space. Schofield has found that given certain realistic features of a multiparty system, cycling may be confined to a small subset of the issue space called the "cycle set." In a paper entitled "Political Competition and Multiparty Coalition Governments" Schofield (1993) shows how the extent of cycling in a multiparty context depends on the relative strength (number of seats) and the ideological location of the participating parties. Even in a multiparty context, the presence of partisan groups (usually political parties) may reduce the incidence of cycles, in this case because it limits the size of the policy space in which cycling can occur.

Schofield's work is particularly helpful to my study because he provides a tractable method for determining the potential for cycling – the presence of a cycle set. It is one thing to identify and describe an isolated cycle (as I do in Chapter 2), but another thing entirely to determine in a systematic way the periods of time in which cycling is expected. In fact, I did not discover the example of cycling that I discuss in Chapter 2 until after I had carried out the systematic analysis of cycle sets that I now report in Chapter 7. Intuitively, I suspected that cycling was possible after the collapse of the Soviet Union. As I have already stated, conditions were similar to the stylized features of McKelvey's model. However, as my analysis in Chapter 7 shows, cycling was possible in only part of that period, only until the end of 1992. After that, no cycle set existed. Furthermore, Schofield's model provides a way to look for cycling in the voting behavior of partisan groups, a much more tractable alternative to analyzing the voting behavior of 250 individuals.

McKelvey showed that cycling will almost always be a problem in a majority-rule institution with three or more members and a multidimensional policy space, but Schofield's model shows how, once again, the structure of deputies' preferences will influence the scope and incidence of cycles. In this sense, I find the work by Aldrich and by Schofield to be complementary. When institutional design alone cannot prevent cycling, everything depends on the organization of deputy preferences.

SINCERE VERSUS SOPHISTICATED VOTING

Throughout this study, my analysis of the voting behavior of Russian deputies requires two important assumptions that bear directly on my use of the theoretical framework presented above: (1) I assume that deputy preferences are exogenous, and (2) I assume that deputies vote sincerely and thus always choose the alternative that is closest to their ideal point.

My own analysis of the voting record of the parliament as well as the judgment of many observers and scholars suggests it is realistic to assume that Russian deputies voted sincerely during these first three years of democratic politics. Because they were unable to coordinate their members' votes, factions had little organizational influence in the parliament; therefore, deputies were weakly organized (Sobyanin 1994). In a legislature of over 200 deputies, uncoordinated strategic behavior would have had no predictable effect, and it is hard to imagine individual deputies engaging in such behavior. I believe that when deputies voted together, they did so because of shared preferences and not because group leaders coordinated their behavior.[8]

So what then of deputy organizations? Let me reiterate that partisan groups in the Russian parliament were based solely on preferences. When deputies voted together, it was because they thought alike on key issues. Of course, deputies tended to join a particular group, a faction, because the goals of the faction coincided with their own policy goals. Faction leaders were spokespersons for their factions. Members of factions tended to vote alike, some more so than others. In these ways, factions were like political parties anywhere.

CONCLUSIONS

In this chapter, I have highlighted the institutional mechanisms that prevent cycling in highly institutionalized legislatures, namely, committees (design) and political parties (preferences). In the following chapter, I detail the institutional design of the Russian Parliament, leaving a discussion of the role of preferences to later in the book. As I would do for any democratic legislature, I discuss the rules governing the legislative process as well as the details of the committee system. In addition, however, I describe a unique institutional feature of the Russian Parliament, the Presidium, paying particular attention to the ways in which the Presidium provided the parliament's chairman with the power to control the legislative agenda.

---

[8] According to a survey of Russian Supreme Soviet deputies carried out by Timothy Colton in the spring of 1991, about half of the deputies surveyed believed that it is a deputy's duty to vote according to what he thinks is best (Colton 1994). Slightly less than half thought that the deputy should carry out the wishes of the voters. However, because parties were weak, ties to voters were also weak, implying that most deputies would have little knowledge about what voters wanted them to do. In point of fact, most deputies were left to vote according to their consciences or according to their assessment of what was in their own best interest. Finally, at this stage of democratic development, with the memory of the unanimity that the Communist Party of the Soviet Union had demanded of deputies in past, undemocratic, Supreme Soviets, very few deputies could have believed that in a democracy a deputy was obligated to vote with his party.

4

Institutional Design and Implications for Majority Rule

Working within the framework of rational choice theory, scholars have found that certain features of legislatures reduce the likelihood of cycling. In particular, "[i]n legislative settings, the answers invariably center on committees and rules" (Krehbiel 1991, p. 32). Shepsle's 1979 study was the first in a series of studies of the U.S. Congress that investigate how institutional design – the rules governing the legislative process – prevents cycling and enables a legislature to enact coherent and stable policies.[1] At the end of over a decade of research, it was common to refer to a "textbook" Congress, a stable legislature dominated by committees and characterized by its rules (Shepsle and Weingast 1995, p. 3).

The argument of this book hinges on the implications of changes in the organization of deputy preferences; the reason that everything depends on deputy preferences is because at no time was the institutional design of the Russian Parliament sufficient to prevent cycling. In this chapter, I explore the most important rules of procedure, those that affected how the legislature made its decisions.

COMMITTEES AND PRESIDIUM IN THE RUSSIAN PARLIAMENT

The Russian Parliament inherited several features from its predecessor, the Supreme Soviet of the Russian Republic, the most significant of

[1] See classic empirical studies by Fenno (1973, 1978), Ferejohn (1974), and Cooper and Brady (1981); and see the pioneering work in the neo-institutional tradition by Weingast (1979), Denzau and Mackay (1981), Shepsle and Weingast (1984a, 1987), Ferejohn, Fiorina, and McKelvey (1987), Weingast and Marshall (1988), Baron and Ferejohn (1989), Gilligan and Krehbiel (1990), Krehbiel (1991), Snyder (1992), Londregan and Snyder (1994), and Tsebelis and Money (1998), to name only a few.

which were a jurisdiction-based committee system and a central organizing body known as the Presidium. Before Soviet leader Mikhail Gorbachev introduced competitive elections to the Soviet Union, the Russian Supreme Soviet was a rubber-stamp institution that met rarely and, when it did, was dominated by its Presidium. The Presidium was authorized to meet throughout the year and to fulfill the duties and functions of the Supreme Soviet when it was not in session (Hough and Fainsod 1979). In addition, the Presidium fulfilled an organizational role in that it was responsible for preparing and distributing materials to deputies for the several days per year that the full Supreme Soviet met.

Committees existed in the Communist-era Supreme Soviet, and their jurisdictional designations corresponded to important legislative categories such as the budget, agriculture, consumer goods, and youth affairs. However, like the actual sessions of the Supreme Soviet itself, committees were not independent organizations responsible for drafting legislation; they met rarely, and the results of their infrequent consultations came in the form of recommendations rather than draft legislation.

As part of his attempt to increase the democratic character of the soviets, Gorbachev's 1988 changes to the Soviet Union constitution made committees the center of legislative activity. Committees were authorized to work on legislation, and committee chairmen were given seats on the Presidium, both to aid them in organizing legislative activity and to empower them in the legislative process (See Remington 2001, pp. 53–56). Notice, however, that Gorbachev did not abolish the Presidium; instead his reforms were intended to make it a seat of committee strength.

When the newly elected Supreme Soviet of the Russian Republic, soon to be dubbed the Russian Parliament, met for the first time in June 1990, one of the first orders of business was to write the "Rules of Procedure," or *reglament*, that would govern activity in the new legislature.[2] One of the most important changes that deputies made was to expand signifi-

---

[2] The *Reglament*, or Rules of Procedure, signed on October 24, 1990, was published in *Vedomosti*, 1990, No. 26, pp. 383–410, the official journal of record for all laws, resolutions, and other decisions made by the Russian Parliament. *Vedomosti Sezda narodnykh deputatov Rossiiskoi Federatsii i Verkhovnogo Soveta Rossiiskoi Federatsii*. Moscow: Supreme Soviet of the Russian Federation.

cantly the number and variety as well as the responsibility of the committees. In the spirit of Gorbachev's reforms, the committees were empowered to draft legislation and to present their draft to the parliament along with detailed accompanying reports for consideration and possible passage. In addition, although committees were not the only body with the right to initiate legislation, laws were not to be passed until they had been given at least a preliminary reading in the appropriate committee.[3] Presumably this was to ensure that laws initiated by some other body than the committees always passed through the hands of the appropriate committee before being brought to the floor for debate by members of the parliament.

Deputies did not seriously consider altering the role of the Presidium from Gorbachev's vision, although they could have done so. The presence of the Presidium and aspects of its role in the Russian legislature were specified in the constitution; however, the Russian Parliament, in conjunction with the Congress of People's Deputies, made many radical changes to that constitution, including creating the office of Russian President. Deputies could have eliminated the Presidium altogether if they had chosen to do so. The fact that no deputy tried to eliminate the Presidium and there was no debate about whether the Presidium ought to be retained or altered suggests that deputies either (a) did not anticipate the anti-democratic role that the Presidium could play in a legislative setting or (b) simply did not question something that had always been a part of Soviet legislative structure.

After extensive debate during the first session of the Russian Parliament, the structure of the legislature ultimately laid out in the rules and regulations combined both old and new elements. The parliament was divided into two chambers (*palaty*), as it had been in the past, and further divided into committees and commissions, some of which originated in one chamber, some in the other, and some in the legislature as a whole. The activity of the two chambers and of the committees and commissions was coordinated by the Presidium, which, as in the past, served as

---

[3] According to Article 110 of the April 21, 1992 Constitution of the Russian Federation, various persons and organizations had the right to introduce draft legislation to the Supreme Soviet, including the chairman of the parliament, the President of Russia, the Presidium, the committees, individual People's Deputies, and the Constitutional Court. Article 117 of the same version of the Russian Constitution specifies that laws and other decisions of the parliament will "as a rule" be discussed in the parliamentary sessions after a preliminary discussion in the appropriate committee or commission.

the central, organizing body, in charge of such tasks as assigning legislation to committees, distributing committee materials to deputies, ensuring that committees were given the necessary resources to do their work, and scheduling discussion of committee draft proposals and legislation in the sessions of parliament.[4] The members of the Presidium included all committee chairmen, in addition to the chairman of the parliament, his deputy chairmen, and the chairmen of the parliament's two chambers. Because most of the work on draft legislation occurred in the committees, the Presidium's role as coordinator of committee activity was significant. Nonetheless, deputies do not seem to have anticipated the amount of control that the Presidium could amass over the activity of the committees.[5]

There were over thirty committees and commissions[6] in the Russian Parliament, each with jurisdictional responsibilities that were specified in general terms in the rules of procedure. Committees (as distinct from commissions) were formed by the parliament as a whole and were concerned specifically with the preparation of legislation on broad issues pertaining to the Russian Federation, such as the organization and activity of the state, economic reform, and the use of natural resources. The permanent or standing commissions of the parliament were organized according to the different jurisdictional responsibilities of the two chambers that made up the parliament. Before proceeding, a note is required on the parliament's two chambers.

Although the Russian Parliament was divided into two chambers, it was *not* a bicameral legislature. The two chambers (*palaty*) of the Russian Parliament, the Soviet of the Republic[7] and the Soviet of

---

[4] Information on the Presidium is gleaned from Articles 37 through 45 of the *Reglament*.

[5] It is clear that such seemingly innocuous organizational powers could easily become a source of influence. For scholars of the former Soviet Union, it is interesting to note the analogy between Khasbulatov's control of the Presidium and Joseph Stalin's control of the Secretariat of the Communist Party of the Soviet Union. In each case, ideological individuals naively overlooked the powers inherent in a position that gave its occupant control over the agenda of the parent organization.

[6] Information on the committees is gleaned from Articles 26 through 36 of the *Reglament* and from the Law on the Standing Commissions of the Palats and on the Committees of the Supreme Soviet of the RSFSR, signed on November 21, 1991, Law No. 1914-I. The text of this law was published in *Vedomosti*, 1991, No. 4, pp. 152–161.

[7] The members of the Soviet of the Republic were deputies who had run in any of the 900 territorial districts, which were based on the entire territory of Russia.

Nationalities,[8] were a holdover from the Soviet past. The purpose of having a Soviet of Nationalities as distinct from the Soviet of the Republic was to provide visible and distinct representation to the autonomous regions and republics within the Russian Federation. Thus, the two chambers were jurisdictionally but not procedurally distinct.[9] Major parliamentary debates and votes occurred in joint meetings of the chambers; and even when working separately, chambers considered identical versions of draft legislation. Thus, the procedural means by which bicameralism can induce stability, as Tsebelis and Money (1998) describe, could not work in the Russian Parliament.

The commissions of the Soviet of the Republic were formed around issues having to do with the social and economic development and culture of the Russian Federation as a whole. The commissions of the Soviet of Nationalities were formed around issues of equal rights for all peoples in the Russian Federation. In particular, these commissions were concerned with the autonomous *oblasts*, autonomous *okrugs*, and minority peoples of the Russian Federation. Thus, the two chambers each had a different set of commissions, whereas the committees were located specifically in neither chamber. Because differences among the committees and commissions were jurisdictional but all procedural rules and rights were the same, throughout the rest of the book I lump the committees and commissions together and call them simply "committees."

Committees were the basic legislative unit in the Russian Parliament. Because all legislation that was debated in the parliament had first to be discussed in committee, all legislative proposals had first to be assigned

---

[8] The members of the Soviet of Nationalities were deputies who had run in any of the 168 national-territorial districts. These districts were designed to represent the 89 administrative units in Russia and to give extra weight to those administrative units based on a distinct nationality, such as in the case of most of the autonomous regions and territories.

[9] For the Soviet of the Republic, the population of the region determined the number of deputies from each region; but for the Soviet of Nationalities, the number of deputies was based on the minority population of Russia. Therefore, in the Congress of People's Deputies, there were far more deputies from territorial districts than from national-territorial districts; but in the Supreme Soviet, the number of deputies from each type of district was the same, because each chamber had equal numbers of members. Therefore, it was far easier for a deputy elected from a national-territorial district to become a member of the approximately 250-member Supreme Soviet than for a deputy elected from a territorial district.

to a particular committee. After a draft law was first submitted to the Presidium for registration, it was the Presidium's job to choose a head committee and to assign the draft to that committee as well as to the Committee on Legislation. The Presidium's power to appoint a head committee and to assign draft legislation to that committee was clearly laid out in Article 67.[10] The head committee was responsible for preparing the project for consideration by the parliament. In many cases, more than one committee worked on the preparation of draft legislation; it was the head committee's responsibility to facilitate the work of multiple committees (if they existed) and to present the final report on the draft when the law was submitted to the legislature. The success or failure of draft legislation, especially controversial legislation such as that bearing directly on economic or political reform, depended very much on the predisposition of the chairman of the head committee; hence, it depended on the Presidium's choice of head committee.

As Joel Ostrow's study of the parliamentary budget committee suggests, committees were given a great deal of deference by their fellow deputies, especially on complex or technical issues (Ostrow 1996). The strong support of the relevant committee was important, if not essential, to the passage of legislation, especially legislation that originated outside of the parliament. Many of the most important and controversial pieces of legislation that the parliament considered originated in the Russian government; and without the support of the head committee, such legislation was almost certain to fail.

For example, the Law on Privatization, which the parliament debated in June 1992, was submitted by the Ministry of Privatization under the auspices of its minister, Anatoly Chubais; the head committee to which it was assigned was the Committee on Economic Reform. The Law on Privatization was a controversial piece of legislation that the parliament came close to defeating. A key reason why the law passed was because in this instance the chairman of the head committee, Sergei Krasavchenko, was a strong supporter of market reform, and his favorable supplementary report and active lobbying influenced deputies.

This example underscores the powerful role that committees and committee chairmen played in making sure that legislation passed or was

---

[10] See changes to Article 67 of the *Reglament* in the Law on Changes and Additions to the Rules of Procedure of the Supreme Soviet of the Russian Federation, passed in June 1992 and published in *Vedomosti*, 1992, No. 10.

defeated. It also demonstrates the importance of the assignment process. So long as the Presidium enforced jurisdictional distinctions among committees, the Presidium maintained an essential characteristic of the equilibrium-inducing committee system. However, if the Presidium assigned legislation to committees based not on a committee's particular jurisdiction but on whether or not the committee chairman was a political ally, then the deference paid to committees by deputies would become a source of power for the Presidium, thus compromising the ability of the committee system to induce equilibria.

A second important source of committee vulnerability, the admissibility of nongermane amendments, was a product of the legislative process. In the Russian Parliament, legislation was passed in two steps, or "readings." In the first reading, the parliament, as a body, decided whether or not to accept the draft legislation and its basic elements or to reject it. During the discussion, deputies could suggest changes; however, the forum in which these suggestions were considered was the second reading. Finally, if a majority of deputies passed the law in the first reading – called passing the draft law *as a basis* – the parliament decided on the time necessary for preparation of the final draft and the holding of the second reading (*Reglament,* Article 76).

In preparation for the second reading, deputies submitted amendments in written form to the Presidium. Article 77 of the Rules of Procedure describes the Presidium's role in collecting amendments and disseminating these to the committees. It was the Presidium's job to submit all amendments to the head committee at least two weeks before the draft was scheduled for review in the parliament. Each amendment, unless the committee incorporated it into the text of the law, had to be affixed to the draft for consideration by the parliament during the second reading. Thus, committees could not reject amendments, even those that were nongermane or which gutted the legislation under consideration. Also significant, the Presidium acted as a conduit from deputies to the head committee so that the head committee did not have direct access to amendments.

A second reading occurred in joint sessions of the chambers. First the draft had to be passed as a basis by a majority from each chamber. Next, each article, section, or chapter of a draft law was voted on separately. If the article, section, or chapter was first passed as a basis, then all amendments (which had been received by the Presidium in written form and then passed along to the head committee) were put to vote one by one. When all amendments had been discussed, the amended articles, sections, or chapters were discussed and passed as a whole.[11] Finally, the draft law was put to vote as a whole. At this stage, every part of the draft law had already been approved, so that the final vote was almost always unanimously in favor.

Although committees were, according to the rules of procedure, allowed to read all amendments before presenting their version of a draft law, committees were not authorized to omit amendments from the text presented to deputies unless the amendment was already subsumed in the text or similar to some other amendment. In other words, the committee could not reject hostile amendments. Thus, it was not only possible for an amendment that gutted the draft law under consideration to be brought to the floor along with the draft law, but it was also possible for this amendment to pass.

There were numerous examples, especially in Sessions 4 and 5, where such hostile amendments were debated on the floor. For example, a conservative deputy[12] offered an amendment that would have ruined the intent of the Law on Privatization. The amendment did not pass because the chairman of the parliament as well as the main supporter of the law, Minister of Privatization Anatoly Chubais, pointed this out to the deputies. In this case, politicians outside of the committee used their clout to prevent the committee from being "defeated." In cases where politicians did not interfere, there was little that a committee chairman could do other than appeal to the legislature. In general, however, most amendments were either trivial or on point, and they were subsumed into the text between the first and second readings.

A third weakness of committees concerned access to the information and resources necessary to prepare draft legislation. In his book on legislative organization, Krehbiel (1991, p. 2) stresses that "resources . . . are necessary conditions for success in the legislative arena. Without resources – such as time, money, and staff support – a legislator cannot study and learn about the content and consequences of legislative policies." Because the Presidium was responsible for organizing the activity of the committees, committees depended on the Presidium for access to the resources and information necessary to prepare draft legislation. The Presidium's control over the information and resources necessary to committees was clearly specified in the rules of procedure.

---

[11] *Reglament*, Article 79.   [12] Vladimir Isakov, the head of Russian Unity.

According to Articles 41 and 42 of the Rules of Procedure, it was the responsibility of the Presidium to support the work of the parliament, including the parliamentary committees. "[I]n connection with the coordination of the activity of the ... committees, the Presidium renders legal, organizational, material, technical and other necessary assistance to their work."[13] In addition, the Presidium "supports the people's deputies by means of official publications and materials about the activity of the Congress of People's Deputies, the Supreme Soviet, and its Presidium, the standing committees, and also by means of references and other materials."[14] In other words, the Presidium allocated office space, office equipment (including a phone), office supplies, administrative support, and even passes to enter the building (critical to outside experts).

The Presidium's role in allocating parliamentary resources is implied in Articles 24, 41, and 42 of the Rules of Procedure. Article 24 indicates that remuneration of the activity of specialists who are working in the committees is drawn from the budget of the Supreme Soviet. However, according to Articles 41 and 42, it is the Presidium that is responsible for supporting the work of these specialists; hence it is the Presidium that will make sure they are paid. Thus, although its power over the budget is only vaguely discussed in the rules of procedure, its mandate to "support" the working of the parliament provided the legal basis for the Presidium's control over the parliament's budget.

Just as the Presidium's control over committee assignments and the amendment process could work to weaken committees, the Presidium's budgetary control could serve the same purpose. By withholding funds for the remuneration of specialists and by denying office space, staff, phones, and other necessary sources of support for the activity of a particular committee, the Presidium could prevent any committee from fulfilling its duties. Interviews with former deputies indicate that after the collapse of the Soviet Union the Presidium was able to abuse its control over resources to impede the work of certain committees in just those ways. When discussing the problems that committees in the Russian Parliament faced, at least two former deputies (one the chairman of a committee, the other the chairman of a subcommittee) said that their biggest problem was gaining access to resources and information.[15]

---

[13] Article 41 of the *Reglament*. [14] Article 42 of the *Reglament*.
[15] Viacheslav Bragin and Lev Ponomarev in interviews with author in June 1996.

Notice that committees were vulnerable only so long as the Presidium used its powers to violate committee autonomy. The powers of the parliament's Presidium, although formidable, were not in themselves sufficient to ensure that committees were weak. Committee chairmen, who made up the overwhelming majority of members of the Presidium, could use the organizational and budgetary powers of the Presidium to mitigate the potential weaknesses of the committees. If a majority of the committee chairmen acted in concert, they could ensure that the Presidium enforced rather than manipulated committee jurisdictions; in this way, a strong Presidium could have contributed to strong committees. In addition, the fact that amendments were submitted first to the Presidium could have provided committee chairmen with the means to challenge amendments before they were submitted to the relevant head committee, thus ensuring that nongermane amendments had as little impact on committee-generated legislation as possible. And, of course, the Presidium could make certain that committees had the necessary resources to prepare legislation.

Thus, the Presidium could have served – and, judging from the intent of Gorbachev's original legislation to increase the autonomy of committees in Soviet legislatures, probably was meant to serve – as a means to enforce committee autonomy. Because the committee chairmen constituted by far the majority of the Presidium's members, the Presidium could have enforced committee strength and helped create the conditions for the existence of a structure-induced equilibrium (SIE). Prior to the collapse of the Soviet Union, when cycling did not occur, the committee system in conjunction with the Presidium appears to have done so; however, after the collapse of the Soviet Union, the Presidium became the means by which the power and autonomy of the committees was undermined. Given that the basic structure of the committee system and its relationship with the Presidium did not change over the life of the parliament, why did an institutional design that was able to prevent cycling before the collapse fail to do so afterwards?

So long as a two-party dynamic characterized the parliament (and its Presidium), the legislature was organized *by parties into committees*, in a fashion similar to that in the U.S. Congress. The majority coalition used the Presidium to promote a democratic agenda. However, once the two-party dynamic broke down, the lack of a stable majority left the Presidium open to domination by its chairman.

Committee chairmen constituted over two-thirds of the members of the Presidium. In a significant difference with the U.S. Congress, these chairmen were not chosen by a majority party; instead the members of their committees elected them. Therefore, the partisan affiliations of the committee chairs were determined by the majorities in each committee rather than by a parliamentary majority party. For the most part, deputies were assigned to the committee of their choice, and the lists of committee members were approved by the parliament as whole during its first session.[16]

According to parliamentary scholar Alexander Sobyanin,[17] because Boris Yeltsin (the chairman of the Parliament for its first one and a half years) was a strong democrat, the democrats had a slight advantage over the conservatives in getting their allies onto committees, especially onto key committees such as the Legislation Committee and the Committee on Economic Reform. Remington et al. (1994, p. 165) note that Yeltsin and his allies had some success in stacking committees with more reform-minded deputies. If we use Sobyanin's index (discussed in Chapter 1) to assess whether or not committee members were democrats or conservatives in this period, we find that more committees had a majority of democratic members than the other way around.[18] And, as we would expect, a substantial majority of the committee chairs (which translated into more than half of the members of the Presidium) could be classified as democrats before the collapse.[19]

The remaining members of the Presidium – the chairmen and deputy chairmen of the parliament and its chambers – were elected by the deputies at large and, not surprisingly, were almost evenly split between reformers and conservatives in the period before the collapse. On the whole, before the collapse of the Soviet Union, the partisan makeup of the Presidium reflected the partisan structure of the legislature as a whole; that is, it was characterized by a quasi-two-party dynamic, and the democrats were in the majority. After the collapse of the Soviet

---

[16] Lev Ponomarev in interview with author, June 1996, Moscow.

[17] Personal interview with author, June 1996.

[18] In the period before the collapse of the Soviet Union (when definitions of "democrat" and "conservative" had meaning), democrats dominated the important Committee on Legislation, as well as committees on Economic Reform, Defense, Social Policy, Foreign Affairs, Freedom of Conscience, Human Rights, and Mass Media. Conservatives also dominated certain committees – for example, the Committees on Agrarian Questions, Industry and Energy, Cultural Heritage of Peoples', and Women's Affairs. Other committees were fairly evenly split between democrats and conservatives.

[19] The median Sobyanin index for members of the Presidium was 63. This index is relevant only for the period before the collapse of the Soviet Union.

Union, as the result of a dramatic change in the number of issues and policy dimensions facing the deputies, the preferences of Presidium members became heterogeneous, just as did the preferences of the parliament as a whole.[20]

Before the collapse of the Soviet Union, the chairman's ability to dominate the Presidium was limited both by his own coalition, on which he was dependent for his position, and by a strong and active opposition; however, when the number of deputy groups and the number of dimensions of debate increased after the collapse of the Soviet Union, no stable majority existed that could block a chairman's misuse of power. Thus, the chairman's ability to dominate the Presidium depended on the structure of deputy preferences. The institutional problem of the parliament was not simply the presence of the Presidium; it was the presence of a Presidium that provided significant powers to the chairman when the preferences of deputies were heterogeneous and the policy space was no longer limited to one dimension. Even in the absence of multiple issue dimensions, such a chairman would have been able to exert enormous influence; but, in the presence of multiple issue dimensions and cycling, such a chairman was able to dominate legislative outcomes in the way that McKelvey (1976) predicts.

While a stable majority existed on the Presidium, committees were strong and active, and cycling did not occur. However, once the two-party dynamic disappeared, the Presidium failed to enforce committee autonomy, and so the conditions for the existence of an SIE disappeared; the committee chairmen were incapable of organized activity and thus could not prevent the chairman of the parliament from gaining more and more control over the activity of the Presidium and, ultimately, of the parliament.

THE POWERS OF THE CHAIRMAN AND AGENDA CONTROL

Interestingly, in the rules and regulations of the Russian Parliament, the chairman's role is described in fairly innocuous terms. Based only on a reading of the rules of the parliament, one would conclude that the most important duty of the chairman was to conduct the joint sessions of the

---

[20] Evidence for the heterogeneity of Presidium member preferences is presented in Chapter 6.

chambers of the parliament.[21] The person chairing a particular meeting had the sole right to call on speakers during the meeting and to dismiss speakers under certain circumstances. It was the responsibility of the person chairing a meeting to summarize the issue being voted on, to organize the vote, and to report the results of the vote. There is no question that the chairman was at a distinct advantage in getting himself heard; however, while the power that accrued to the chairman as a result of his role in conducting the meetings of the parliament was important, it was trivial when compared to those powers that accrued to him in his capacity as chairman of the Presidium. And, although the particular powers of the Presidium were well described in the rules, nowhere in the rules were the powers of the chairman of the Presidium made explicit. He is, simply, the head of the Presidium.[22]

According to all observers, both inside and outside the parliament, Yeltsin and Khasbulatov were very different kinds of chairmen. In comparing the styles of the two chairmen, Ponomarev described Yeltsin as more of a "leader" and described Khasbulatov as more of a "manipulator." It was precisely because he was *not* the head of a majority coalition that Khasbulatov relied much more on his ability to manipulate the Presidium and its resources than did Yeltsin. Differences in the structure of deputy preferences had a direct bearing on the means by which each influenced the parliamentary agenda.

As the leader of the democratic majority, Yeltsin's position as chairman of the Presidium gave him important powers with which to pursue his agenda, so long as that agenda was supported by the majority democratic coalition on the Presidium. The democratic committee chairs supported the democratic agenda in the Presidium, spearheaded democratic legislation in their respective committees, and shepherded democratic legislation on the floor. That is, the parliament's agenda reflected that of the majority coalition. Also, just as important, a unified conservative opposition, which utilized similar tactics to resist the democratic majority, consistently opposed Yeltsin and the democrats. So long as he maintained the democrats' support, Yeltsin was immune to attacks from the conservative opposition. If Yeltsin had tried to deviate from the agenda of the democratic coalition, he would have risked losing the support of at least some of its adherents and thus jeopardized policies

---

[21] It is relevant to note that both Yeltsin and Khasbulatov frequently delegated responsibility for chairing meetings of the parliament.

[22] Article 37 of the *Reglament*.

near and dear to him, in particular the creation of the office of Russian President.[23]

Thus, during the period of Yeltsin's tenure, the parliamentary agenda was monopolized by items having to do with Russia's political and economic sovereignty from the Soviet Union; these items included several resolutions condemning the Soviet government, passage of separate treaties between Russia and other republics of the Soviet Union, a series of laws establishing economic independence from Moscow including the transfer of formerly Soviet enterprises to Russian control, an actual declaration of sovereignty, and the creation of a Russian Presidency.

During this period, the communist conservative opposition attempted to remove Yeltsin from his position as chairman on several occasions, a reflection of their size (a near-majority) and unity (homogeneity of preferences). Of course, because the communist and democratic coalitions were so nearly even in size, the communists could never muster the required two-thirds vote to remove the chairman.

After the collapse of the Soviet Union, the preferences of Presidium members were heterogeneous, and, as in the legislature as a whole, there was no longer a stable majority among the members of the Presidium. Ruslan Khasbulatov, chairman of the parliament and its Presidium from November 1991 until its dissolution in September 1993, was elected with the grudging support of democratic deputies in recognition of his prominent role in defending the Russian Parliament during the August coup attempt, but he was never the leader of any parliamentary group, certainly not of a majority. At first, in the absence of a stable majority on the Presidium, the chairman had no success in pursuing a coherent political agenda. He vacillated repeatedly from supporting to opposing reform.

Although his lack of majority support at first limited Khasbulatov's ability to pursue a particular political agenda, the fact that no stable majority existed on the Presidium or in the parliament also meant that there was no majority to oppose a chairman's behavior. Khasbulatov was able to abuse the levers of power provided by the Presidium because there was no majority to prevent it. As one would expect, his violations of procedural rules increased over time.

Over the course of his tenure as chairman, Khasbulatov used control over the budget to undermine committees whose chairmen resisted his efforts to control their activities and who criticized him for doing so.

---

[23] The logic of this argument is similar to that offered by Krehbiel (1991, pp. 18–19) in his discussion of "the remote majoritarian postulate."

Observers[24] acknowledge that Khasbulatov withheld necessary operating funds from committees of which he did not approve, thereby reducing their staff, their access to phones and other equipment, and their office space. He denied admittance passes to experts that such committees needed. Some observers[25] claim that Khasbulatov bribed members of the Presidium with summer houses, apartments in Moscow, and trips abroad.

Khasbulatov's attack on committee autonomy and strength grew as his power over Presidium members increased. According to Viacheslav Bragin, chairman of the Committee on Mass Media and thus a member of the Presidium, it was during the year of 1992 (Khasbulatov's first year as chairman) that "there was a reduction in the role of the committee chairmen in the Presidium, because Khasbulatov increasingly usurped this power." Ponomarev, who was occasionally present at Presidium meetings, agreed. "The meetings of the Presidium gradually changed." While Yeltsin was chairman, in meetings of the Presidium, questions were decided by vote. While Khasbulatov was chairman, gradually fewer and fewer questions were decided by vote. "Khasbulatov simply directed the Presidium." Matters were approved by fiat, because there were no objections. "Since to object is always harder than to acquiesce, the members gradually ceased objecting. Thus, a distressing silence arose."[26]

While he was chairman, Khasbulatov was the subject of intense and wide-ranging criticism not only from his peers in parliament, but from the government, the press, and academic circles.[27] Despite the fact that it was widely acknowledged that Khasbulatov was abusing his position as head of the Presidium, there was no serious threat to remove him from office. The only effort to punish Khasbulatov for his transgression of parliamentary rules never made it out of the Presidium; committee chairmen could not agree even to discuss the chairman's violations of parliamentary rules.

There was simply no group large or unified enough to sustain an effort to remove Khasbulatov.

---

[24] Sergei Markov, interview with author, Moscow, December 1993.
[25] Bragin and Ponomarev in interviews with author in June 1996.
[26] Bragin in interview with author in June 1996.
[27] In interviews with me, three former deputies (two of Khasbulatov's critics as well as one ally) as well as two legislative scholars (Markov and Sobyanin) described Khasbulatov's violation of procedural rules. Throughout his tenure as chairman, Khasbulatov was the subject of countless articles in the press – especially in the newspaper *Izvestia*, which discussed his violation of parliamentary rules.

By gaining control over the Presidium, Khasbulatov also gained control over the parliament's agenda, but his agenda control differed from that of Yeltsin. As chairman, Yeltsin controlled the parliament's agenda in the manner that the majority party in the U.S. Congress controls the congressional agenda. He was the head of a majority coalition, and as such he was both empowered and limited by the majority – his agenda reflected the political goals of the majority. Khasbulatov controlled the agenda in the absence of a stable majority; hence, his agenda reflected the political goals of no one but himself.

FROM DOMINANCE OF THE PRESIDIUM TO DOMINANCE OF THE PARLIAMENT

While Yeltsin was chairman, there was no discord between the chairman's agenda and the goals of the *parliamentary* majority. So long as the two-party dynamic continued, Yeltsin's major role as chairman was to articulate the democratic agenda and to make certain that his slight majority held together when it came down to a vote. Yeltsin, an extremely charismatic and persuasive leader, excelled in this role. With each legislative victory, his stature rose. It is accordingly easy to forget that although Yeltsin led the parliament, he did not dominate it. Yeltsin was limited in what he could achieve by the same majority from which he derived his power. When he took a position too far from that of the centrist democrats, he was defeated. Yeltsin achieved his legislative success by recognizing the limits that the parliamentary majority imposed on what he, as chairman, could achieve.

Lacking the support of a parliamentary majority, it might seem at first blush that despite his dominance of the Presidium, Khasbulatov ought to have had no success in pursuing his personal agenda. However, the same conditions that made it difficult for the parliament to get things done – shifting majority coalitions and an increase in the relevant issue dimensions – allowed him to manipulate the parliament's agenda to achieve his own ends. Khasbulatov was able, working through the committees, to influence the content of legislation and the timing of its consideration by the legislature. In addition, he was able to influence the amendment process on particular pieces of legislation, ordering agenda items in a manner exactly analogous to McKelvey's theoretical example. I discuss examples of how Khasbulatov wielded both these kinds of agenda control in Chapter 8.

While it did not cause the conflict between president and parliament, the lack of clarity in the Russian Constitution regarding the distribution of power between the legislative and executive branches of government provided a framework for the confrontation between the two leaders. Recall that at that time the constitution in use was a much-amended version of the 1978 Soviet-era constitution. Although it had been amended to include the office of president, the constitution continued to give prominence and importance to the head, or chairman, of the "Supreme Soviet," the precursor to the parliament.[28] At the same time, the new Russian President was labeled the country's highest official and the head of the executive branch of government.[29] Thus, both the president and the parliament's chairman could, according to the constitution, claim to be preeminent; it was all a matter of interpretation. As Ponomarev explains, although the president was the highest official in Russia, the parliament had the power to decide any question affecting Russia. "[Khasbulatov] thought that since such a point existed [in the constitution] and he was the chairman of the Supreme Soviet [parliament], he might vie with Yeltsin for power."[30]

As Robert Sharlet (1993, p. 319) has described, the essential problem in Russia was the fact that an executive institution, the Russian Presidency, which was created in early April 1991, was simply tacked onto a constitution that emphasized parliamentary powers. "At worst, Russia's system comprised a presidency badly grafted onto a cumbersome parliamentary system. . . . Pure presidentialism and pure parliamentarism were incompatible, even without the reciprocal hostility between Yeltsin and Khasbulatov."

Flaws in the design of executive–legislative relations exacerbated the flaws in the parliament's design. When conditions permitted the chairman of the Presidium to dominate the parliament's agenda and thus control legislative outcomes, ambiguity in the constitutional specification of presidential versus parliamentary powers created an incentive for him to use this control to increase his power vis-à-vis the president.

---

[28] See Article 115 of the April 21, 1992 version of the Russian Constitution (Basic Law). 1992. Moscow: *Izvestia*.
[29] See Chapter 13 and especially Article 131 of the April 21, 1992 version of the Russian Constitution (Basic Law). 1992. Moscow: *Izvestia*.
[30] Quote is from personal interview with author, June 1996, in Moscow.

CONCLUSIONS

Institutional features that prevent cycling in stable, long-lived legislatures may not yet exist in newly created legislatures. In the U.S. Congress, for example, the complex Congressional committee system that organizes the legislative process today was not delineated in the rules of procedure of the earliest Congresses. Committee jurisdictions, prerogatives, and responsibilities instead evolved over time.[31] Paralleling this, I found that in the case of Russia's first national legislature, the rules of procedure, which were written by deputies after the legislature had first convened, were by no means exhaustive. These rules provided no more than a basic framework upon which the parliament could proceed, leaving much of the work of committees, speaker, and other parliamentary bodies unspecified and thus subject to constant reinterpretation. Indeed, an absence of complex rules and norms is a predominant characteristic of all transitional institutions that have been studied so far in the former Soviet Union.[32]

In this chapter, I described the institutional design of the Russian Parliament, paying particular attention to features highlighted by work on the U.S. Congress, namely, committees and rules of procedure. Like the U.S. Congress, the Russian Parliament was organized into committees according to jurisdiction, and all legislation had to pass through the committees before being considered by the legislature as a whole. Also, like Congress, preference-based coalitions worked through the committees to try and achieve their policy goals. Before the collapse of the Soviet Union, when a two-party dynamic dominated the parliament, the interaction of committees and coalitions worked much as Aldrich's model described. However, once the number of partisan groups increased beyond two, it became clear that the committee system alone was unable to induce an SIE.

---

[31] For a history of the evolution of the congressional committee system, see McConachie (1989). For an analysis of the period in which the basic characteristics of the committee system in the modern Congress came into being, see Gamm and Shepsle (1989).

[32] There is now a significant literature on transitional institutions in the former Soviet Union. Work by political scientists on emerging currency markets (Frye and Shleifer 1997), economic development in Russia's regions (Prokop 1996), and the role of informal networks in local governments (Stoner-Weiss 1997) and by economists on privatization (Blasi, Kroumova, and Kruse 1997; Frydman, Rapaczynski, and Turkewitz 1997) underscores the extreme lack of rules and norms that characterizes the institutional environment of a country in transition.

The key to the breakdown in the workability of the democratic institutions of Russia's first three years of transition was a change in the structure of deputy preferences. If there are any lessons to be learned from Russia's experience, one of these must be that in designing democratic institutions, constitutional engineers must pay attention to the fit between institutional design and preferences. Legislatures that are capable of dealing with the difficult problems of a transition are not only the product of well-crafted rules; they are also dependent on the preferences of the participants. In the next chapter I begin my examination of the role that deputies' preferences played in Russia's legislative problems.

5

Issue Dimensions and Partisan Alliances

In the first two chapters, I argue that changes in the structure of deputy preferences transformed the Russian Parliament from a purposive vehicle for political and economic reform into the obedient dupe of an ambitious politician. As the key to why Russia's transitional parliament failed as a democratic, representative institution, it is important to investigate the origins of deputies' preferences as well as how and why they changed.

Philosophers and scholars have focused on two possible sources of the preferences of elected representatives; either the preferences of deputies reflect their ideology or they reflect the collective desires of the constituents who elected them. As philosophers and scholars have noted, either alternative has important implications for the meaning of representative democracy (Burke 1774; Fenno 1973, 1978). It seems likely that the preferences of deputies consist of a combination of (a) personal ideology and (b) attentiveness to constituent demands, and that these will exert greater or lesser influence depending on the strength of the deputy's personal ideology (Budge 1994; Ansolabehere, Snyder, and Stewart 2001) and the strength of the electoral connection (Mayhew 1974, Fiorina 1977, Strom 1990). In stable, long-lived democracies, in which elections to the national legislature have been held for decades or even generations, the electoral connection between citizens and representatives is strong. Voters reelect candidates who successfully represent their interests, and they reject candidates who do not (Fiorina 1981).

Political parties reinforce this electoral connection. By crafting a party program in which the party takes a position on a broad array of distinct issues, political parties provide an informational link between voters and their representatives (Downs 1957). Voters don't need to know how each of their representatives stands on every issue; they need only be familiar with the platform of the party or parties to which their representatives belong. Furthermore, they can rely on the party organization, which has the ability to withhold resources that candidates need, to help compel representatives to vote according to the party platform (Aldrich 1995b).

The fundamental idea behind the electoral connection is that the most important mechanism to inform representatives about what constituents want is the election itself. Almost by definition, in the first few years of a democratic transition, very few elections (usually only one or two) have been held.[1] Deputies may not yet have faced the threat of removal from office. Indeed, deputies may not yet have decided whether or not they will run for office a second time.[2] In the very early years of a transition, the primary motive for doing what constituents want may be absent.

Furthermore, in many countries of the former Soviet Union, political parties did not survive several decades of communist rule; therefore, in the first few years of the transition, political parties were generally unorganized and resource-poor.[3] They were limited in their ability to disseminate information to voters; and, as a result, especially in the first election, voters knew very little about the candidates who were running.[4] Even if voters were aware of candidates' party affiliations (if they had any), they could not be certain that a candidate would adhere to the platform he ran on. Without the organization and financial resources to help candidates get elected, parties could not threaten to withdraw future resources and thus could not force deputies to support the party's platform once elected.

Ian Budge (1994) suggests that when deputies are uncertain that voters know about, understand, or remember the actions of their representatives, they are more likely to behave according to their own or their party's ideology than to constituent demands. Therefore, ideology plays a greater role in determining what policies parties and deputies support than has usually been assumed. Budge's criticism of the basic Downsian

---

[1] During the period in Russia that forms the basis of this study, only one parliamentary election had been held. From March 1990 until December 1995, three elections were held. In Hungary, two parliamentary elections were held between 1990 and 1994. In Poland, two elections were held between 1991 and 1993.

[2] In a 1991–1992 survey of 159 deputies in the Russian Parliament, Timothy Colton found that at that time only 21% were planning to run for reelection (Colton 1994).

[3] At first even the communist parties were not at an advantage, because they tended to be even less adept at electoral politics than the brand-new opposition parties; and, in many cases, communist parties did not have access to their considerable resource base for months or years.

[4] For a discussion of local conditions during the 1990 elections see Andrews and Vacroux (1994), Colton (1990), and Embree (1991).

assumption has direct implications to analyses of representatives during the first few years of a democratic transition, when uncertainty about what voters want and what they will do if they don't get what they want is very high.[5]

Limited electoral experience, weak political parties, and poorly informed constituents lead to only one conclusion: In the first 2–4 years of a democratic transition, the electoral connection is either weak or nonexistent. If representatives either don't know or don't care what their constituents want them to do, and if they owe no allegiance to political parties, it is logical to assume that they will support policies based on their own ideology.[6] This means that once elected, deputies will join parties based solely on the degree to which they agree with a party's position on the issues. If the issues change, a deputy may change his or her partisan affiliation.

At the time of the 1990 parliamentary elections, the first competitive national election in over seventy years, the electoral connection in Russia was weak indeed. The political alliances that formed in the parliament after the election were based solely on shared ideology – they were affiliations of deputies who thought alike on the major issues of the day. These groups were only loosely organized and played very little formal role in parliamentary deliberations. The result was that group leaders had very little control over their members, and members could not be relied upon to vote together. When the issues changed, the groups changed as well. In the following section, I discuss partisan affiliations in the Russian Parliament and describe the changes in these affiliations that occurred over time.

PARTISAN AFFILIATIONS IN THE RUSSIAN PARLIAMENT

Historical Background

At the time of the elections and until December 1991, Russia was a republic of the Soviet Union; indeed, it was the cornerstone of the Union. When Gorbachev launched *glasnost'* in 1988, Russia became the seat of

---

[5] Some scholars emphasize uncertainty as the critical characteristic of transitions to democracy; see, for example, Bunce and Csanadi (1993).

[6] In his 1991–1992 survey of 159 Russian Parliament deputies, Timothy Colton found that 49% of those surveyed believed that a deputy should "do what he considers necessary" rather than "carry out the wishes of voters," an option supported by 36% of respondents (1994). Of those who said they had experienced a conflict of interest between what voters wanted and what they thought was right, 55% said that they did what they thought was right.

a great public debate about the fate of the Soviet Union. Confronted for the first time with the truth about the economic failures, terrible crimes, and overwhelming dishonesty of the Communist regime, people from all walks of life, but especially the Russian intellectuals, wondered what course Russia should adopt for the future (Remnick 1993, Shane 1994). Radicals within the Communist Party of the Soviet Union (CPSU) and intellectuals throughout the scientific and artistic community urged the country to democratize its polity and marketize its economy. The majority of the communist party's bureaucrats dug in their heels, more in resistance to change than in support for any coherent alternative. Gorbachev supported a middle course, a radically reformed version of communism. It was within this political context that the 1990 elections were held.

At the time of the elections, political parties other than the CPSU were illegal. There were, however, tens of clubs, groups, and semipolitical organizations that had emerged during "*glasnost.*" In preparation for the elections, many of the groups that supported democratization united loosely under an "umbrella" organization called Democratic Russia (McFaul and Markov 1993). Democratic Russia became the champion of the position in support of democratization and marketization. The Communist Party opposed the goals of Democratic Russia; however, it was somewhat hampered in its ability to develop an opposing platform because its ostensible leader, Gorbachev, was actively promoting a course of radical reform. In actual fact, fewer and fewer people supported Gorbachev's position (Dunlop 1993). Despite the fact that parties were illegal, the Russian election resembled a two-party contest.

Democratic Russia was at an enormous disadvantage vis-à-vis the CPSU. Because political parties other than the Communist Party were illegal up until a week after the election, Democratic Russia did not begin overt campaigning until it had become clear that such activity would soon be legalized, about a month before the election. Even then, it had little money and no grassroots organization, and it was generally barred from access to the media, which was almost completely controlled by the Communist Party.

Despite its serious handicaps, Democratic Russia campaigned quite successfully for pro-democracy candidates, especially in Russia's largest cities. In Moscow and St. Petersburg (then Leningrad) as well as several other regional capitals, Democratic Russia distributed, posted, or, in the very few cases where a sympathetic newspaper existed, published lists of the candidates that they supported. In some cities and regions, candidates debated on live TV and were able to inform viewers of their political affiliations. One of the main signals that candidates used to let voters know they supported Democratic Russia was by mentioning Yeltsin in their campaign literature and in their public appearances. Candidates supported by Democratic Russia were extremely popular in Moscow, St. Petersburg, and a few other regional capitals (Colton 1990, Embree 1991, Kiernan 1993, Hahn 1993, Andrews and Vacroux 1994, Friedgut 1994). Although Democratic Russia was largely unsuccessful in influencing the vote in areas outside these few large cities, about one-third of the deputies elected in March 1990 had been supported by or were supporters of Democratic Russia (Remington et al. 1994).

Although the Communist Party of the Soviet Union had almost no experience competing in elections (Urban 1990, Kiernan and Aistrup 1991), and it did not have a timely and attractive political message as did Democratic Russia, the Communist Party relied on its huge grass-roots organization and its clout in smaller cities and rural areas to ensure that a sizable number of dedicated communists were elected, about the same number as Democratic Russia deputies. A "dedicated" communist was not merely a member of the CPSU – most of the candidates were members of the Communist Party, but this was to be expected in a country were membership in the Party was an important career credential (Hough 1977) – but someone who worked within the Communist Party organization or who occupied a Communist Party post in the state economic bureaucracy.[7]

Before the Collapse of the Soviet Union – Two Grand Coalitions

When members of the parliament met for the first time in June 1990, the deputy corpus was characterized internally and in the press by members' allegiance to either of the two political organizations that had organized the electoral campaigns of most of those elected: Deputies were described either as "democratic reformers" (i.e., supporters of Democratic Russia) or as "communist conservatives" (i.e., supporters of the CPSU). There were also a sizable number of deputies who had not been supported by either Democratic Russia or the CPSU. A majority of

---

[7] In fact, most of the supporters of Democratic Russia were members of the Communist Party, at least at the time of the election. Many of these soon renounced their membership, and all had done so by the beginning of 1992 (after the aborted coup).

these so-called "independents" consistently supported the policies of Democratic Russia, starting with the election of Boris Yeltsin to the post of chairman.

Neither of the two grand coalitions had an official list of its members, nor was either group capable of forcing its affiliates to vote a certain way. Rather, the coalitions were made up of like-minded individuals who shared positions on the two major issues of the day: (a) reform of the moribund command economy (Colton 1986, Aslund 1991) and (b) reform of the discredited and undemocratic Soviet political system.

Citing Gorbachev's inability or unwillingness to deal with the country's economic crisis, Yeltsin and the democratic coalition called for dismantling the command economy and building a market economy in its stead. In addition, as Gorbachev attempted to roll back the basic freedoms he launched in 1988, such as freedom of speech and assembly and freedom of the press, the democrats pushed for a dramatic overhaul of the political system as well. The conservatives were united in supporting a continuation of the Soviet command economy along with a continuation of the political power of the Communist Party. Thus, the political platform of each of these two groups combined a position along the dimension of political reform with a position along the dimension of economic reform. In this way, although the issues of economic and political reform were not aligned along a single dimension, the location of the two coalitions was such that the issue space was one-dimensional.

The dimension that spanned the positions of the two coalitions can be termed Russian sovereignty (Figure 5.1). For the democrats, who supported Russian sovereignty, an end to the Soviet Union meant an end to Party rule as well as an end to the command economy, providing them with the opportunity to build a democratic polity and a market economy within Russia's borders. Russian sovereignty spelled disaster for the conservatives, who predicted that it would bring about the dismantling of the Soviet Union and an end to their commanding role as leaders in the CPSU; therefore, the communist coalition strongly opposed Russian sovereignty. Throughout the period before the collapse of the Soviet Union, a quasi-two-party structure existed, and the issue space was effectively one-dimensional.

As the conservatives feared, Russia's declaration of sovereignty and the election of a Russian President led to the collapse of the Soviet Union at the end of 1991, rendering moot the issue dimension that

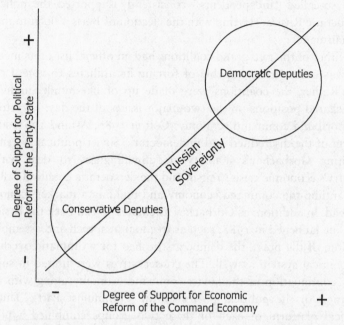

Figure 5.1. Spatial representation of dimensions and deputy positions before the collapse of the Soviet Union. Democratic deputies are those that support both political and economic reform; they believe that the primary means of achieving this reform is the achievement of Russian sovereignty. Conservative deputies are those that do not support reform and thus do not support Russian sovereignty.

had characterized partisanship for the parliament's first year and a half. With the appalling state of the Russian economy, and Russia's new independent statehood a fact, deputies were forced to contend with an array of political and economic problems that had been overshadowed before the breakup. As the deputies attempted to rewrite Russia's Constitution, they considered many new issues such as the definition of human rights, the rights of Russia's minority populations, the distribution of power between the legislative and executive branches of government, and the creation of an independent judiciary. To the extent that one of the central questions they faced was how to reform the command economy, they had to decide how to allocate pieces of the huge state-owned economic pie (e.g., whether to maintain a safety net for the poor, privatize state industry, or allow private ownership of land). According to Baron and Ferejohn (1989), when politics becomes distributive, the number of issue dimensions increases.

Immediate Aftermath of the Collapse – Parliament Split into Multiple Factions

Once sovereignty as a unifying issue was gone, it turned out that "democrats" and "conservatives" differed in their responses to these new economic and political questions, and the coalitions that characterized parliament prior to the collapse broke down. The quasi-two-party structure was replaced by a quasi-multiparty structure based on parliamentary groups called *fraktzii*, or factions.[8]

Most of the factions formed in the first few weeks after the deputies were elected, and most were associations of deputies from identifiable social groups, such as workers, middle managers in the industrial complex, members of the military, non-CPSU members, or representatives of minority populations, and they formed to support the particular interests of their group. Before the collapse of the Soviet Union, these factions supported the policy program of either of the two grand coalitions, the democratic reformers or the communist conservatives.

Accounts by observers such as Alexander Sobyanin as well as results of roll call analysis suggest that the democratic coalition of deputies included the factions Democratic Russia, Radical Democrats, Left of Center, Free Russia, Civil Society, and the Non-Party faction. The conservative coalition included the factions Russia, Fatherland, Agrarian Union, and the Communists of Russia. The centrist factions, Change-New Policy, Workers' Union, Industrial Union, and Sovereignty and Equality, tended to support the democratic coalition during this period.

Once the dimensional basis for the grand coalitions was gone, the two coalitions ceased to exist. As a result, the individual factions began to play a greater role in the parliament. Fourteen factions, including factions that had formed at the First Congress as well as several others that had formed in reaction to political events and government policy, officially registered at the Sixth Congress in April of 1992.[9] They were: Democratic Russia,

---

[8] *Fraktzii* have an old and important historical tradition in Russia as described in Emmons (1983) and Radkey (1950). At the only other time in Russia's history that an elected assembly existed, party politics was carried out by the factions. . . . Lenin strove to eliminate factions, and so he eliminated dissent.

[9] There are conflicting reports as to the names and number of the parliamentary factions. The reason for this confusion is due to frequent changes that occurred in the number and composition of a few of the factions over the life of the parliament. I have chosen to base my account of the factions (and other deputy groups) on the official publication of the Press Center of the Supreme Soviet (*Rossiiskii Parlament: Ot Pervogo k Sed'momy S'esdy*. 1992. Moscow: *Izvestia*) as well as on the

Radical Democrats, Left of Center, Non-Party Deputies, Free Russia, Civic Society, Change-New Policy, Industrial Union, Workers' Union, Sovereignty and Equality, Communists of Russia, Agrarian Union, Russia, and Fatherland.

At this time, the factions published official platforms. Not only do these platforms reflect the factions' positions on issues of political and economic reform, they identify the major dimensions of debate that existed at that time. In the next section, I briefly discuss the major policy positions of each of the factions as well as some general characteristics of faction members. (See Appendix 5A for a tabular summary of faction platforms, membership, and coalition alliances.) Following this discussion, I present a graphical representation of the major issue dimensions that emerge from the platforms and the location of each faction along these dimensions.[10]

Democratic Russia

The faction Democratic Russia was one of only two factions (the other being the Communists) with ties to a political organization outside the parliament, and its political platform was that of the national organization. The coordinator of Democratic Russia within the parliament was Lev Ponomarev, also a leader in the national movement. Up until the collapse of the Soviet Union, Democratic Russia worked closely with Yeltsin, first while he was chairman and then while he was president, to define the parliament's democratic agenda. The faction supported a

---

categorizations made by INDEM, an analytic group focusing on parliamentary groups, deputies, and votes. The accounts by INDEM and the Press Center, which are in agreement, are based on the official registration of factions that took place in April 1992 at the Sixth Congress of People's Deputies. Differing accounts seem to be based on publications by Alexander Sobyanin (see, for example, Sakwa, 1993), who has himself published at least two different accounts of the number and names of factions in the parliament (Sobyanin and Yur'ev 1991, Sobyanin 1994). Sobyanin's accounts are based on the exact composition of factions at the time of writing, and, as noted above, the exact composition and titles of some of the factions changed over time. One thing to note: The discrepancies all concern minor, centrist factions. All accounts include the most active and important factions: Democratic Russia, Radical Democrats, Left of Center, Free Russia, Workers' Union, Industrial Union, Change-New Policy, Fatherland, Sovereignty and Equality, Agrarian Union, Russia, and the Russian Communist Party.

[10] Use of party manifestoes to identify issue dimensions and place parties along those dimensions has a long tradition in comparative research on party systems (Budge et al. 1987, Laver and Schofield 1991, Budge 1994, Budge et al. 2001).

Western model of liberal democracy and a *laissez faire* market economy. A certain inconsistency crept into the faction's program after Yeltsin launched his program of "shock therapy" market reform. Because of its close ties to Yeltsin's government, in the parliamentary debate over the balance of power between president and parliament, Democratic Russia became an advocate for a strong, almost imperial presidency.

Members of the Democratic Russia faction were highly educated, each having had at least a college education, with five holding candidate degrees and two with doctorates. About half of the members were employed in research institutes or in medicine. These deputies were members of the traditional Russian "intelligentsia."

Radical Democrats

The faction Radical Democrats was a close ally of Democratic Russia. Like the members of Democratic Russia, the Radical Democrats supported liberal democracy and a market economy. Yet, they differed from Democratic Russia in two respects. The Radical Democrats were not closely associated with President Yeltsin and his reform program; therefore, they were much freer to criticize him when he compromised on rapid and radical free market reforms. In addition, Radical Democrats were more critical of Yeltsin's imperial presidency than were members of Democratic Russia. Like the members of Democratic Russia, the Radical Democrats were highly educated. They each had a college education and held jobs in the technical professions.

Left of Center

Members of Left of Center were self-described social democrats. They supported an end to political oppression and were strong supporters of human rights and multiparty competition. However, they did not support laissez faire capitalism, believing in the necessity of maintaining a social safety net. Also, while they supported privatizing small and medium enterprises and the service sector, they did not support the privatization of large state enterprises and heavy industry. A group as highly educated as that of Radical Democrats, members of Left of Center were employed in quite different spheres of the economy. Several worked in the militia, one in the KGB, others in engineering and teaching, and a contingent came from the medical professions. Well-educated and intellectual, Left of Center deputies were not, however, members of the Russian scientific elite, the traditional "intelligentsia." Their views were similar to those of other Western European social democrats.

Non-Party Deputies

The group of *Bespartiinye* or Non-Party Deputies first organized to stand up for the rights of the tens of millions of Russians who were not members of the Communist Party. The name *bespartiinye deputaty* came from the word *bespartiinye*, meaning not a member of the CPSU, which appeared in the short paragraph accompanying the announcement of each candidate published in the local and national newspapers. The importance of being *bespartiinye* was short-lived. Soon after the 1990 elections, almost all reform-minded deputies renounced their membership in the communist party. Also, once President Yeltsin outlawed the CPSU after the August 1991 coup, the faction's constituency – the tens of millions of Russians who were not Party members – disappeared.

The platform of the Non-Party faction included positions on other issues as well, most important of which were human rights, defined in terms of individual rights, and the creation of multiparty competition. Members were less supportive of economic reform, although they advocated a moderate course of market reform, in which state industry would be maintained, along with the privatization of small and medium enterprises. Like the members of Left of Center, members of this faction were highly educated and intellectual – they were employed in the social sciences, engineering and industry – but they were not members of the Russian "intelligentsia."

Members of the four factions reviewed so far were the most consistently likely deputies to support radical reform of the old system, but they were by no means a unified group. Although each of these factions shared a commitment to individual rights, important socioeconomic differences prevented them from being natural allies. Intellectuals in Democratic Russia and Radical Democrats, mostly scientists and engineers from Moscow and St. Petersburg, supported the theoretical principles of shock therapy, whereas the newer and more geographically dispersed free-thinking elite, members of Left of Center and the Non-Party Deputies, were harshly critical of shock therapy's practical hardships. It was this issue, shock therapy and the president's association with this unpopular program, that destroyed any chance of a unified democratic coalition after the collapse of the Soviet Union.

Free Russia

Free Russia, originally called "Communists for Democracy," was formed in part as a vehicle for its leader Alexander Rutskoi, who became Russia's Vice-President in June 1991. As expressed in their platform, members of Free Russia were particularly concerned about the struggle between the president and parliament, and they supported a balance of forces between the legislative and executive branches. While the faction supported a strong presidency, they became more and more critical of the sitting president, Boris Yeltsin. Rutskoi, who declared himself president when Yeltsin disbanded the parliament extraconstitutionally in the fall of 1993, clearly had ambitions of his own regarding that office. As a faction, Free Russia was not particularly concerned with individual rights or fostering political competition. It supported market reforms, but only so long as a strong social safety net was maintained. Members were highly educated and employed in the same kinds of professions as members of Left of Center, engineering, teaching, and medicine.

Civic Society

Members of Civic Society were originally members of the Radical Democrats, but they broke from Radical Democrats because they disagreed with their support for Yeltsin and his administration. Members of this faction supported economic reform, but they strongly disapproved of Yeltsin's radical program. Civic Society lacked a unique political program of its own. Like members of Left of Center, Civic Society wanted to maintain a social safety net. By emphasizing local and regional government, they also held some views in common with Sovereignty and Equality. Of all the factions, members of Civic Society were perhaps the least likely to act as a group.

Sovereignty and Equality

Deputies from the various non-Russian regions formed the faction Sovereignty and Equality. In their platform, they spoke only of the human rights of minorities and other collectives. About half of the members were employed in government work or worked directly for the Communist Party. This helps explain why the voting profile of a faction that considered itself part of the democratic center looked so much like that of the Communist and Agrarian factions.

Change – New Politics

Members of the faction Change-New Policy considered themselves political pragmatists, impatient with the confrontation between president and parliament. The faction supported a "civilized" market and declared its goal to pass legislation to promote workable economic reform. (In practice, this meant that faction members generally supported privatization, but opposed market reforms absent social guarantees of the sort supported by the faction Left of Center.) The faction was patriotic and considered itself centrist.

Half of Change-New Policy's members were employed in various spheres including Party work, the military, research institutes, and medicine, but the other half was employed in industry. According to Aslund (1995), it was precisely these people, *nomenklatura* industrialists, that gained the most from privatization; thus, it was possible for a deputy to support privatization but to oppose other aspects of radical economic reform.

Industrial Union

The Industrial Union of Russia, first formed at the second Congress, was one of the parliament's smallest factions. All members of this faction were employed in industry or by the Communist Party. Like those members of Change-New Policy who worked in industry, members of Industrial Union were generally supportive of privatization but opposed many other aspects of Yeltsin's shock therapy program. Members supported a strong presidency, but were generally critical of President Yeltsin.

Workers' Union

Another small faction, the Workers' Union of Russia, was first formed in May 1990 under the name "Workers-peasants Union." Members of Workers' Union held positions similar to those of Industrial Union. They supported privatization, especially that plan that benefited workers, but they strongly opposed market reforms that eliminated social programs that had traditionally benefited workers. All but one member of this faction was employed in industry.

Each of the last five factions discussed (Free Russia, Sovereignty and Equality, Change-New Policy, Industrial Union, and Workers' Union) supported the democratic coalition before the collapse of the Soviet Union. Free Russia and Change-New Policy were self-declared democratic factions. However, after the collapse, none of these factions maintained a democratic profile. Except for Sovereignty and Equality, none of these factions was particularly concerned with issues of human rights; their primary concerns were the economy and presidential power. While they opposed some of Yeltsin's economic initiatives and supported others, members of each of these factions became strong opponents of Yeltsin himself by the end of 1992.

Communists of Russia

Like Democratic Russia, the Communists of Russia faction was tied to a national organization, but one that was outlawed after the August coup. While the CPSU reconstituted itself as the Communist Party of the Russian Federation, the parliamentary faction continued to support the traditional platform of the Communist Party, a working Russian's right to a job, a pension, a place to live, free health care, and free education. The Communist faction opposed privatization and supported only limited market reform. They supported the class-based rights that form the core of communist ideology.

One of the most striking characteristics of the Communist faction is that the Communist Party employed the overwhelming majority of its members. About half of the members were in governmental work, which meant that they held their posts at the behest of the Communist Party, and more than one-third were employed directly by the Communist Party. Employees of the Communist Party were members of an elite group called the *nomenklatura*, people who received special privileges *gratis* from the Party. Such people had the strongest vested interest in maintaining the status quo of any group in the country.

Agrarian Union

The Agrarian Union was a close ally of the Communist faction, especially after the collapse of the Soviet Union. (According to many, the Agrarian Union was little more than the agricultural wing of the Communists of Russia.) Most of its members were managers in the huge Communist Party-dominated collective and state farm sector of the economy. Like the members of the Communist faction, members of Agrarian Union were from the Party *nomenklatura*.

Russia

The faction Russia was formed in the fall of 1990 as an alternative to Democratic Russia and the Communists of Russia. The faction Russia opposed "shock therapy" and was strongly critical of Yeltsin and the government. It opposed the dissolution of the USSR and the loss of Russia's international clout and prestige. In its platform, Russia claims to occupy a position in the political center; however, according to the voting behavior of its members, Russia emerged as one of the most extreme of the factions. All but one member had a higher education; and the leader, Sergei Baburin, was the equivalent of an associate professor at a university. Other members were employed in a variety of spheres including medicine, industry, government, and Communist Party work.

The faction Russia, like the faction Free Russia, was very much centered on its charismatic leader Baburin. While leader of the faction Russia, Baburin was Yeltsin's loudest critic. He initiated impeachment proceedings against President Yeltsin several times, and he blamed Yeltsin for the collapse of the Soviet Union. Although the faction claimed that its aggressive criticism of Yeltsin was in reaction to his destruction of the Soviet Union and the excesses of shock therapy, it seems plausible that the attempts to impeach President Yeltsin were intended more to support Baburin's political ambitions than from any clear policy objective. Even Ruslan Khasbulatov, another strong critic of President Yeltsin, blamed Baburin for his unbridled provocation of Yeltsin.[11]

Fatherland

This faction was overtly patriotic and strongly opposed to the collapse of the Soviet Union. The military or the militia employed almost half of the members of the faction Fatherland; the rest were employed in government or Communist Party work. Like the members of the Communist faction and Agrarian Union, most members of Fatherland were members of the *nomenklatura*. The head of the faction was Boris Tarasov, a political member of the military.

Each of the last four factions discussed were part of the conservative coalition prior to the collapse of the Soviet Union. Although Russia and Fatherland were primarily nationalist factions, and the Communists of

[11] Personal interview with author, June 1996.

Russia and the Agrarian Union were based primarily on the economic principles of socialism, all four factions were strongly opposed to the disintegration of the Soviet Union, and they opposed Russian sovereignty. On issues that surfaced after the collapse, these four factions were not always in agreement. Russia was more supportive of economic reform than were the other three factions. In addition, while they opposed President Yeltsin, the faction Russia championed a Russian republic, distinguishing it from the Communists, Agrarian Union, and Fatherland, which never supported any truly democratic regime.

A comparison of the members of Russia versus the Communists, Agrarian Union, and Fatherland helps explain the differences among these factions. While some members of Russia belonged to the *nomenklatura*, many others were members of the new educated elite (like members of the Non-Party faction or Left of Center); and the faction's leader, Baburin, was an intellectual. Almost all members of the other three factions belonged to the *nomenklatura*. While the Communists, Agrarian Union, and Fatherland supported a return to a past in which the Communist Party dominated economic and political life, Russia supported a different vision. Members of Russia united with the other three factions only on the issue of Russian statehood (a desire to reconstitute the USSR) and on opposition to President Yeltsin.

Unaffiliated Members

A substantial number of deputies (about 75) were not affiliated with any of the fourteen factions. There was no single reason why some deputies chose not to join any faction, nor were the unaffiliated deputies unified on any particular issue. They came from all walks of life and all political persuasions. As a group, the unaffiliated deputies occupied mostly centrist positions along each of the six dimensions; thus they were generally in favor of modest reform and opposed to a return to communism – that is, typical Russian "Independents."

ISSUE DIMENSIONS IN THE RUSSIAN PARLIAMENT

Based on a careful study of the political platforms of the fourteen factions, I have identified six issue dimensions that appeared in almost all of the platforms and were emphasized by at least half of the factions. These dimensions correspond well with those discussed by parliamentary analyst Alexander Sobyanin (1994) and by legislative scholar

Thomas Remington (1994). Following Budge et al. (1987), Laver and Schofield (1991), and Budge (1994), I analyze the platforms of each of the factions in order to locate it along each of the six dimensions (see Figures 5.2 through 5.7). Because the programmatic information published by the factions was limited (I had access to only a page or two for each faction, whereas, for example, the Manifesto Project Research Group (Budge et al. 1987) based its analysis on hundreds of documents and thousands of detailed pages), the placements represent my own subjective reading of the platforms and are intended only to show the relative positions of the factions. If a faction name does not appear on a dimensional scale, it is because that faction did not indicate a position along that dimension.

After the collapse of the Soviet Union, several other issue dimensions concerning economic and political reform of the new Russia joined the issue of Russian sovereignty in saliency (Figure 5.2). To the extent that Russian sovereignty remained salient, it did so because several factions advocated a return to the old USSR boundaries, and two factions were particularly concerned with maintaining Russia's superpower status. The remaining factions merely reasserted their continued support for a free Russia. Along this dimension, alliances among the factions very much resembled those that had existed before the dissolution of the USSR.

The most important new issues concerned economic reform, which began in earnest on January 2, 1992 when Yeltsin's government liberalized prices, and the definition of Russian democracy. Deputies were faced with important new questions. How deeply should market mechanisms penetrate the economy? Should all property be privatized? Should Russia become a presidential or parliamentary democracy? Should individual or

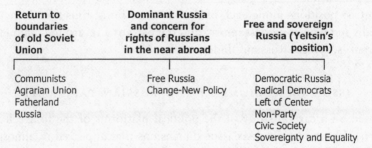

Figure 5.2. Russian statehood dimension. Factions on the left support a return to the boundaries of the old Soviet Union. Factions on the right support a contained and sovereign Russia.

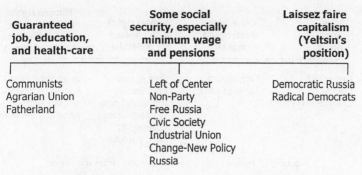

Figure 5.3. Market reform dimension. Faction locations indicate the extent to which each faction supports full market reform. Factions on the left support only limited market reform. Factions on the right support full market reform.

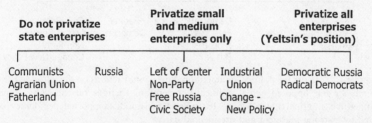

Figure 5.4. Privatization dimension. Faction locations indicate the extent to which each faction supports the transfer of state property into private hands. Factions on the left do not support privatization of state property. Factions on the right support privatization of the entire economy. Factions in the middle support limited privatization.

class-based rights be placed in the forefront of the new constitution? How factions stood on these issues are captured in Figures 5.3 through 5.6.

As the dimensional scales presented in Figures 5.3 through 5.6 reveal, factions that had worked together to support Russian sovereignty took quite different positions on the new economic and political issue dimensions. Many of the factions that had aligned with the democratic reformers before the Soviet Union's collapse no longer did so afterwards. Furthermore, different sets of factions voted together on different issues, which means that the composition of winning coalitions differed depending on the issue.

An examination of the two economic dimensions (Figures 5.3 and 5.4) reveals that there was little variation in how factions stood on the issues of market reform and privatization. Factions that supported laissez faire

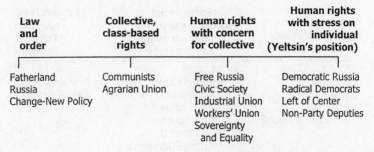

Law and order	Collective, class-based rights	Human rights with concern for collective	Human rights with stress on individual (Yeltsin's position)
Fatherland Russia Change-New Policy	Communists Agrarian Union	Free Russia Civic Society Industrial Union Workers' Union Sovereignty and Equality	Democratic Russia Radical Democrats Left of Center Non-Party Deputies

Figure 5.5. Human rights versus law and order dimension.

"Democracy" without competition	Presidential republic (Yeltsin's position)		Multi-party democracy
Communists Agrarian Union Fatherland	Democratic Russia Free Russia Industrial Union Russia	Radical Democrats	Civic Society Left of Center Non-Party Change-New Policy

Figure 5.6. Support for political competition dimension. Factions on the left used the term *democracy* but opposed actual political competition. Factions on the right supported competitive, multiparty democracy. Factions in the middle supported democracy dominated by a strong president and presidential party.

capitalism (Democratic Russia and Radical Democrats) also supported a completely privatized economy; those that rejected privatization (Communists of Russia, Agrarian Union, and Fatherland) also rejected most market reforms, because these would eliminate the traditional guarantee of a communist economy – a job. With three exceptions, factions that supported a social-welfare state (Left of Center, Non-Party Deputies, Free Russia, Civic Society, and Russia) opposed the privatization of state industry and large enterprises. The exceptions were the factions Change-New Policy and Industrial Union, which were generally supportive of large-scale privatization but opposed to the harsh market reforms of shock therapy. In general, there were three coalitions of factions: One supported radical economic reform, one opposed economic reform, and the largest one advocated a moderate middle ground.

Compared to the economic reform dimension, there was considerably more variation in how factions stood on the two dimensions that concerned the constitution of Russian democracy (Figures 5.5 and 5.6).

Figure 5.7. Balance of power between president and parliament dimension.

Some factions that supported individual rights (Democratic Russia and Radical Democrats) were strong supporters of a presidential republic, a position they shared with one faction dedicated to law and order (Russia). At least one faction that supported multiparty competition (Change-New Policy) also supported law and order over individual or even collective human rights. The Communists expressed a strong commitment to traditional class-based rights, but shared an opposition to party competition with the strictly law and order faction Fatherland. Although Russia emphasized law and order, and its members were outspoken enemies of Yeltsin, they supported a presidential republic, in contradiction to the Communists and Fatherland, the other most outspoken of Yeltsin's critics. Not only was there no consistent coalition of deputies across the two dimensions concerned with Russian democracy, there was little relationship between a faction's position on economic reform and its position on democratic reform.

The last dimension depicted had nothing to do with the theoretical question of the relative merits of parliamentary versus presidential democracy; rather it was based on the factions' positions on the power struggle between President Yeltsin and the parliament. The struggle began almost immediately after the Congress of People's Deputies in November 1991 granted Yeltsin enormous leeway to carry out economic reform by decree. Once Yeltsin's government began the actual process of economic reform, clearly many deputies regretted their hasty decision to abdicate parliamentary power in this area. Factions that supported the president did so because they supported Yeltsin. Factions that supported the parliament did so not because they supported multiparty parliamentary democracy, but because they supported their own powerbase. Also, factions that supported a "balance of forces" supported a pragmatic compromise. As the program of Free Russia put it, they supported "a political union with the President," but they reserved "the right to criticize constructively . . . the decisions and methods of the President and government."

The analysis of faction platforms suggests that after the collapse of the Soviet Union, the issue space was multidimensional. As described in an official document of the parliament's press center, "The orientations of the people's deputies of the Russian Federation defined a motley political spectrum."[12] In this environment, the coalitional structure of the parliament was complex, and it changed from issue to issue. If deputies considered legislation that encompassed any two of these six dimensions (the draft Russian Constitution was an example of such legislation), we would expect outcomes to cycle.

Attempt to Reduce Deputy Groups and Stabilize Outcomes: The Formation of Three Blocs of Factions

While faction leaders did not discuss the problem of shifting majorities in technical terms, they were well aware of the difficulty of forging a stable majority in the parliament at this time. In an effort to influence more effectively legislative decision making, faction leaders formed two new coalitions of factions, or *blocs* as they were officially called, in April 1992: Russian Unity (which included the factions Communists of Russia, Agrarian Union, Russia, and Fatherland) and Constructive Forces (which included Change-New Policy, Workers' Union, Industrial Union, Civic Society, and Sovereignty and Equality). They were joined by the Coalition for Reform[13] (which had formed at the First Congress, and

---

[12] *Rossiiskii Parlament: Ot Pervogo k Sed'momy S'esdy.* 1992. Moscow: *Izvestia*, p. 94.

[13] There are different interpretations of the proper membership of the bloc Coalition for Reform. (According to the Press Center documents, Coalition for Reform included Democratic Russia and the Radical Democrats.) A coalition by that name existed prior to the Sixth Congress of People's Deputies, when all factions and blocs were officially registered, and when the practice of belonging to more than one faction was prohibited. When the coalition was officially registered in April 1992, it was made up of members from all of the democratic factions including Democratic Russia, Radical Democrats, Left of Center, Free Russia, and the Non-Party Faction. No members of Industrial Union, Fatherland, Russia, Agrarian Union, Communist Party of Russia, or Change-New Policy were in the Coalition for Reform. Only one member each from Sovereignty and Equality, Civic Society, and the Workers' Union joined. However, there were 13 members of Coalition for Reform who were unaffiliated with any faction. Thus, membership in the

which included the factions Democratic Russia, Radical Democrats, Left of Center, Non-Party Deputies, and Free Russia).[14] I summarize faction and bloc membership for Sessions 2 through 6 in Table 5.1.

In Figure 5.8, I present a graphical representation of two of the six issue dimensions and plausible locations for the three blocs, Coalition for Reform, Constructive Forces, and Russian Unity. In this representation, the indifference curves represent the set of points that each bloc prefers to the status quo. Areas of intersection represent sets of points that are preferred by two of the three blocs; these sets contain points that can defeat the status quo, and they are accordingly called the *win sets* of the status quo. As can be seen, the status quo can be defeated by any of three coalitions: one containing Coalition for Reform and Russian Unity, one containing Russian Unity and Constructive Forces, and one containing Constructive Forces and Coalition for Reform. It is clear from this diagram that there are many points that can defeat the status quo; hence, it is not stable. Furthermore, if there is no means to prevent alternatives to the status quo being raised, no matter what alternative is

Coalition for Reform did not necessarily coincide with membership in one of the democratic factions. However, in an internal publication of the Russian parliament, Alexander Sobyanin published a list of the blocs and their member factions, which designated the bloc Coalition for Reform as including the factions Democratic Russia, Radical Democrats, Left of Center, Free Russia, and the Non-Party Faction; this list is published in Sakwa (1993, p. 62). Thus, according to Sobyanin, an "insider" in the parliament and with the democratic deputies, all of the democratic factions were part of the Coalition for Reform. My main purpose in presenting information about the blocs is to illustrate the voting behavior of three broad groups of deputies with nonoverlapping members. Considering that factions were the fundamental deputy group throughout the three-year life of the parliament, I have chosen to use Sobyanin's designation, as published in Sakwa (1993), of the Coalition for Reform.

[14] The bloc Democratic Center was created in an attempt to provide a parliamentary vehicle for an important extraparliamentary centrist coalition called Civic Union. Civic Union was an organization created by several democratic leaders, including Nikolai Travkin, head of the Democratic Party of Russia, Alexander Rutskoi, Russia's vice-president and head of the Free Russia Party, and Volsky, head of the Russian Union of Industrialists and Entrepreneurs. During the tense period in the fall of 1992 when the president and parliament struggled to work out a division of labor in the Law on the Government, Travkin, Rutskoi, Volsky, and others organized Civic Union in an attempt to help broker a compromise between Yeltsin's government and the parliament. While Civic Union was greeted in the press and by Yeltsin himself as a promising new centrist political force, its parliamentary counterpart, Democratic Center, played almost no role in the parliament. According to Sobyanin (1994, pp. 189–199), Democratic Center was never active in the parliament.

Table 5.1. *Summary of Faction and Bloc Membership in the Russian Parliament*

Membership	Session 2	Session 3	Session 4	Session 5	Session 6
Democratic Russia	14	14	16	15	19
Radical Democrats	6	6	7	6	6
Left of Center	17	15	17	14	13
Non-Party Faction	9	9	14	14	14
Free Russia	12	12	11	13	15
Bloc Coalition for					
Reform	**58**	**56**	**65**	**62**	**67**
Workers Union	9	9	9	8	10
Civil Society	7	6	7	6	6
Change-New Policy	16	16	19	19	22
Industrial Union	8	7	3	4	4
Sovereignty and Equality	24	24	21	21	23
Bloc Constructive					
Forces	**64**	**62**	**59**	**58**	**65**
Fatherland	7	7	11	11	12
Agrarian Union	23	19	15	16	19
Russia	15	13	11	11	14
Communists of Russia	16	16	16	15	16
Bloc Russian Unity	**61**	**55**	**53**	**53**	**61**
Unaffiliated Deputies	61	53	49	48	52
TOTAL	**244**	**226**	**226**	**221**	**245**

proposed, there will always exist some other alternative that can defeat it. In theory, outcomes are not stable and cycling will occur.[15]

The spatial representation of partisan alliances and issue dimensions depicted in Figure 5.8 is a reasonable model of political reality for the first six months of 1992. (Additional dimensions only complicate the picture, making it even more likely that conditions for cycling exist.) The locations of the three blocs roughly correspond to the locations of their constituent factions depicted in Figures 5.3, 5.4, and 5.5. Coalition for Reform occupies a position strongly in favor of human rights (a position shared by four of its five member factions) and supportive of privatization (two of its member factions supported privatizing the entire

---

[15] If cycling occurred in two dimensions, then it also occurred in higher-dimensional spaces.

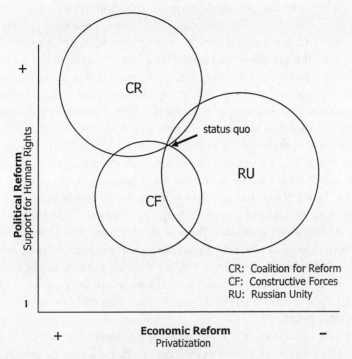

Figure 5.8. Spatial representation of two important issue dimensions and three deputy blocs after the collapse of the Soviet Union. The areas of overlap between the preference curves for the three blocs, Coalition for Reform, Constructive Forces, and Russian Unity, are areas in which majority-preferred alternatives to the status quo are located.

economy, while three supported privatizing only part of the economy). Constructive Forces occupies a position supporting law and order over human rights (which corresponds to the position of its dominant member, Change-New Policy) and supporting privatization. Its position along the economic reform dimension is fairly similar to that of Coalition for Reform (again reflecting Change-New Policy's platform). Russian Unity occupies a position strongly opposing privatization (which corresponds to the position of three of its four member factions) and weakly supporting human rights over law and order (reflecting the position of its two largest members factions, the Communists and Agrarian Union).

Obviously, the positions shown in Figure 5.8 are only approximations, but the diagram illustrates three theoretical propositions that I test rigorously in succeeding chapters: (1) The issue space was multidimensional after the collapse of the Soviet Union, (2) deputy groups were dispersed in such a way that no stable majority coalition existed, and (3) cycling occurred after the collapse of the Soviet Union. I test the first two propositions in Chapter 6 and test the third proposition in Chapter 7.

Given the agenda-setting powers that could accrue to the parliament's chairman when the two-party structure broke down, a multidimensional policy space and shifting majority coalitions created the conditions for Chairman Khasbulatov to manipulate the parliament for his own purposes. Notice that among the dimensional scales presented in Figures 5.2 through 5.7, there is only one dimension on which Yeltsin holds a position that is at the extreme end from that of the majority: the issue of the balance of power between president and parliament. On all other dimensions, Yeltsin's position and that of the majority are the same, or his position is to the right of a centrist majority position. Therefore, on all but one of the dimensions identified by the factions, Yeltsin either held the majority position or was in a position to bargain with the majority center – he had room to maneuver. Only on the dimension of the balance of power between president and parliament is Yeltsin isolated. As I argue in Chapter 2, this was the dimension that Khasbulatov used to achieve his ideal point.

Using as an example the Law on the Government, which in the fall of 1992 was the most important item on the parliament's agenda, I illustrate hypothetically how Khasbulatov could have manipulated the two-dimensional nature of the debate to achieve his own most-preferred outcome – a reduction in executive power. The Law on the Government encompassed a two-dimensional issue space, and the positions of the deputy blocs were such that Khasbulatov could manipulate the agenda to obtain an outcome that altered economic reform only moderately, but harshly challenged the power of Russia's president. The spatial representation shown in Figure 5.9 illustrates the relevant issue dimensions, plausible locations of the three blocs, and a series of hypothetical alternatives, each of which is supported by a parliamentary majority (I include only the first set of indifference curves in the diagram), which leads to an outcome favorable to the chairman, especially along the dimension of parliamentary versus executive power. In Chapter 8, I test the theoretical proposition depicted in Figure 5.9.

In October, the parliament rejected the government's initial version of the Law on the Government, which gave the president full authority to appoint his Cabinet without parliamentary approval. The legislative version, which the parliament adopted in November and the Seventh Congress adopted in December, granted parliament the right to approve

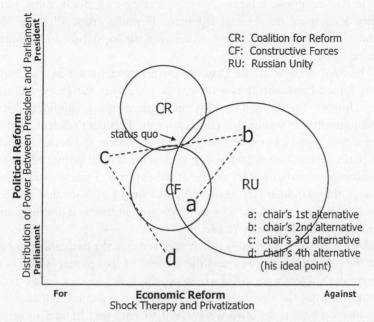

Figure 5.9. Spatial representation of a chairman's manipulation of three deputy blocs in two issue dimensions. Because majorities are unstable, a chairman with agenda-setting powers can propose alternatives to the status quo, *a*, *b*, *c*, and *d*, and move the majority position from the centrally located status quo to the more extreme position of alternative *d*. This is essentially what Khasbulatov did during the debate on the Law on the Government. By the end of the debate, the parliament supported a position quite hostile to the president.

all major Cabinet appointments. While President Yeltsin interpreted the legislative version of the Law on Government as an attempt to weaken his power and halt radical economic reform by removing the architects of shock therapy from his Cabinet, deputies supported their version for a variety of reasons.

Whether the Law on Government was an attack on executive power or on economic reform depended on one's point of view, because these two issues were separable in many deputies' minds. From the point of view of Russian Unity members, by supporting the legislature's right to approve Cabinet appointments, they were hoping to replace key reformers in Yeltsin's administration and thus change dramatically or even halt the course of economic reform. But, from the point of view of the many moderate members of the Coalition for Reform, by supporting the legislature's version of the Law on the Government, they were hoping not to halt economic reform or even to change its general course but to soften its impact on average Russians. Deputies from all three blocs believed that the balance of power between the legislature and executive needed to be restored.

The final version of the Law on Government passed by the parliament forced President Yeltsin to replace his choice for Prime Minister, the reformer Yegor Gaidar, with the parliamentary candidate Victor Chernomyrdin. It was at this point, after the President's defeat, that the parliament began its extraordinary attack on Yeltsin and his allies within the parliament. Once Khasbulatov achieved his ideal point, which was an increase in parliamentary power at the expense of presidential power, he kept the parliamentary agenda focused only on issues that could be couched in these terms, thereby using the parliament as a platform from which to attack President Yeltsin.

One of the most noticeable differences between the parliament in 1992 and the parliament in 1993 was the content of its agenda. Whereas the parliament's agenda included votes on the full array of issues facing deputies during the first half of 1992, during the second half the array of issues on which deputies were asked to vote was limited mostly to attempts to decrease executive power.

Throughout 1993, the parliament's final year, few roll call votes were taken, and most of these concerned resolutions either to repudiate Yeltsin's political goals or to increase the chairman's power vis-à-vis the president and the president's democratic supporters in the parliament. Khasbulatov had shifted the parliament's agenda to reflect his own ideal point.[16]

CONCLUSIONS

In this chapter, I have presented graphical representations of four theoretical propositions that underlie my explanation of changes in how the parliament functioned: (1) A two-party dynamic and a one-dimensional policy space characterized the parliament before the collapse of the Soviet Union (see Figure 5.1); (2) in response to dramatic changes in the kinds of issues facing deputies, a multiparty dynamic in a multidimensional policy space characterized the parliament after the collapse (see Figures 5.2 through 5.7); (3) outcomes cycled for several months after

[16] Both Lev Ponomarev and Viacheslav Bragin expressed these views in interviews with me in June 1996.

the collapse (see Figure 5.8); and (4) a chairman with the power to set the parliamentary agenda manipulated deputies within the multidimensional policy space (see Figure 5.9).

In the following three chapters, I test each of these four propositions empirically. In Chapter 6, I examine changes in the structure of deputy preferences, studying the organization of deputy preferences – that is, whether they were homogeneous or heterogeneous; I also study changes in the dimensionality of the issue space. In Chapter 7, I address systematically the question of when cycling was possible and whether or not it occurred during the predicted periods – that is, after the Soviet Union collapsed. I also consider the issues over which cycles existed. In Chapter 8, I compare the agenda-setting powers of Yeltsin versus Khasbulatov.

The basis for all three empirical discussions is the parliamentary voting record. Following Poole and Rosenthal (1985, 1987, 1991) and Heckman and Snyder (1992, 1996, 1997), I use the complete set of roll call votes of the Russian deputies to determine the ideal points of the legislators. Taking seriously the argument that roll call votes alone cannot be used to identify coalitional arrangements (Budge et al. 1987, Laver and Schofield 1991), in this chapter I have based my theoretical arguments regarding changes in the structure of preferences on the electoral platforms of the two grand coalitions and the published platforms of the deputy factions, but I use the actual legislative activity of the deputies – how they voted – to test my theories. The true measure of a deputy's preferences (that complex combination of ideology and self-interest) is how he or she votes.

Appendix 5A

Here, I summarize the important deputy groups that existed in the parliament as of the Sixth Congress. Although most of the factions were formed at the First Congress, membership in the factions was not officially registered until the Sixth Congress, which occurred in April 1992. At the Sixth Congress, many of the factions chose to form blocs of factions; thus, by the spring of 1992, deputies had two partisan affiliations, one with their faction and one with a larger bloc of factions.

In Table 5A.1, I show which factions belonged to which blocs. In addition, I summarize the main points of the political platforms of each faction.

Table 5A.1. *Summary of Political Platforms of the Factions*

Faction	Membership (April 1992)	Grand Coalitions (1990–1991)	Blocs (1992–1993)	Main Points of the Platform
Democratic Russia	16	Democratic coalition	Coalition for Reform	1. Followed the national program of the movement "Democratic Russia," which stood for liberal democracy and a free market economy. 2. Supports the right of all individuals to realize the fruits of their labor without regard to class or party membership. 3. Free market; laissez faire style. 4. Strong advocate of multiparty democracy. 5. Strong supporter of equal rights.
Radical Democrats	7	Democratic coalition	Coalition for Reform	1. Defense of human rights and freedom of the individual. 2. Support for private property and an end to the state's monopoly on property. 3. Support for sovereignty of Russia.
Left of Center	17	Democratic coalition	Coalition for Reform	1. Support for a free Russia and the development of a new union of free republics. 2. Opposition to the harsh privatization measures of the administration and support for state regulatory intervention to protect ordinary Russians from its effects. 3. Privatization must include small and medium enterprises, as well as the service sector, but not including the huge state industrial complex.

Bespartiinye Deputaty (Non-CPSU Deputies)	14	Democratic coalition	Coalition for Reform	4. Support for new constitution, a democratic order, and basic human rights. 1. Goal is to represent the interests of the millions of non-Communist Party members in Russia. 2. Support for the elimination of the Communist Party's monopoly on the political life of Russia. 3. Support for private property, including private land. 4. Support for increased role of factions in the parliament. 5. Support for a market economy, but with a guaranteed minimum wage and pensions. 6. Support for private property while preserving state and collective property. 7. Support for creation of a tax system to stimulate industry. 8. Support the agrarian sector. 9. Equal rights for all subjects of the Federation, especially support for representation of minority peoples. 10. Support for creation of a new constitution.
Free Russia (Originally, the faction was called "Communists for Democracy.")	11	Democratic coalition	Coalition for Reform	1. Support for a balance of political forces and parties. 2. Support for radical economic reform but with social guarantees for the population. 3. Support for the president, but will continue to offer parliamentary criticisms and corrections to help move the country out of crisis.

Table 5A.1 (continued)

Faction	Membership (April 1992)	Grand Coalitions (1990–1991)	Blocs (1992–1993)	Main Points of the Platform
Civic Society (Deputies from the Radical Democrats who were disaffected by that faction's pro-administration stand formed this group at the Sixth Congress.)	7	Democratic coalition	Constructive Forces	1. Support for the consolidation of the "healthy forces" in society in order to solve the problems of the newly consolidated Russia without conflict. 2. Support for radical economic reform. 3. Privatization under strong state and social control. 4. Equality of all forms of property including land. 5. Reform of agriculture. 6. Support for all people of Russia, mainly through development of local government.
Sovereignty and Equality (Originally, the faction was formed by deputies from republics, autonomous *oblasts* and *okrugs* within Russia.)	21	Democratic coalition	Constructive Forces	1. Defense of the rights of all peoples to self-determination including the minority populations in the Russian Federation. 2. Support for international documents on the rights of individuals. 3. Support for a new constitution in which the rights of the various peoples and parts of the Russian Federation will be spelled out: equality of peoples, self-government, fairness to all.

Industrial Union (Originally, the faction was called "Organizers of the National Economy." They describe themselves as leaders of industry who hold centrist or left-centrist political positions.)	3	Democratic coalition	Constructive Forces	1. Support for a market economy and the development of small businesses. 2. Decisions about the principal economic problems should be decided on the basis of consensus of the union of leaders of state enterprises and entrepreneurs along with the administration and the trade unions. 3. Support for privatization of state property in the interests of the workers' collectives. 4. Supports a strong presidential republic. 5. Equality of all political parties and movements.
Workers' Union (Originally the faction was called the "Workers–Peasants' Union.")	9	Democratic coalition	Constructive Forces	1. Support for the professional and regional interests of the workers. 2. At the Third, Fourth, and Fifth Congresses, the faction worked with the faction "Left of Center," in the democratic block. However, at the Sixth Congress, they joined the new bloc "Constructive Forces."
Change-New Policy (Originally, the faction supported the movement Democratic Russia, but later they detached themselves for ideological	19	Democratic coalition	Constructive Forces	1. Supports a democratic alternative, parliamentary professionalism, and pragmatic politics. 2. Supports a balance of power. 3. Civilized market. 4. Patriotism. 5. Goal is to pass legislation that will promote economic, political, and social reform in Russia and to distribute and explain this legislation.

Table 5A.1 *(continued)*

Faction	Membership (April 1992)	Grand Coalitions (1990–1991)	Blocs (1992–1993)	Main Points of the Platform
reasons and joined the "centrist" bloc "Constructive Forces."				6. To render assistance in the execution of legislation. 7. To render assistance in the creation of political forces with a centrist orientation.
Russian Communist Party	16	Communist conservative coalition	Russian Unity	1. Support for the rights and interests of the workers of Russia. 2. Conditional support for the transition to a market economy; however, it is imperative that the right to a job, a place to live, a pension, free education, and free health care be maintained.
Agrarian Union (The faction was originally called "Food-Stuffs and Health.")	15	Communist conservative coalition	Russian Unity	1. Support for the agricultural complex of Russia. 2. Support for the peasants, both individually and collectively. 3. Support for giving the peasants the right to choose the management of the collective farms and to ensure that the state create equal conditions for the introduction of private farms.
Fatherland	11	Communist conservative coalition	Russian Unity	1. Main supporters/members were deputies who were also members of the military, and the main reason for the formation of the faction was disquiet with the fate of the Russian state.

138

11	Russia (The faction was formed as an alternative to Democratic Russia and the Communists of Russia. It was formed in reaction to and against events and decisions of the parliament.)	Communist conservative coalition	Russian Unity	2. Goal is to rally patriotic forces in support of the "fatherland." 3. To maintain the integrity of the RSFSR as a member of the renovated Union. 4. Opposed a free and sovereign Russia, separate from the USSR. 5. Opposed to the chaos of "sovereignty." 6. Stood for law and order and a strong and effective state. 1. Opposed to the ill-conceived actions of the parliament, which killed the Soviet Union and encouraged separatism within the Russian Federation. 2. Opposed to "shock therapy" and the impoverishment of the majority of the Russian people. 3. Supports a market economy that promotes all types of property, especially "people's enterprises." 4. Supports a law-based state, local self-government, rule of law, and three branches of government (legislative, executive, and judicial).

Source: Information summarized in this table comes from *Rossiiskii Parlament: Ot Pervogo k Sed'momy S'ezdy*. 1992. Moscow: *Izvestia*, pp. 94–108.

139

6

The Structure of Preferences

In this and the succeeding two chapters, I investigate systematically the voting record of the Russian deputies in order to test the key theoretical components of my account of what went wrong in the Russian legislature. For my explanation to be persuasive, I must show that (1) the structure of deputy preferences and the dimensionality of the policy space differed before and after the collapse of the Soviet Union, (2) cycling occurred only after the collapse, and (3) the achievements of Chairman Yeltsin and Chairman Khasbulatov were compatible with the hypothesized differences between the Soviet period parliament and the post-Soviet parliament. I test the first assertion in this chapter, the second assertion in Chapter 7, and the third assertion in Chapter 8.

The first theoretical premise I defend is that the conditions for cycling existed after the collapse of the Soviet Union but not before. In this chapter, I investigate empirically the structure of deputy preferences and the dimensionality of the policy space. If deputies were divided into two grand coalitions whose members had homogeneous preferences, or if the issue space was one-dimensional, cycling could not occur. If deputies were divided into many groups with heterogeneous preferences and if the issue space was multidimensional, cycling could have occurred. Using the roll call votes of the parliamentary deputies, I test the following two propositions: (1) Deputy preferences were homogeneous before the collapse of the Soviet Union and heterogeneous afterwards, and (2) the issue space was one-dimensional before the collapse and multidimensional afterwards.

I use principal components analysis to estimate the preferences of the Russian deputies. (In Appendix 6A, I discuss in detail the exact procedure I followed to obtain the estimates of deputy ideal points.) In a series of papers, Heckman and Snyder (1993, 1996, 1997) rigorously justify using a linear factor model (such as principal components or principal factors analysis) to determine the dimensional structure of a set of roll call votes as well as the ideal points of the deputies voting.[1] One can represent deputy preferences in factor analytic form in the following way: "The factors are the unobserved attributes of two potential options for choice setting (i.e., "for" or "against"), and the factor loadings are the preferences of the decision makers (Heckman and Snyder 1996, p. 14)." Thus, the factors (or in the terminology of principal components analysis, the components) correspond to the underlying issue dimensions that drive deputy voting, and the loadings (principal components scores) are estimates of the deputies' ideal points.[2]

In the first section of this chapter, I describe my data, namely, the roll call votes of the Russian Parliament. In the next section, I examine the ideal points of deputies. The graphs of deputy ideal points show that before the collapse of the Soviet Union, preferences were grouped into two relatively homogeneous coalitions, but after the collapse the two-party structure disintegrated as deputy preferences became heterogeneous. Maps of the ideal points of members of the Presidium demonstrate that the preferences of Presidium members were structured very much as the preferences of the parliament as a whole. Before the collapse a two-party dynamic characterized the Presidium; and as the graphs demonstrate, the democratic reformers had a majority on the Presidium while Yeltsin was Chairman. After the collapse the preferences of Presidium members became heterogeneous – there is no majority coalition visible in the graphs – rendering it very unlikely that the Presidium could have collectively resisted the chairman's misuse of power.

In the final section of the chapter, I investigate the dimensional nature of the issue space before and after the collapse. A graphical presentation

---

[1] Prior to Heckman and Snyder's recent work (1993, 1996, 1997), analysts interested in estimating the ideal points of deputies as well as the dimensional structure of the underlying policy space relied on Poole and Rosenthal's NOMINATE methodology, and many researchers continue to do so (Cox and McCubbins 1993, Myagkov and Kiewiet 1994, Londregan 1996). However, because of its better-understood statistical properties as well as its ease of estimation, I follow Heckman and Snyder and use principal components analysis to determine the dimensionality of the underlying issue space and to estimate the ideal points of deputies.

[2] According to Heckman and Snyder (1996, p. 3), so long as there are a sufficient number and variety of roll call votes, estimates of decision-maker preferences are consistent. The appropriate number of roll call votes appears to be around 200; therefore, throughout my study I draw most of my conclusions based on an analysis of roll call votes in Sessions 3, 4, and 5, in each of which there were approximately 200 roll call votes. I am more tentative in my conclusions regarding Sessions 2 and 6, which had about 70 and 30 roll call votes, respectively.

of the median ideal points for each of the factions provides particularly clear evidence of a change from a one-dimensional issue space to a multi-dimensional issue space. These final graphs correspond remarkably well with the theoretically motivated spatial representations that I presented in Figures 5.1 and 5.8 of the preceding chapter. An interpretation of the first and second dimensions recovered by the principal components analysis suggests that before the collapse of the Soviet Union, the first and dominant dimension was the issue of Russian sovereignty. After the collapse of the Soviet Union, the major issue dimension was that of reform, both economic and political, and it appears to have been mostly a reaction to the reforms implemented by the executive branch rather than an alternative program of reform originating in the legislature.

STRUCTURE OF DEPUTY PREFERENCES

Roll Call Votes of the Russian Deputies

From June 1990 until September 1993, the parliament met in six distinct sessions. Three of the sessions – Session 1, which ran from June to July of 1990, Session 2, which ran from September to December of 1990, and Session 3, which ran from January to July of 1991 – occurred before the collapse of the Soviet Union. Except for the last month of Session 3, Boris Yeltsin was chairman throughout this period. Session 4, which ran from September to July of 1992, Session 5, which ran from September 23 to December of 1992, and Session 6, which ran from February to September of 1993, occurred after the collapse of the Soviet Union. (Technically, the first three months of Session 4 occurred before the official end of the Soviet Union; however, for all practical purposes, the Soviet Union began to collapse after the failed coup of August 1991.) Ruslan Khasbulatov was chairman for these last three sessions. Starting in Session 2, roll call votes were regularly taken.

Most votes were not roll call votes. A roll call vote was taken only if a deputy motioned to do so, and one-fifth of the deputies present supported the motion. Asking for a roll call vote was a routine matter, and the motion was almost always supported. As in the U.S. Congress, roll call votes in the Russian Parliament were important votes. As noted by Snyder (1992), this means that roll call data is almost always biased. However, if the set of issues covered by the roll call votes is representative of all issues in the policy space, then it is still possible to use principal components analysis to determine the dimensionality of the underlying issue space. Based on a comparison of the issues discussed in the platforms of deputy groups, which I presented in Chapter 3, with the issues debated in the parliament, I conclude that roll call votes were representative of the broad set of issues facing the deputies in Sessions 2, 3, and 4, but that roll call votes were somewhat restricted in Session 5 and highly restricted in Session 6. This would be expected given that the chairman exerted increasing control over the parliamentary agenda in the legislature's last two sessions.

The number of roll call votes changed from session to session.[3] In Session 2, there were 68 roll call votes, in Session 3 there were 203, in Session 4 there were 181, in Session 5 there were 222, and in Session 6 there were 30 roll call votes. Notice that the number of roll call votes in Sessions 2 and 6 was much lower than the number in Sessions 3, 4, and 5. Session 2 was the first session in which roll call votes were held; deputies took some time to get used to the electronic equipment and to the idea that they could request a roll call vote at any time. In Session 6, the number of roll call votes was extremely low because the parliament had ceased to function in an open, deliberative manner. The number of roll call votes held in Sessions 3, 4, and 5 was comparable to the number of roll call votes held in individual U.S. Congresses.

Voting rules in the Russian Parliament were unusual. First of all, a quorum (two-thirds of the members of each of the chambers) was required before a vote could count. Second, according to Article 111 of the Russian Constitution, a law of the Russian Federation was considered passed only if it passed in each chamber[4] by a majority of the members of that chamber, not just those present. The arithmetic is such that even if two-thirds of the chambers' deputies were present and accounted for, the resolution would not pass unless substantially more than a majority of those present voted in favor of the resolution.

The absolute majority rule meant that it was possible to vote against something simply by not showing up. The implications of this fact seem

[3] The number of deputies in the Russian Parliament changed from session to session due to retirement or due to the periodic rotation of members. Every year, one-fifth of the members of each of the chambers was to be rotated out, and new members from the Congress of People's Deputies who had not yet served in the Supreme Soviet were to be voted in to replace them. During the three and one-half years that the parliament existed, the rotation occurred at the beginning of Sessions 4 and 6. The total number of deputies in Session 2 was 247, in Session 3 the number was 229, in Session 4 the number was 227, in Session 5 the number was 222, and in Session 6 the number was 246.

[4] Recall from Chapter 4 that the parliament was divided into two chambers, the Soviet of the Republic and the Soviet of Nationalities.

to have been obvious to all deputies. According to Alexander Sobyanin, a noted expert on the Russian Parliament, deputies absented themselves strategically.[5] He said that they understood full well that being absent was equivalent to voting "no."

Analysts of Congressional roll call votes typically either (a) eliminate data for representatives who are missing or (b) use some form of imputation to supply the missing values. In the Russian case, an atypical voting rule makes the problem of coding missing values somewhat easier. I assume that deputies were strategic when absenting themselves from votes; therefore, I code all absences or examples of nonvoting as "no." Evidence from the roll call record as well as from the stenographic reports of the meetings of the parliament support this decision.

For example, Sergei Shakhrai, a leading liberal deputy in the parliament, head of the commission responsible for ensuring compliance with the rules of procedure, and a man who was intimately acquainted with the rules governing the parliament, would typically absent himself for some votes on a given day. Being absent (i.e., talking in the hall) was a way to vote "no" without going on record for that vote. Throughout the voting record, there are hundreds of examples of deputies skipping certain votes on a given day.

On March 26, 1992 during the discussion of the draft Russian Constitution, another deputy, Viacheslav Liubimov, a conservative member of the faction Russia, explained that he had decided not to vote on any of the amendments to the new constitution, because he disagreed with the whole project.[6] By deciding not to vote on anything having to do with the draft constitution, this deputy rightly concluded that he would be casting a uniformly negative vote. Although the motivations of deputies varied, it seems fair to conclude that all deputies were aware that being absent was equivalent to voting "no." This should have become clear to even the less politically savvy of the deputies, especially because the issue of deputy absences was a frequent subject of criticism in the press, something about which the chairman and deputy chairmen did not fail to scold the deputies.[7]

In Table 6.1, I show that the average number of deputies who absented themselves from votes changed from session to session. The act of

---

[5] Interview with this author in Moscow, June 1996.
[6] Liubimov's remarks are recorded on page 40 of Bulletin No. 48 of the stenographic report of the Supreme Soviet of the Russian Federation.
[7] Khasbulatov frequently chastised the deputies for not showing up to vote.

Table 6.1. *Average Absences in Sessions 2–6*

Session 2	Session 3	Session 4	Session 5	Session 6
0.263701	0.218298	0.321039	0.436123	0.3421

Note: The average Sobyanin index (see Chapter 1 for a discussion of this index) for those absent is negative in Session 2 and positive in Session 5. Also, the average, at least in Sessions 2 and 3, is about 0 for uncontested votes. This suggests that deputies absented themselves strategically. Democratic deputies were absent more in Session 5, when debate focused on an attempt to reduce Yeltsin's power to carry out reforms, and conservative deputies were absent more in Sessions 2 and 3, when debate centered around attempts to establish a democratic Russian Federation. In Session 4, the average Sobyanin index varies with the subject of the vote; thus, given that Khasbulatov had not yet consolidated his control over the agenda, we see that different groups of deputies absented themselves depending on the day's agenda.

absenting oneself from a vote was not, therefore, a random event, nor were there deputies who were always absent.[8] In particular, during Session 5, when almost all roll call votes had to do with a law that would diminish Yeltsin's powers to continue the economic reform program, the average number of absences was at its highest point.

In order to carry out statistical analyses of the roll call votes in the parliament, I have had to make some changes in how votes are coded. In all analyses presented in this and succeeding chapters, I eliminate roll calls for which fewer than 2.5% of those present voted for or against the winning outcome.[9] I code positive votes as "1" and code negative votes as "0." In addition, I code abstentions as well as absences as "0."

Homogeneous Versus Heterogeneous Preferences

Whatever the official partisan organization of a legislature, it is the structure of deputies' preferences that determines whether or not cycling may occur (Aldrich 1995a). Deputies with homogeneous preferences tend to share the same political values and, presumably, vote alike. Deputies with heterogeneous preferences hold different preferences and do not vote

---

[8] I considered eliminating deputies who never or almost never showed up to vote, but there were no such deputies, a fact that supports my assertion that deputies absented themselves strategically.

[9] I follow Heckman and Snyder (1993, 1996) in choosing the 2.5% threshold for eliminating unanimous votes.

alike. If a legislature is organized into two parties and the members of those parties vote alike, cycling will not occur because there are, in effect, only two decision makers in the legislature.[10] However, if the members of the two parties do not vote alike, implying that there are many decision makers in the legislature, cycling may occur.[11] Likewise, if a legislature is organized into several parties, but the preferences of the deputies are tightly organized into two grand coalitions, cycling will tend not to occur.[12] Finally, and obviously, if a legislature is organized into several parties, and deputy preferences are also organized into several partisan groups, cycling may occur.

In the Russian Parliament, there were always several official partisan groups. In fact, the factions, the basic partisan groups in the parliament, did not change over the three years of the parliament's existence. However, the structure of deputy preferences changed dramatically after the collapse of the Soviet Union. Before the collapse, preferences were organized into two coalitions; after the collapse they were organized into many groups. Also, unlike in the U.S. Congress, when the two-party dynamic disintegrated, the institutional design (in particular, the parliamentary committee system) was incapable of preventing cycling. Thus, in the Russian parliament, stability depended on the structure of preferences.

The partisan organization of the Russian Parliament was complex, as it was in the early years of all the post-Communist democracies.[13] As I described in Chapter 5, the Russian deputies entered the parliament with very loose partisan affiliations. For most deputies, a partisan identity was forged only after they entered parliament. Most of the deputies joined one of several factions. These factions were, in turn, organized into larger coalitions. Before the collapse the factions were organized into two unofficial coalitions, and after the collapse they were organized into three

---

[10] This is Aldrich's point. When Congressional party members have homogeneous preferences, it is as if there were only two decision makers in Congress, and cycling cannot occur.

[11] According to Aldrich, this is where institutional design comes in. In the U.S. Congress, even if party members' preferences are heterogeneous, the Congressional committee system can and does prevent cycling. However, this is certainly not the rule. The Philippines provides an excellent example of a two-party system in which party members hold heterogeneous preferences and thus cannot prevent cycling (Montinola 1999).

[12] This would appear to be the case in France's Fifth Republic.

[13] For a detailed discussion of parties in several post-Communist countries see Kitschelt et al. (1999).

official blocs. Although the organization of the factions into two grand coalitions before the collapse was mostly informal, and the organization into three blocs was recorded and entered as part of the official structure of the parliament, the evidence I present in this chapter shows that the preferences of the members or affiliates of these two grand coalitions were much more homogeneous than the preferences of members of the blocs. Despite the lack of formal organization, deputy preferences were much more highly organized before the collapse than afterwards.

Thus, to understand the nature of the partisan dynamic in the Russian Parliament, we cannot rely on the official record; instead we must investigate the structure of deputy preferences.

Mapping Deputy Ideal Points Using Principal Components

As Heckman and Snyder (1996) discuss, principal components scores are consistent estimates of deputy ideal points.[14] The scores for the first principal component represent deputy ideal points along the most important issue dimension in a given session of the parliament, the scores for the second principal component represent deputy ideal points along the next most important issue dimension, the scores for the third principal component represent ideal points along the third dimension, and so on.

Throughout the rest of this chapter, I use the first two principal components to graph deputy ideal points. The presentation of ideal points based on only two coordinates is uncontroversial for Sessions 2, 3, 5, and 6, because roll call data in these sessions appears to be of low-dimensionality; but, there were certainly more than two issue dimensions in Session 4. However, presenting more than two dimensions graphically is impractical, and, ultimately, one of the goals of this mapping exercise is to provide a means to test whether or not cycling occurred in any of the sessions. If I can show that cycling occurred in two dimensions, then we can conclude that it occurred in more dimensions. (I use the mapping exercise presented in this chapter to test for cycling in Chapter 7.)

---

[14] As Heckman and Snyder (1996) have shown, a principal components analysis on the covariance matrix of roll call votes produces estimates of ideal points that are extremely highly correlated with those estimated by NOMINATE. In addition, starting from precise behavioral assumptions about voter behavior, Heckman and Snyder have shown that the linear model used in standard factor analytic techniques provides appropriate and consistent estimates of legislator ideal points.

Deputy Ideal Points

In Figures 6.1a through 6.1e, I plot the first two principal components for each deputy in each of the five sessions. Each point on the graphs is an estimate of a particulars deputy's ideal point. Because I carried out a separate principal components analysis for each of the five sessions, the ideal points of the deputies change from session to session; however, they remain constant within any given session. In each graph, points that are close together represent deputies with a similar voting record. The closer the points, the more similar the deputies' voting records. The farther the points, the less similar the deputies' voting records.

In Sessions 2 and 3, the two sessions that occurred before the collapse of the Soviet Union and while Yeltsin was still chairman, deputies are clearly divided into two groups (see Figures 6.1a and 6.1b). In particular, there is a core of democratic deputies with similar preferences. Although the conservative deputies are less unified in Session 3 than in Session 2, still there are two recognizable groups of deputies, especially with regard to the first dimension.

The array of deputy positions in Sessions 4 and 5, the two sessions that occurred after the collapse of the Soviet Union but before Khasbulatov had begun to seriously limit the parliament's agenda, is strikingly unorganized (see Figures 6.1c and 6.1d). The core of democratic

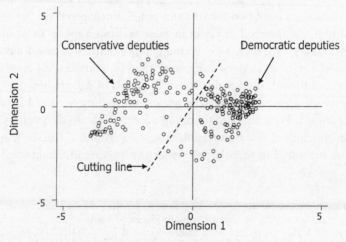

Figure 6.1a. Deputy ideal points in Session 2. Democratic deputies are located to the right of the origin, with conservatives to the left, along the first dimension. The cutting line shows the approximate dividing line between these two coalitions.

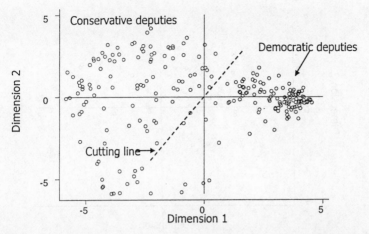

Figure 6.1b. Deputy ideal points in Session 3. As in Session 2, democratic deputies are located to the right of the origin, with conservatives to the left, along the first dimension. Notice that for the conservative deputies, a second dimension was important in Session 3. On the other hand, the democratic deputies are even more tightly clumped along the first dimension.

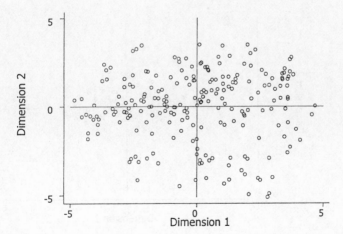

Figure 6.1c. Deputy ideal points in Session 4. Ideal points are well-dispersed throughout the two-dimensional issue space in Session 4. It is no longer possible to identify two distinct coalitions based on preferences. This illustration shows clearly that the two coalitions that existed prior to the collapse of the Soviet Union no longer exist afterwards.

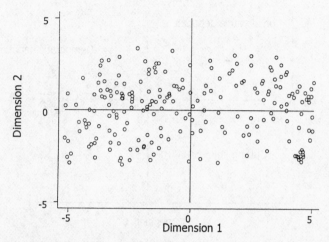

Figure 6.1d. Deputy ideal points in Session 5. As in Session 4, ideal points are well-dispersed throughout the two-dimensional issue space, although they are slightly more constrained along the second dimension than was the case in Session 4. It is clear, however, that the two coalitions that existed prior to the collapse of the Soviet Union no longer exist afterwards.

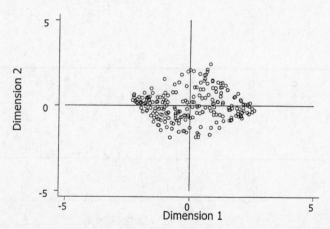

Figure 6.1e. Deputy ideal points in Session 6. Ideal points in Session 6 were constrained along both dimensions. Remember that only 30 roll call votes were held in Session 6, which means that the dimensional picture uncovered by the principal components analysis is less reliable than those uncovered for prior sessions.

deputies has dissolved, and the group of conservative deputies has become even more dispersed.

I have argued that in 1993, the year in which the parliament's sixth session met, Khasbulatov limited the number and scope of topics on which deputies were asked to vote. The fact that deputy ideal points are tightly located and do not cover as much area in the issue space as votes from earlier sessions supports this argument (see Figure 6.1e). As in Sessions 4 and 5, there are no identifiable deputy groups within the larger whole.

The graphs of ideal points of the entire deputy corpus (Figures 6.1a through 6.1e) are supportive of my argument that deputy preferences were homogeneous before the collapse and heterogeneous afterwards. The deputies appear to have been polarized along one dimension in Sessions 2 and 3, but dispersed across both dimensions in Sessions 4, 5, and 6. Not only am I interested in the number of partisan organizations in the parliament, I am also interested in the ideological content of these organizations. If we break down the deputy corpus into the fundamental partisan units, the factions, we get a sense of the ideological content of the two grand coalitions before the collapse. We can also see which deputies were most susceptible to the changes that occurred after the collapse of the Soviet Union. As we will see, deputies in only a couple of the factions (Democratic Russia, Radical Democrats, and Russia) continued to vote as a group after the collapse. I present graphs of deputy ideal points broken down into factions in Figure 6.2.

Sessions 2 and 3 (Figures 6.2a and 6.2b)

Looking first at the graphs for Sessions 2 and 3 (Figures 6.2a and 6.2b), we see that the ideal points for members of the Communist faction are located far from the ideal points for members of Democratic Russia.[15] Deputies in Democratic Russia are located to the right of the origin along the first dimension, and deputies in the Communist faction are located to the left of the origin. In fact, in Sessions 2 and 3 there are four factions that appear to be solidly organized to the right of the origin along the first dimension: Democratic Russia, Radical Democrats, Left

---

[15] Only 68 nonunanimous roll call votes were taken in Session 2, as opposed to 203 in Session 3. The variety of issues was equally great in either session; therefore, the principal component scores more precisely measure the location of deputies for Session 3.

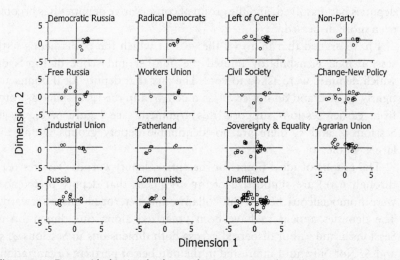

Figure 6.2a. Deputy ideal points by faction for Session 2. Each circle represents the ideal point of a particular member of a faction. Members of the more democratic factions (Democratic Russia, Radical Democrats, Left of Center, and Non-Party faction) tend to be located to the right of the origin along one dimension. Members of the most conservative factions (Russia and the Communist faction) tend to be located to the left of the origin. Members of other factions, including the unaffiliated deputies, are located equally to the left and right of the origin. A weak left–right dimension seems to be present in this period before the collapse of the Soviet Union.

of Center, and the Non-Party faction. As I discussed in Chapter 5, these were the factions most committed to radical political and economic reform before the collapse. There are three factions whose members are consistently located to the left of the origin in Sessions 2 and 3: the Communists, Russia, and Fatherland. In Session 3, they were joined by Sovereignty and Equality and the Agrarian Union. These were the five factions most opposed to reform of the Soviet system.

As the confrontation between the Russian Republic and the Soviet Union as well as the power struggle between Boris Yeltsin and Mikhail Gorbachev heated up, the positions of democrats and conservatives became more polarized. Therefore, the role of the two coalitions in structuring the issue space is most apparent during Session 3. The graphs of faction ideal points in Session 3 show clearly that two groups existed in the parliament: (a) factions whose members are located to the right of the origin formed the basis of the democratic coalition and (b) factions whose members are located to the left of the origin formed the basis of the conservative coalition.

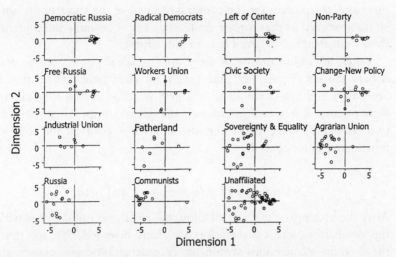

Figure 6.2b. Deputy ideal points by faction for Session 3. In Session 3, members of the more democratic factions (Democratic Russia, Radical Democrats, Left of Center, and Non-Party faction) are tightly clumped to the right of the origin along the first dimension. Members of the conservative and moderately conservative factions (Russia, the Communist faction, Fatherland, Sovereignty and Equality, and Agrarian Union) are located to the left of the origin; however, they are dispersed along a second dimension. The position of the democratic deputies appears to be one-dimensional, whereas that of the conservative deputies is two-dimensional. This apparent difference in the distribution of democratic and conservative deputies can be seen in the dispersion of the unaffiliated deputies as well. A strong left–right dimension exists among the democratic deputies, whereas a weaker one exists among the conservative deputies.

In addition to the core factions of each of the two coalitions, there were five factions whose members are dispersed around the origin: Change-New Policy, Civic Society, Workers' Union, Industrial Union, and Free Russia. Some of the deputies in these factions voted consistently with either the democratic or conservative coalition; a minority voted with either coalition on various occasions.

For the core members of the democratic coalition – Democratic Russia, Radical Democrats, Left of Center, and the Non-Party Deputies – one dimension dominated debate; thus the ideal points of members of these factions are tightly clumped to the right of the origin along only one dimension. Among the core members of the conservative coalition, a second dimension was also important. This second dimension seems to have tapped into divisions within the conservative coalition on the issue of economic reform. Because conservatives were not united in supporting or opposing economic reform, the second dimension was relevant;

therefore, the picture for the conservative end of the spectrum is not as straightforward as that for the democratic end. I examine the content of these "dimensions" in detail later in the chapter.[16]

Taken in conjunction with the graphs of ideal points for the entire deputy corpus (Figure 6.1), the graphs of ideal points by faction for Sessions 2 and 3 provide additional evidence that at that time deputies were organized into two groups and that these groups corresponded to two distinct ideological positions, one in favor of political and economic reform and one opposed.

Sessions 4 and 5 (Figures 6.2c and 6.2d)

After the breakup of the Soviet Union, the preferences of deputies within the democratic and conservative coalitions diverged. We see this in the diversity of positions within the core democratic and conservative factions. This diversification of deputy opinion was caused by the increase in the number and complexity of issues facing deputies after the collapse of the Soviet Union.

Not only was it necessary for deputies to address problems that they had previously been able to avoid, such as the status of Russia's regions and the need for a new constitution, deputies were faced with a new issue, namely, radical reform of the Russian economy. Deputies had initially given the major responsibility for enacting economic reform to President Yeltsin, who had chosen a radical plan known as "shock therapy." However, once Yeltsin's radical reforms began, deputies reacted in a variety of ways.

Although most democratic deputies continued to support a market economy, many did not support Yeltsin's "shock therapy" program. Most conservative deputies continued to oppose dismantling the Soviet party-state, but the special interests they sought to protect differed from deputy to deputy. The collapse of the Soviet Union and the introduction of market mechanisms began to change the traditional support groups for these two groups of deputies. As the interests that they supported began to diversify in the population at large (as old industrialists got rich

---

[16] Results of the principal components analysis suggest that one dimension dominated debate before the breakup of the Soviet Union but that a second dimension was present and important. A graphical presentation of the principal components scores supports this conclusion, but suggests that the second dimension was more important in Session 2 than in Session 3, and that in Session 3 it was important only to conservative deputies.

through privatization; as democrats began to see the suffering that capitalism caused average Russians), deputies' positions on the right way to reform the economy became much more varied than could be captured by a simple dichotomy between reform/no reform.

Some hard-liners in the Communist Party faction, collective farm chairmen in the Agrarian Union, and extreme nationalists in the Russia faction dug in their heels and resisted reform. But others, especially enterprise managers who benefited from privatization, developed a more complex attitude toward market reforms. The deputies with ties to these enterprise managers supported privatization while at the same time supporting subsidies for failing and unprofitable enterprises.

Members of the moderately democratic factions such as Left of Center and Free Russia found that although they supported a market economy, they did not support the draconian measures adopted by Yeltsin and his government. Thus, during Session 4, as the economy diversified due to economic reform, deputies' interests diversified, and their voting reflected this proliferation of options and tastes.

An examination of faction member ideal points shows that the democratic and conservative coalitions broke apart as their more moderate members came to hold increasingly complex positions (Figures 6.2c and 6.2d).

In Session 4, the only faction whose members all remained firmly committed to reform – that is, they are located to the right of the origin on the first dimension – was Radical Democrats. As my later analysis shows, the first dimension in Session 4 has to do with support or opposition to economic reform. In most of the democratic factions, some members move to the left of the origin, which means that they reacted negatively to the economic and political reforms implemented by Yeltsin following the collapse of the Soviet Union. Many members of the communist and nationalist factions move to the right of the origin, which means that they supported Yeltsin's reforms.

In Session 5, ideal points of members of all factions except Democratic Russia, Radical Democrats, and Industrial Union are as unorganized or more so than in Session 4.

The other important change in the location of deputy ideal points in Sessions 4 and 5 is the importance of a second dimension. This second dimension is important to all deputies, including members of the more democratic factions. If one compares the mappings for members of the fourteen factions in Session 3 with those in Sessions 4 and 5 (Figures 6.2b, 6.2c, and 6.2d), it is clear that in none of the democratic

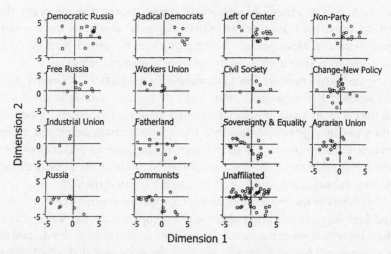

Figure 6.2c. Deputy ideal points by faction for Session 4. In these figures for Session 4, it is difficult to distinguish the dispersion of deputy ideal points by faction. Members of the more democratic factions as well as members of the conservative factions are located in all quadrants of the issue space. It is no longer possible to identify even a week left–right dimension among the deputies.

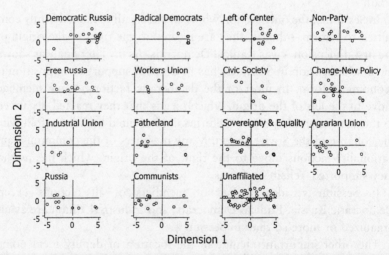

Figure 6.2d. Ideal points by faction for Session 5. As in the figures for Session 4, it is difficult to distinguish the dispersion of deputy ideal points by faction in these figures.

factions are the deputies as tightly clumped as they were in Session 3. Even in the case of the Radical Democrats, the only democratic faction in which no members move to the other side of the origin, deputies begin to disperse along the second dimension. Among the members of Communists of Russia, Russia, and Agrarian Union, more members are located on the reform side of the origin in Sessions 4 and 5 than in Session 3.

An examination of the ideal points of faction members in Sessions 4 and 5 illustrate clearly how the coalitions of democrats and conservatives "dissolved" after the breakup of the Soviet Union. We see that the number of factions whose members remain passionately committed to or passionately opposed to political and/or economic reform diminishes over time.

Ideal Points of Presidium Members

In this book, I argue that while Yeltsin was chairman, he was the leader of a majority coalition both in the parliament and in the Presidium, but Khasbulatov was the leader of no majority, either in the parliament or in the Presidium. In addition, I argue that because the preferences of Presidium members were heterogeneous after the collapse of the Soviet Union, Presidium members were incapable of mounting unified opposition to Khasbulatov. Although there were several attempts within the Presidium to remove Khasbulatov (mounted both by members of the Coalition for Reform and members of Russian Unity), each such attempt died due to lack of a majority to support the motion. In Figure 6.3, I map the ideal points of Presidium members in Sessions 2, 3, 4, and 5. I identify the Presidium members by their affiliation with one of the three deputy blocs or as an independent.

It is clear from the graphs of Presidium members in Sessions 2 and 3 that before the collapse of the Soviet Union, members of the Presidium were polarized in the same way as members of the parliament as a whole. Furthermore, before the collapse, many more members of the Presidium were democrats than were conservatives, giving Yeltsin a clear and substantial majority while he was chairman. Although it is difficult to decipher the codes for Sessions 2 and 3, most of the Presidium members located to the right of the origin are members of the Coalition for Reform. As you can see in the graphs for Sessions 4 and 5 (and even Session 3), there were more members of the Coalition for Reform in the Presidium than members of Russian Unity, even after the collapse of the Soviet

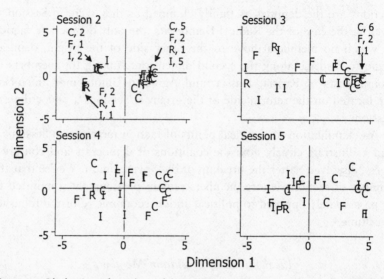

Figure 6.3. Ideal points of members of the Presidium in Sessions 2, 3, 4, and 5. To improve legibility, Coalition for Reform is abbreviated as C, Constructive Forces as F, Russian Unity as R, and the independent deputies as I. (In the graphs for Sessions 2 and 3, particular ideal points are noted in those places where it is difficult to distinguish among ideal points.) From this figure we see that the ideal points of the members of the Presidium are dispersed in a way similar to that of the ideal points of the members of the legislature as a whole.

Union. As I discussed in earlier chapters, because the democrats had a majority in the first meeting of the Congress, the committees were slightly stacked in favor of the democrats, and the committee chairmen (who were members of the Presidium) were, consequently, mostly early supporters of reform. The graphs for Sessions 4 and 5 show that among the members of the Presidium (as among the deputies as a whole), being a member of the Coalition for Reform after the collapse of the Soviet Union did not mean that a deputy was a supporter of reform. Notice that in Sessions 4 and 5 there are several members of the Coalition for Reform that are located to the left of the origin along the first dimension, and one member of Russian Unity located to the right of the origin. Also, while most Presidium members who were also members of Russia Unity are located beneath the origin along the second dimension, members of Constructive Forces and the Coalition for Reform are located on either side. There is little apparent structure among the preferences of the Presidium members in Sessions 4 and 5.

DIMENSIONALITY OF THE ISSUE SPACE

In this section, I use the results of the principal components analysis to explore the number of policy dimensions that were present at various times in the Russian Parliament. In particular, I am interested in the number of dimensions that were present in three key periods: (1) before the collapse of the Soviet Union (Sessions 2 and 3), (2) immediately after the collapse (Session 4), and (3) the period of Khasbulatov's increasing control over the parliamentary agenda (Sessions 5 and 6).

The purpose of principal components analysis, as originally conceived, is to reduce a large number of variables to a smaller subset that encompasses most of the variance of the original data. Deciding how many dimensions exist in a set of roll call votes is analogous to deciding how many principal components to retain when the goal is to use only a few principal components to capture the essential information in a large group of variables. Although Heckman and Snyder have devised a method for estimating the number of dimensions present in a set of roll call votes, their method requires far more roll call votes than exist in my data set (Heckman and Snyder 1996, 1997).

Given that a method for estimating the number of dimensions in my data does not exist, I rely on three types of evidence, which taken together provide convincing evidence that the dimensionality of the issue space increased dramatically after the collapse of the Soviet Union. The evidence also supports the contention that the issue space was one-dimensional before the collapse and multidimensional afterwards.

The three kinds of evidence I present are: (1) an analysis of the percentage of the original roll call votes that models of increasing dimensionality correctly predict, (2) spatial presentation of the median ideal points of relevant deputy groups (factions and blocs), and (3) an interpretation of the policy content of the estimated components (dimensions).[17]

In Table 6.2, I report the percent of the total number of roll call votes correctly predicted by the first principal component, the first two principal components together, the first three, and so on, for each session of the Russian Parliament (for a full description of this summary procedure, see Appendix 6A).

---

[17] Poole and Rosenthal use this method to support their important conclusion that throughout the history of the U.S. Congress only one or two dimensions are needed to characterize deputy voting. In their comparison of the results of principal components analysis with the NOMINATE model and method, Heckman and Snyder

Table 6.2. *Percent of Votes Correctly Predicted by a Model that Includes 1, 2, 3, 4, 5, and 6 Dimensions*[a]

Number of Components Retained	Session 2	Session 3	Session 4	Session 5	Session 6
1	76.7	76.0	69.5	77.6	75.4
2	79.5	80.0	73.7	80.6	79.6
3	80.7	81.9	75.8	81.9	82.8
4	82.5	83.1	77.7	82.9	
5	83.7	83.8	79.1	83.5	
6			80.5		

[a] I coded numbers less than .5 as 0 and numbers greater than or equal to .5 as 1.

According to Koford (1989, 1990), the first principal component must correctly predict more than 75% of the votes to justify the conclusion that the issue space is one-dimensional.[18] In Sessions 2, 3, 5, and 6, the first dimension alone correctly predicts between 75.4% and 77.6% of the votes, slightly more than the 75% threshold that Koford proposes. In Session 4, the first dimension correctly predicts only 69.5% of the votes, and an additional two dimensions are needed to pass the 75% threshold. These results demonstrate that there was a dramatic increase

(1993, 1996) report the percent correctly predicted as a means to verify that principal components analysis uncovers the same dimensional structure as the method used by Poole and Rosenthal (1991). Thus, Heckman and Snyder also show how the percent correctly predicted can be used to identify the number of issue dimensions. Heckman and Snyder also provide a method to *estimate* the number of issue dimensions in a set of roll call data. Other methods are essentially ad hoc. Unfortunately, the Heckman and Snyder technique requires hundreds more roll call votes than are present in my data set.

[18] Koford (1989, 1990) derives an appropriate null hypothesis against which to measure the percent correctly predicted by the first dimension in a dimensional analysis. Even if the true number of dimensions is two, the first principal component will correctly predict 75% of the votes; therefore, the first dimension must predict more than 75% of the votes to justify the conclusion that the issue space is one-dimensional. In an exhaustive response to Koford's concerns, Poole and Rosenthal (1991, p. 245) conclude that if a single dimension correctly predicts about 80% of the roll call votes, then it is highly unlikely that the underlying issue space is two-dimensional or higher. Therefore, if the first dimension accurately predicts 80% of the votes, one dimension is sufficient to describe the data. Poole and Rosenthal (1991, p. 243) also find that voting in particular Congresses can either be accounted for by low-dimensional models (i.e., one or two dimensions) or be spatially chaotic. "There appears to be no middle-ground."

in the number of issue dimensions in the first months after the collapse of the Soviet Union, the period corresponding to Session 4.

In none of the sessions does the first dimension predict much more than 75% of the votes. The second dimension adds an additional 2.8% to 4.2%. According to Poole and Rosenthal (1991), a more appropriate threshold for concluding that one dimension is sufficient to describe the data may be 80%. Under this rule of thumb, in none of the sessions was the issue space strictly one-dimensional; it was two-dimensional in Sessions 2, 3, 5, and 6 and "spatially chaotic" in Session 4. An interpretation of the percent correctly predicted does not lead to a conclusive answer to the question of the dimensionality of the issue space. We can say that in the Russian Parliament either a low-dimensional model (one or two dimensions) accounts for roll call voting (as it does in Sessions 2, 3, 5, and 6), or voting is spatially chaotic (as it is in Session 4).

Let us now interpret the policy content of the dimensions uncovered by the analysis.

Interpretation of Issue Dimensions

Examining the correlation of the roll call votes with the dimensions uncovered in the principal components analysis gives additional information about the issue space. Characterizing the first dimension in Sessions 2 and 3 is straightforward (see Table 6.3). Of the seventeen votes in Session 2 that were highly correlated with the first dimension, all concerned the issue of Russian sovereignty.[19] For example, a series of fifteen

---

[19] Interpretation of the components resulting from a principal components analysis is not an exact science. Typically, one examines those variables that are highly correlated with the component to get a sense of its meaning (this is the method that Poole and Rosenthal, Heckman and Snyder, and many others use). Indeed, this is a standard way to "interpret" dimensions.

As do most researchers, I interpret the first principal component in Sessions 2, 3, 5, and 6, by referring to those votes that are correlated with the component at .6 or greater. In all five sessions, there are very few votes correlated with the second principal component at .6 or greater; therefore, in order to interpret the second dimension, I look at votes that are correlated with the principal component at greater than .3 (or less than −.3). In Session 4, it is difficult to interpret either the first or second dimension. There are few votes correlated with the first principal component at .6 or greater, therefore I also look at votes correlated at .5 or greater. Although there are many votes correlated at .3 or greater with the second component, no single issue or set of issues seems to describe these votes. For this reason, it is almost impossible to characterize the dimensions in Session 4 based on the principal components analysis.

Table 6.3. *Votes Highly Correlated with First Principal Component in Sessions 2 and 3*

Date of Vote	Correlation of Vote(s) with First Principal Component	Content of Vote
SESSION 2		
		Votes on Russian sovereignty: 17
October 23–24, 1990	.60 to .89	Series of votes (15) on the draft law of the USSR concerning the effect of laws of the USSR on the territory of the Russian Republic (RSFSR).
October 24, 1990	.72	Vote on a draft resolution on the rights of the Russian government to decide how to distribute paper products produced exclusively in the Russian Republic.
October 31, 1990	.60	Five votes on a resolution guaranteeing the economic basis for the sovereignty of the Russian Republic.
SESSION 3[a]		
		Votes on Russian sovereignty: 41
February 7, 1991	.67 and .67	Two votes on treaties with Kazakstan and Belorussia.
February 27, 1991	.70 to .77	Five votes as part of a general discussion of Russia's need for its own radio and television stations, separate from those controlled by the Soviet government. The question was repeatedly raised: How can Russia be a sovereign state without its own mass media?
April 24, 1991	.60 to .83 and −.61 to −.68	Sixteen out of the 53 votes on the draft law on the election of the President of the Russian Republic.
April 24, 1991		Fifteen out of 63 votes on the draft law on the Russian President.
May 16, 1991	.66	Vote to debate the role of the Soviet Army in Armenia and Azerbaidjan. Deputies are concerned about the role of Russian soldiers in the conflict.
July 5, 1991	.62	Within a larger discussion of the Union Treaty, the deputies vote on whether or not the fifteen republics (of which Russia is one) should no longer be considered the property of the USSR.

Date of Vote	Correlation of Vote(s) with First Principal Component	Content of Vote
June 21, 1991	.62	Vote to publish a document sharply critical of key USSR government leaders (Pavlov, Iazov, Kriuchkov) for not following the 500-day program and for holding a secret session of the USSR Congress of People's Deputies.
		Votes on Economic reform: 1
January 31, 1991	.69	Vote to debate Gorbachev's decree concerning the struggle against economic sabotage. This decree was an anti-market, anti-competition decree.
		Votes on other subjects: 7
January 21 and 24, 1991	.68 to .75	Three votes within a larger discussion of the report of the Chairman of the Russian Parliament, Boris Yeltsin.
February 21, 1991	−.74	Vote to hold a future extraordinary Congress of People's Deputies on March 4.
February 21, 1991	.63	Vote to hold the extraordinary Congress of People's Deputies on April 25.
March 1, 1991	−.65	Vote to bring a criminal case (for libel) against deputy A. M. Tarasov.
April 18, 1991	.60	Votes on a draft law on the militia. These votes concern Section 5 of the law, which has to do with the depoliticization of the organs for internal affairs (the militia).

[a] Five votes from Session 3, held on March 1, 1991, were not included in the table due to the difficulty in deciding the content of the votes based only on the transcript of debate.

votes, which were correlated with the first dimension at .60 to .89, concerned a draft law on the effect of USSR laws in the Russian Republic. Five votes on a resolution guaranteeing the economic sovereignty of the Russian Republic were correlated with the first dimension at .60. Of the forty-nine votes highly correlated with the first dimension in Session 3, forty-one concerned Russian sovereignty (over thirty were votes on the creation of a Russian president). Undoubtedly, the most important dimension before the breakup of the Soviet Union was Russian sovereignty.

Because no votes are even moderately correlated with the second principal component in Session 2, it is difficult to interpret this second dimension; hence its relevance is suspect. However, in Session 3, several votes are moderately highly correlated (at .5 or greater) with the second principal component. Most of these are votes on amendments to the draft law creating the office of Russian President, such as an amendment that would give to the chairman of the parliament rather than to the president the right to sign laws into effect. Other votes were on amendments to constrain the president's ability to choose his own prime minister (head of Cabinet), or to make the president follow the laws of the USSR as well as Russian laws. Another set of votes concerned the protocol for impeachment. Therefore, I interpret the second dimension in Session 3 as support versus opposition to a strong executive.

Interpreting the first dimension in Session 4 is difficult, because few votes are highly correlated with the first principal component. In order to provide some interpretation, I relax the correlation criteria. If one examines the first principal component in Session 4 by looking at all votes that are moderately highly correlated with the first dimension,[20] it is clear that many different issues are moderately highly correlated with the first principal component (see Table 6.4). Votes on constitutional guarantees of human rights, on delineating the powers of the public prosecutor, and on privatization and bankruptcy are all included in the first dimension, capturing aspects of both political and economic reform. Support for economic and political reform is negatively associated with the first dimension; therefore, I interpret the first dimension as a general reaction *against* reform. Interpreting a second dimension in Session 4 is impossible, because there were no votes even moderately highly correlated with this dimension.

In Session 5, all fifty-four votes highly correlated with the first dimension concerned the parliament's version of the Law on the Government, which was designed to increase the parliament's power vis-à-vis the president (see Table 6.5). For example, the final vote on the draft law was correlated with the first dimension at .68. Again, it is impossible to interpret the second dimension. Clearly, the most important dimension during Session 5 was the balance of power between president and parliament. Of course, as I argue in earlier chapters, a major reason why the

---

[20] By moderately highly correlated, I mean a level of .5 or greater.

Table 6.4. *Votes Highly Correlated with the First Principal Component in Session 4*

Date of Vote	Correlation of Vote(s) with First Principal Component	Content of Vote
January 17, 1992	.50 to .58	Series of votes (11) on the draft law of the Russian Federation on the office of the public prosecutor.
March 26, 1992	.56 to .71	Series of votes (10) on the second section of the draft constitution of the Russian Federation, which concerned the basic rights, freedoms, and responsibilities of the individual and citizen.
March 27, 1992	.50 to .54	Three votes on the third section of the draft constitution. The third section was titled "Citizen's Society."
May 28, 1992	−.52	Vote to pass the draft law on bankruptcy.
May 29, 1992	−.51	Vote to pass as a basis the program on privatization of state enterprises of the Russian Federation.
June 5, 1992	3: .50 to 54 2: −.51, −.53	Five votes on the Law on Privatization.
June 11, 1991	.56	Vote on amendment to the Law on Privatization that contradicts the entire law (proposed by head of the Russian Unity bloc).
June 19, 1992	.54	Draft law on consumer cooperatives.

parliament wished to increase the powers of the legislature was to increase the legislature's role in making economic reform policy. Some analysts interpreted the legislature's efforts to restrict the president's powers solely as an effort to alter the course of economic reform that had been chosen by the president.

Of the seven votes in Session 6 that are highly correlated with the first dimension, five are directed against Khasbulatov's enemies both inside and outside the parliament. Two are votes to disband parliamentary committees whose chairmen dared to challenge Khasbulatov's misuse of power, and three are votes to restrict freedom of the press, especially of the

Table 6.5. *Votes Highly Correlated with the First Principal Component in Sessions 5 and 6*

Date of Vote	Correlation of Vote(s) with First Principal Component	Content of Vote
SESSION 5		
November 6, 1992	.62 to .68	Eleven votes (out of 48) on the draft law of the Russian Federation on the Council of Ministers; this version of the law eliminates the president's ability to appoint members of his Cabinet.
November 11, 1992	.60 to .82	Forty-two votes (out of 131) on the draft law of the Council of Ministers.
November 13, 1992	.68	Vote to approve the draft law on the Council of Ministers as a whole.
SESSION 6		
April 29, 1993	.63 and .65	Two votes on the reorganization of committees dominated by democratic deputies – the committees on mass media and legislation, in particular.
June 24, 1993	.61	Not enough information to discern content.
June 25, 1993	.61	One vote on an investigation into corruption among Yeltsin's government.
June 25, 1993	.78 to .79	Three votes on Article 21 of the draft law on the media. Article 21 concerns the publisher's rights. These votes should be seen in the context of an attack by Khasbulatov on the newspaper *Izvestia*, formerly the official organ of the USSR Presidium of the Supreme Soviet.

newspaper *Izvestia*, which was harshly critical of the parliament and of Khasbulatov's chairmanship. The main issue dimension in Session 6 seems to have been related to Khasbulatov's efforts to consolidate his autocratic position. Insofar as Khasbulatov used the issue of parliamentary power to justify his attempt to increase his own power, the main dimension in Session 6 can be thought of as a variant on the balance of power issue.

The Sobyanin Index

Two sophisticated analysts of the Russian Congress of People's Deputies, Alexander Sobyanin and D. Yur'ev, created the index, which I am calling the "Sobyanin index."[21] These two scholars were committed Westernizing democrats. They created their index by selecting 105 key (*kliuchevoi*) votes from the first four sessions of the Congress of People's Deputies.[22] Sobyanin and Yur'ev defined key votes as those that were decisive in either creating democracy or hindering the creation of democracy. They calculated their index based on the proportion of the 105 key votes in which a particular deputy sided for or against democracy. Thus, their index is analogous to many interest group ratings created in the United States or in other Western democracies. In fact, Sobyanin and Yur'ev refer to their index as a rating (*reiting*), borrowing from Western vocabulary.

I use the Sobyanin index in the same way that students of the U.S. Congress use interest group ratings: I consider it as a biased but informed measure of the particular trait of concern to the interest group – in this case, "support for liberal democracy." The fact that Sobyanin and Yur'ev created their index based on votes within the Congress of People's Deputies is especially useful to me, because it is an index created on a *different set of votes* than those used in my principal components analysis. The deputies in the parliament were, of course, a subset of those in the Congress of People's Deputies. Thus, I have an independent measure against which to compare the scores generated by the principal components analysis.

By design, the Sobyanin index is a measure of the degree to which a deputy's votes on key issues reflects his or her support for democracy versus support for the old Soviet command system. Prior to the collapse of the Soviet Union, the first principal component appears to capture much the same dimension as does Sobyanin and Yur'ev's index. As I discuss above, Russian sovereignty was very much seen as synonymous with democratic reform and as opposition to the Stalinist command system. Many of the votes that Sobyanin and Yur'ev choose in creating their index are those votes in the Congress of People's Deputies that

---

[21] Sobyanin and Yur'ev's analysis of the makeup of the Russian Congress of People's Deputies along with some of the crucial decisions considered by this institution are summarized in their important book, *S'ezd narodnyh deputatov RSFSR v zerkale poimennyh golosovanii*, 1991, Moscow.

[22] Recall that the Congress of People's Deputies was the larger parent body of the parliament.

Table 6.6. *Correlation of Sobyanin Index with First Principal Component for Sessions 2–6*

Session 2	Session 3	Session 4	Session 5	Session 6
0.4652	0.8640	−0.5529	−0.3825	−0.4454

have to do with Russian sovereignty and with the creation of the post of President of Russia – the same kind of votes that correlate highly with the first principal component in my analysis.

As can be seen in Table 6.6, the first principal component correlates highly with the Sobyanin index *before the breakup* of the Soviet Union. The fact that the Sobyanin index is correlated at .86 with the first principal component in Session 3 supports my conclusion that before the breakup of the Soviet Union the first principal component captures the dimension of Russian sovereignty and democratic reform. There are two reasons why the correlation in Session 2 is not as high as in Session 3: (1) There were only 68 roll call votes in Session 2, and (2) the issue of Russian sovereignty as well as democratic reform became more defined and more salient by Session 3.

After the breakup of the Soviet Union, the correlation of the first principal component and the Sobyanin index is negative, which supports my contention that after the collapse the first principal component measures an anti-reform reaction. The fact that the correlation is weaker in Session 5 than in Session 4 supports my argument that while the main issue dimension in Session 5 was associated with many deputies' reactions to Yeltsin's economic reform program, it mostly concerned the balance of power between president and parliament.

Median Faction Ideal Points

So far, I have discussed the ideal points of individual deputies, as measured by the first and second principal component score for each deputy. We can also think of factions as having ideal points. There are several ways in which one could compute a faction's ideal point, based on the principal component scores for the members of the faction. One possible way would be to compute the median first principal component score and the median second principal component score. This definition assumes that factions make decisions based on majority rule and that the two dimensions are separable. Thus, the median position might correspond to a different deputy for each dimension. This measure is more attractive than using the average position of a faction because in every faction except Radical Democrats there were several deputies who really didn't belong, deputies whose ideal point was at the opposite extreme to the majority of members of the faction. These misfits tend to be weighted more in computing an average than in computing a median.

I present median ideal points for each faction in Sessions 2 through 6 in Table 6.7.

In Figures 6.4a through 6.4d, I map the coordinates for the factions from Table 6.7.

Looking only at the location of factions, the dimensional nature of the issue space is starkly depicted. In Session 2, all but three factions are clumped together around a point slightly to the right of the origin (see Figure 6.4a). As I have discussed earlier, this was a time in which the Russian Parliament was beginning to assert the rights of Russia to proceed along a different path than that advocated at the time by the president of

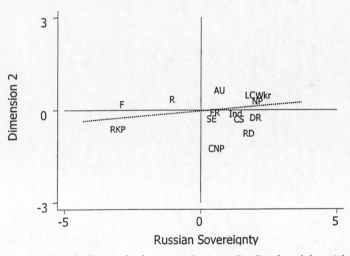

Figure 6.4a. Median ideal points for factions in Session 2. Reading from left to right, RKP stands for the Communist Party faction, F for Fatherland, R for Russia, SE for Sovereignty and Equality, FR for Free Russia, CNP for Change-New Policy, AU for Agrarian Union, Ind for Industrial Union, CS for Civil Society, RD for Radical Democrats, LC for Left of Center, DR for Democratic Russia, NP for the Non-Party faction, and Wkr for Workers' Union. A single dimension (represented by the dotted line) captures fairly well the location of most of the median members of the factions. However, the Radical Democrats and Change-New Policy are located such that two dimensions are necessary to describe their positions.

Table 6.7. Dimension by Dimension Medians for Each Faction in Sessions 2–6

Group Names	Session 2		Session 3		Session 4		Session 5		Session 6	
	pc1	pc2	pc1	pc2	pc1	pc2	pc1	pc2	pc1	pc2
Factions										
Democratic Russia (DR)	2.0	-0.2	4.0	-0.3	2.7	1.2	3.5	0.9	1.8	0.1
Radical Democrats (RD)	1.8	-0.7	4.1	-0.5	3.7	-0.5	4.9	0.2	2.1	-0.2
Left of Center (LC)	1.8	0.5	3.4	0	1.1	1.2	2.3	0.7	0.7	-0.1
Non-Party Faction (NP)	2.1	0.3	3.4	-0.4	1.2	0.8	0	1.9	0.2	0.2
Free Russia (FR)	0.5	-0.3	3.6	0.2	1.0	0.8	-0.3	0.8	0.9	0.2
Workers' Union (Wkr)	2.3	0.5	2.2	0.2	-0.4	0.9	-0.4	1.2	0.1	-0.4
Civil Society (CS)	1.4	-0.3	1.1	0.4	0.9	0.5	1.3	0.2	-0.4	-0.5
Change-New Policy (CNP)	0.6	-1.2	2.2	-0.4	-0.4	0.5	-1.3	0.2	0.4	-0.2
Industrial Union (Ind)	1.3	-0.1	-0.6	0.6	-0.8	1.3	-2.7	-2.1	-0.6	-0.5
Sovereignty and Equality (SE)	0.4	-0.2	-1.8	0.4	-0.7	-0.5	-1.5	0.5	-0.4	-0.4
Fatherland (F)	-2.9	0.2	-2.2	0.3	-0.9	-0.4	-3.0	0	-1.2	0.2
Agrarian Union (AU)	0.7	0.7	-3.0	1.0	-1.5	-0.4	-2.9	-0.9	-1.0	-0.4
Russia (R)	-1.0	0.4	-3.7	0.5	-2.4	-0.7	-2.7	-1.7	-1.6	-0.3
Communists (RKP)	-3.0	-0.6	-4.6	0.7	-1.6	-0.8	-2.4	-0.8	-1.7	0.2

the Soviet Union, Mikhail Gorbachev. Most deputies thought of themselves as democrats, and they understood this term in only a vague way.

In Session 3, when concrete efforts were made by Yeltsin to assert Russian interests over those of the Soviet Union, the factions become quite starkly lined up across the issue space. Thus, even though two dimensions were salient in this period, these issues were joined in such a way that voting occurred along a single dimension only (see Figure 6.4b). This means that one can predict the policy position of a particular faction along one dimension just by knowing their position on the other dimension. Recall the earlier discussion in Chapter 5. In Figure 5.1, I showed spatially how even when two dimensions are salient, deputies may vote as if only one dimension exists, in this particular case the issue of Russian sovereignty. In Figure 6.4b, the representation of faction ideal points in Session 3 looks exactly like the theoretical picture presented in Figure 5.1.

By contrast, Figures 6.4c and 6.4d show that in both Sessions 4 and 5, factions can be differentiated by their positions on at least two dimensions. They do not line up along a single dimension that spans the issue space, as in Session 3. This means that the policy position of a faction along one dimension cannot be predicted based on its position

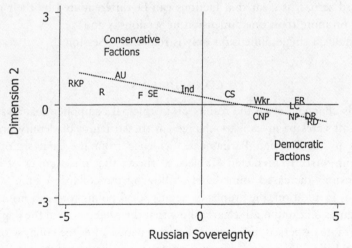

Figure 6.4b. Median ideal points for factions in Session 3. Again, RKP stands for the Communist Party faction, F for Fatherland, R for Russia, SE for Sovereignty and Equality, FR for Free Russia, CNP for Change-New Policy, AU for Agrarian Union, Ind for Industrial Union, CS for Civil Society, RD for Radical Democrats, LC for Left of Center, DR for Democratic Russia, NP for the Non-Party faction, and Wkr for Workers' Union. Clearly, in Session 3, a single dimension (represented by the dotted line) explains the variation among median members of the factions.

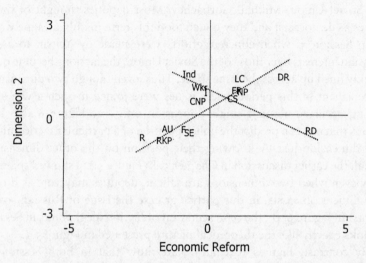

Figure 6.4c. Median ideal points for factions in Session 4. A single dimension is insufficient to capture the dispersion of the ideal points of median members of factions in Session 4.

along the other dimension. Even taking into account the great range in deputy member ideal points, which tends to bias all median positions toward zero, it is clear that factions can be differentiated by their positions on more than one dimension in Sessions 4 and 5.

Finally, a single dimension only is relevant in Session 6.

CONCLUSIONS

In this chapter, I used the results of a principal components analysis of roll call votes to investigate changes in the structure of deputy preferences in the Russian Parliament. Evidence from the analysis of the percent correctly predicted (Table 6.2) shows that the number of issue dimensions increased immediately following the collapse of the Soviet Union. In addition, the graphs of deputy ideal points for Sessions 4 and 5 (Figures 6.2c and 6.2d) clearly show that the preferences of the deputies were more dispersed, hence more heterogeneous, after the collapse of the Soviet Union. A second dimension appears to be relevant in all three post-Soviet sessions, and more than two dimensions are present immediately after the collapse, in Session 4. The graphs of the faction ideal points for Sessions 4 and 5 (Figures 6.4c and 6.4d) provide additional evidence that a second dimension was important for members of most of the factions after the collapse.

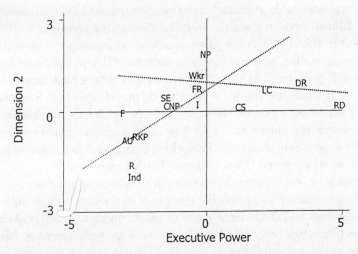

Figure 6.4d. Median ideal points for factions in Session 5. As in Session 4, a single dimension is insufficient to capture the dispersion of the ideal points of median members of factions in Session 5.

Evidence for the presence of only one dimension *before* the collapse of the Soviet Union is not as clearcut. The analysis of the percent correctly predicted suggests that one dimension may be sufficient to describe the data, but the results are not conclusive. The graphical representations of faction ideal points (Figures 6.4a and 6.4b), however, are highly supportive of my contention that one dimension (that of Russian sovereignty) dominated the debate before the collapse of the Soviet Union.

I have argued that the reason deputy ideal points are more dispersed after the collapse of the Soviet Union is that following the collapse of political and economic institutions, deputies were faced with an array of issues and problems that they had never before encountered. New dimensions became relevant, and alliances that had been relevant before this institutional collapse were no longer relevant afterwards.

In an interview on March 11, 1992, published by *Nezavisimaya Gazeta*, First Deputy Chairman of the Parliament, Sergei Filatov, discusses the changes in deputy alliances and voting. Filatov describes a parliament in which the democratic deputies, so unified before the collapse of the Soviet Union, have broken down into a number of rival factions. He mentions the defection of Change-New Policy and the growing independence of the Radical Democrats and Free Russia. In his opinion, "The emergence of more and more new disagreements among democrats was inevitable after the defeat of communism . . . [and] it will be very difficult even to unite the so-called democratic factions."

Filatov also discusses the general lack of organization in all factions and in particular in the democratic factions. "[D]eputies come to the session ill-prepared," he says. "Sometimes they do not have time even to read the law they are voting for. So what do they do then? . . . Some listen – they try to get a grip on the issue – others watch their neighbors. But most watch the chairman . . . [I]t has to be admitted that this applies mostly to economic questions. Everything changes when a political problem is being discussed. Then everyone has his own view."

In such an atmosphere, a chairman with no strong partisan ties had ample opportunity to exploit the ignorance of the centrist and independent deputies and the indecisiveness of the democratic deputies. Aldrich argues that when party members' preferences are heterogeneous, parties can be only weakly influential; and, in a legislature with powerful committees, the balance of influence shifts away from parties toward committees. However, in a legislature with weak committees and a strong chairman, power shifts toward the chairman.

As quoted above, Filatov says that deputies pay less attention to the chairman when the issues are political. As I will show in the next chapter (Chapter 7), the voting behavior of deputies in Session 4 was incoherent on precisely those votes having to do with political and social issues. In the next chapter, I review the definition of such a situation, called cycling, and provide evidence that outcomes did indeed "wander" through the space of alternatives after the collapse of the Soviet Union.

Appendix 6A

THE BASICS OF PRINCIPAL COMPONENTS ANALYSIS

Principal components analysis is a factor analytic technique; however, it differs in important respects from traditional factor analysis. Principal components are algebraically fully determined; the researcher makes no choice over possible solutions as occurs in traditional factor analysis.

The Model

We begin with the matrix of roll call votes in which each variable (column) corresponds to a roll call vote and each observation (row)

Table 6A.1. *Example Roll Call Data Set*

	Amendment 1	Amendment 2	Amendment 3	Amendment 4	Amendment 5
Deputy 1	1	0	1	0	1
Deputy 2	0	1	1	1	1
Deputy 3	0	1	0	1	1
Deputy 4	1	0	1	0	1
Deputy 5	1	0	1	0	1
Deputy 6	0	1	0	1	0
Deputy 7	0	1	0	1	0
Deputy 8	1	0	1	1	1
Deputy 9	1	1	1	1	1
Deputy 10	0	1	0	1	0
Mean	.5	.6	.6	.7	.7

corresponds to a particular deputy. For the sake of illustration, I shall create a matrix of data consisting of ten observations (deputies) on five variables (roll call votes). The example data are presented in Table 6A.1. A "1" indicates a deputy's affirmative vote; a "0" indicates a negative vote.

Principal components are linear combinations of a set of weighted variables. There are as many principal components for a given set of data as there are variables. For our example above, there are five variables (five columns corresponding to five votes); therefore, there are five principal components. The three key criteria that determine the principal components are as follows: (1) Each principal component maximizes the remaining variance in the data set, (2) each component is uncorrelated with the other principal components, and (3) the squared elements of the vector of weights must sum to 1.[23] The first principal component is chosen to maximize the variance of the entire data set, the second principal component maximizes the variance remaining after the first principal component has been extracted, and so on.

The primary use of principal components analysis is to reduce a large number of variables to a much smaller subset of principal components. Usually, the first one to two components capture most of the variance in a given set of data. Therefore, a researcher can substitute these

[23] This is the most commonly used means to insure that the model is identified. Heckman and Snyder discuss this issue at length in their 1996 paper.

Table 6A.2. *Example Covariance Matrix*

	Amendment 1	Amendment 2	Amendment 3	Amendment 4	Amendment 5
Amendment 1	.28	−.22	.22	−.17	.17
Amendment 2	−.22	.27	−.18	.2	−.13
Amendment 3	.22	−.18	.27	−.13	.2
Amendment 4	−.17	.2	−.13	.23	−.1
Amendment 5	.17	−.13	.2	−.1	.23

components for the original variables, thereby gaining degrees of freedom and manageability in subsequent analyses. Most criticisms of principal components analysis and factor analytic techniques focus on this use of the method.

The starting point for a principal components analysis is not the matrix of variables in their original form but either the covariance or correlation matrix of the variables.[24] The variances and covariances for the five example variables are presented in Table 6A.2. The diagonal elements in the covariance matrix contain the variances of the individual variables, and the off-diagonal elements contain the covariances between each pair of variables. In most cases, only the bottom half of this matrix is presented, because it is symmetrical. However, I present the whole for completeness.

Let z_i be the ith principal component. Let a_i be the ith eigenvector of the covariance matrix, and let a_{ij} be the jth element of the ith eigenvector. Principal components can be expressed as linear functions of the deviations of the original variables from their respective means and the characteristic vectors, or *eigenvectors*, of the covariance matrix. Let x_p be the deviation of the pth variable from its mean consisting of n observations. In our example, x_{15} would be the vote of Deputy 5 on Amendment 1 minus the mean vote for all deputies on Amendment 1. There are as many components as there are variables, so, using our example, we will compute five principal components.

---

[24] Because the statistical properties of components based on the covariance matrix are better understood than those based on the correlation matrix, when possible it is better to use the covariance matrix. Because the units of analysis are identical in the case of dichotomous variables, and following the recommendation of Heckman and Snyder, all principal components results reported in this book are based on the analysis of the covariance matrix.

$$z_1 = a_{11}x_1 + a_{21}x_2 + a_{31}x_3 + a_{41}x_4 + a_{51}x_5 \tag{1}$$

$$z_2 = a_{12}x_1 + a_{22}x_2 + a_{32}x_3 + a_{42}x_4 + a_{52}x_5 \tag{2}$$

$$z_3 = a_{13}x_1 + a_{23}x_2 + a_{33}x_3 + a_{43}x_4 + a_{53}x_5 \tag{3}$$

$$z_4 = a_{14}x_1 + a_{24}x_2 + a_{34}x_3 + a_{44}x_4 + a_{54}x_5 \tag{4}$$

$$z_5 = a_{15}x_1 + a_{25}x_2 + a_{35}x_3 + a_{45}x_4 + a_{55}x_5 \tag{5}$$

As is clear from equations (1)–(5), principal components can be expressed in terms of the original variables. Note that z_i is a vector with each of its n elements (often called z *scores* or simply *scores*) corresponding to a particular observation, just as x_p is a vector consisting of n observations. Let us take z_1 as an example. The full expression of the first principal component for a data set consisting of ten observations on five variables (our example) is

$$z_{11} = a_{11}x_{11} + a_{21}x_{12} + a_{31}x_{13} + a_{41}x_{14} + a_{51}x_{15} \tag{6}$$

$$z_{12} = a_{11}x_{21} + a_{21}x_{22} + a_{31}x_{23} + a_{41}x_{24} + a_{51}x_{25} \tag{7}$$

$$z_{13} = a_{11}x_{31} + a_{21}x_{32} + a_{31}x_{33} + a_{41}x_{34} + a_{51}x_{35} \tag{8}$$

$$z_{14} = a_{11}x_{41} + a_{21}x_{42} + a_{31}x_{43} + a_{41}x_{44} + a_{51}x_{45} \tag{9}$$

$$z_{15} = a_{11}x_{51} + a_{21}x_{52} + a_{31}x_{53} + a_{41}x_{54} + a_{51}x_{55} \tag{10}$$

$$z_{16} = a_{11}x_{61} + a_{21}x_{62} + a_{31}x_{63} + a_{41}x_{64} + a_{51}x_{65} \tag{11}$$

$$z_{17} = a_{11}x_{71} + a_{21}x_{72} + a_{31}x_{73} + a_{41}x_{74} + a_{51}x_{75} \tag{12}$$

$$z_{18} = a_{11}x_{81} + a_{21}x_{82} + a_{31}x_{83} + a_{41}x_{84} + a_{51}x_{85} \tag{13}$$

$$z_{19} = a_{11}x_{91} + a_{21}x_{92} + a_{31}x_{93} + a_{41}x_{94} + a_{51}x_{95} \tag{14}$$

$$z_{110} = a_{11}x_{101} + a_{21}x_{102} + a_{31}x_{103} + a_{41}x_{104} + a_{51}x_{105} \tag{15}$$

The definition of principal components seems simple enough, but how are they derived?[25] To understand the derivation of principal components, another term from matrix algebra must be introduced – the characteristic root, or *eigenvalue*, of a matrix. As is clear from the above discussion, the first principal component is a linear function of the original variables and the first eigenvector of the covariance matrix. The first eigenvector is chosen such that the sum of each of its elements squared equals 1, and the variance of the first principal component is maximized. The first eigenvalue of the matrix is the variance of the first principal component. The second eigenvalue of the matrix is the variance of the

---

[25] If the reader is interested in a full derivation of principal components, he should refer to one of the many texts on the subject; two of the best are *A User's Guide to Principal Components* by J. Edward Jackson (1991) and *Principal Component Analysis* by I. T. Joliffe (1986).

$$U'SU = L$$

Table 6A.3. *Eigenvalues and Eigenvectors for Example Data*

	Eigenvector 1	Eigenvector 2	Eigenvector 3	Eigenvector 4	Eigenvector 5
Amendment 1	0.50	0.00	0.60	−0.00	0.62
Amendment 2	−0.47	0.41	−0.13	0.57	0.51
Amendment 3	0.47	0.41	0.13	0.57	−0.51
Amendment 4	−0.39	0.57	0.55	−0.41	−0.22
Amendment 5	0.39	0.57	−0.55	−0.41	0.22

	Eigenvalue 1	Eigenvalue 2	Eigenvalue 3	Eigenvalue 4	Eigenvalue 5
Proportion of variance	0.95	0.18	0.07	0.04	0.03
explained	0.75	0.14	0.06	0.03	0.02

second principal component, and so on. The sum of the eigenvalues for the covariance matrix equals the total variance for that matrix. Thus, one can discover the variance explained by a particular principal component simply by dividing its corresponding eigenvalue with the total variance of the covariance matrix. This number is often reported along with each eigenvalue to give a sense of a principal component's relative importance.

Let us derive the principal components for our example data set. The eigenvectors and their corresponding eigenvalues are presented in Table 6A.3.

Using the information presented in Tables 6A.2 and 6A.3, we determine the values of the first principal component of our example data simply by plugging the appropriate values into equations (6)–(15).

First principal component scores:

$$1.11 = .5 * \quad .5 - .47 * -.6 + .47 * \quad .4 - .39 * -.7 + .39 * \quad .3$$
$$-.25 = .5 * -.5 - .47 * \quad .4 + .47 * \quad .4 - .39 * \quad .3 + .39 * \quad .3$$
$$-.72 = .5 * -.5 - .47 * \quad .4 + .47 * -.6 - .39 * \quad .3 + .39 * \quad .3$$
$$1.11 = .5 * \quad .5 - .47 * -.6 + .47 * \quad .4 - .39 * -.7 + .39 * \quad .3$$
$$1.11 = .5 * \quad .5 - .47 * -.6 + .47 * \quad .4 - .39 * -.7 + .39 * \quad .3$$
$$-1.11 = .5 * -.5 - .47 * \quad .4 + .47 * -.6 - .39 * \quad .3 + .39 * -.7$$
$$-1.11 = .5 * -.5 - .47 * \quad .4 + .47 * -.6 - .39 * \quad .3 + .39 * -.7$$
$$.72 = .5 * \quad .5 - .47 * -.6 + .47 * \quad .4 - .39 * \quad .3 + .39 * \quad .3$$
$$.25 = .5 * \quad .5 - .47 * \quad .4 + .47 * \quad .4 - .39 * \quad .3 + .39 * \quad .3$$
$$-1.11 = .5 * -.5 - .47 * \quad .4 + .47 * -.6 - .39 * \quad .3 + .39 * -.7$$

From the above, the first principal component is seen to be a vector of values corresponding to each of the ten observations (deputies) in our example. It is, in effect, a new variable based on the linear combination of the weighted original variables (votes). *Each score corresponds to a particular deputy and is a measure of that deputy's position either for or against the dimension captured by the first principal component.*

A number of techniques exist to determine the number of dimensions necessary to characterize a data set. The method I use in this study is that employed by Poole and Rosenthal (1991) and reproduced by Heckman and Snyder (1993, 1996), in which one assesses the importance of a dimension (or component) by analyzing the percentage of roll call votes that the model correctly predicts. According to this method, one determines the number of issue dimensions in a legislature based on the percent correctly predicted by the estimated components.

For example, if we wish to test the importance of the first dimension as captured by the first principal component, we examine the values for each deputy predicted by that first component. If we compare the predicted values with the true values, we can determine the percent correctly predicted by the analysis; this is a typical way to interpret the results of dimensional analysis.[26] The formula used to compute predicted values is the following:

$$\hat{x}_i = \bar{x} + a_i z_{ij}$$

where x_i is the ith vote, a_i is the ith eigenvector, and z_{ij} is the ith principal component score for the jth deputy.

In our example, if we multiply each of the z scores for the first principal component by the first value in the first eigenvector (.50 in our example; see Table 6A.3), then subtract the mean of the first variable from each of these numbers, we will get a prediction for the first variable. If we multiply each of the z scores for the first principal component by the second value in the first eigenvector (−.47 in our example), then subtract the mean of the second variable from each of these numbers, we will get a prediction for the second variable. If we do the same for each of the remaining three values of the first eigenvector, we get estimates for the values of the five variables. The predicted values of

---

[26] This is the technique used by Poole and Rosenthal (1985, 1987, 1991), upon which they base their conclusion that a single underlying dimension dominates most of the voting in the history of Congress.

Table 6A.4. *Predicted Values for Our Five*
Example Variables

	$\hat{x}_1$	$\hat{x}_2$	$\hat{x}_3$	$\hat{x}_4$	$\hat{x}_5$
Deputy 1	1.06	.07	1.13	.27	1.13
Deputy 2	.37	.72	.48	.80	.60
Deputy 3	.14	.94	.26	.98	.42
Deputy 4	1.06	.07	1.13	.27	1.13
Deputy 5	1.06	.07	1.13	.27	1.13
Deputy 6	−.06	1.13	.07	1.13	.27
Deputy 7	−.06	1.13	.07	1.13	.27
Deputy 8	.86	.26	.94	.42	.98
Deputy 9	.63	.48	.72	.60	.80
Deputy 10	−.06	1.13	.07	1.13	.27

our five example variables based on only the first principal component
are presented in Table 6A.4.

Following standard procedure, I recode all predicted values of .5 or
above as "1" and all other values as "0." If one compares the predicted
values in Table 6A.4, taking into account the recoding just mentioned,
with the original values in Table 6A.1, one finds that only four values
are incorrectly predicted. Therefore, the percent correctly predicted by
the first principal component in our example is $100 - \frac{4}{50} = 99.2\%$.

Finally, it is necessary to have some understanding of the analytical
content of the principal components uncovered by an analysis. The *inter-*
pretation of principal components is not an exact science. It is conventional in dimensional analysis of roll call votes to characterize dimensions
by the particular votes with which they are strongly correlated. By strongly
correlated, it is typical to look at those votes that are correlated with a
certain dimension at greater than .6 and less than −.6. It is conventional to
think of votes correlated at greater than .3 (or less than −.3) as moderately
correlated with a particular principal component (Kline 1994).

To derive the correlation of a particular variable (in this case a particular vote) with a principal component, one uses the following formula;
that is, the correlation, r, of the ith principal component, z_i, and the jth
original variable (vote), x_j, is equal to

$$r_{zx} = \frac{a_{ji}\sqrt{l_i}}{s_j}$$

Table 6A.5. *Eigenvalues and Variance Explained for the First 10 Principal Components for Sessions 2–6*

PC	Session 2 Eigen-value	Session 2 Prop. Variance Explained	Session 3 Eigen-value	Session 3 Prop. Variance Explained	Session 4 Eigen-value	Session 4 Prop. Variance Explained	Session 5 Eigen-value	Session 5 Prop. Variance Explained	Session 6 Eigen-value	Session 6 Prop. Variance Explained
1	3.95	0.27	10.94	0.22	5.36	0.13	10.04	0.25	1.87	0.28
2	1.78	0.08	4.94	0.10	3.78	0.09	2.71	0.07	0.68	0.10
3	0.66	0.04	1.85	0.04	2.15	0.05	1.63	0.04	0.46	0.07
4	0.58	0.04	1.67	0.03	1.56	0.04	1.13	0.03	0.41	0.06
5	0.50	0.03	1.27	0.03	1.37	0.03	0.97	0.02	0.33	0.05
6	0.45	0.03	1.13	0.02	1.26	0.03	0.84	0.02	0.28	0.04
7	0.38	0.03	0.86	0.02	1.14	0.03	0.80	0.02	0.27	0.04
8	0.36	0.02	0.83	0.02	1.07	0.03	0.76	0.02	0.25	0.04
9	0.33	0.02	0.75	0.02	0.94	0.02	0.67	0.02	0.23	0.03
10	0.30	0.02	0.72	0.01	0.91	0.02	0.63	0.02	0.21	0.03

where s_j is the standard deviation of the jth original variable (vote), l_i is the ith eigenvalue, and a_{ij} is the jth element of the ith eigenvector.

The principal component analysis that I present in Chapter 6 follows exactly that which I have presented as an example in this section. Summary results of the analysis are presented in Table 6A.5.

The first thing to note is the small size of the proportion of variance explained by the first two principal components, which ranges from 13% to 28% for the first principal component and from 7% to 10% for the second principal component. Typical values for the U.S. Congress range from 30% to 50% for the first principal component and from 5% to 20% for the second principal component (see Heckman and Snyder 1992). The fact that the proportion of variance explained in my analysis of the Russian Parliament is lower than that found by analysts of the U.S. Congress indicates that the majority of deputies tended not to vote consistently. Voting as a bloc was the exception rather than the rule, especially in Session 4. Thus, issue dimensions within the former Russian Parliament were weaker than in the U.S. Congress. This is not surprising, given the lack of political parties able to enforce voting discipline among the deputies. Clearly, Russian deputies had more trouble than their American counterparts in perceiving their own interests. They did not have long-lived parties to guide them; they had little professional experience; and, in many cases they had great difficulty in understanding the ramifications of bills and amendments, because they had almost no experience with market economics, private property, human rights, and ethnic self-determination, the subject of many important votes.

7

Legislative Instability

Essentially, I begin the book in Chapter 2 with a case study of the most important example of cycling in the Russian Parliament, the cyclical debate on the new Russian constitution. In my story, I emphasize just how seriously cycling disrupted debate on the constitution. Furthermore, I describe how it enabled the chairman to manipulate the agenda, using the problematic constitutional issue to keep deputies focused on reducing the powers of the executive branch. From this story, we know that cycling did occur in the Russian Parliament and that it occurred at precisely that moment when conditions in the parliament conformed to the conditions outlined by formal theory: Deputies were making complex choices involving several policy dimensions at once (i.e., the issue space was multidimensional), the number of partisan groups was large (greater than two), and legislative institutions (such as committees) were weak. The story in Chapter 2 also demonstrates that the impact of cycling was not trivial. It affected the legislature's ability to make collective decisions. It allowed the chairman to monopolize the agenda and thus keep the legislature focused on a power struggle with the executive branch, which in turn reduced the ability of either institution to function. Ultimately, cycling affected Russia's choice of constitutional system.

That said, we still do not know the answers to several questions. Was the cyclical debate on the draft constitution an isolated occurrence, or was the problem of cycling more extensive? Did cycling occur in sessions other than Session 4? Did it affect legislation other than that concerning Russia's new constitution? To answer these questions, we must investigate the phenomenon more systematically. Toward this goal, I develop several methods to uncover evidence for both the potential for and presence of cyclical majorities.

SYSTEMATIC STUDY OF CYCLING IN THE RUSSIAN PARLIAMENT: ADAPTATION OF SCHOFIELD'S MODEL

Since publication of the so-called chaos results (Plott 1967, McKelvey 1976, Schofield 1978), which showed that cycling ought to be a problem in majority rule institutions, researchers have tried to discover the extent to which cycles can exist in a multidimensional legislature with more than two members (McKelvey and Schofield 1986, 1987). In "Political Competition and Multiparty Coalition Governments," Norman Schofield (1993), provides a framework in which to consider both the possibility of and the extent of cycling in a multiparty context.[1]

In Schofield's model, the potential for cycling depends on the number and ideological location of possible coalitions. In his parliamentary model, a coalition is a potential government, which includes some set of political parties such that the coalition is supported by a majority of the parliamentary members. Thus, the potential for cycling depends on the ideological location of the parties in the parliament and on the parties' relative strength – that is, number of seats. Thus, in Schofield's model, a *winning coalition* refers to a coalition of parties that is able to form a government. In my use of the model, a winning coalition, K, is a coalition of *blocs* with enough seats to ensure the passage of a particular vote. A winning coalition must include more than half of the members of parliament. A *minimal winning coalition* is a winning coalition in which the defection of one coalition member will cause the coalition to no longer be a winning coalition. A fundamental assumption of Schofield's model is that party members vote alike. Thus, each party is a single actor with a weighted vote. To adopt his model, I make the same assumption about blocs; the group in the Russian Parliament that I believe was most equivalent to a political party.[2]

---

[1] In his 1993 paper, Schofield assumes that in most European multiparty systems, the issue space is multidimensional. This is not an uncontroversial assumption; however, he presents evidence that coalition behavior does not make sense if one assumes that the issue space is one-dimensional (Schofield 1993, p. 9). Furthermore, the author limits his presentation to two dimensions for the usual reasons: First of all, it is extremely difficult to present graphical representations in more than two dimensions, and Schofield's model of a cycle set is best understood graphically; and, second, Schofield asserts that it is straightforward to extend his model to three or more dimensions. Although I present evidence in Chapter 6 that more than two dimensions were present during Session 4 of the Russian Parliament, I restrict my presentation to two dimensions.

[2] Empirically, of course, no party behaves consistently as a single actor. Parties undergo internal dissension, defection, and debate. In the Russian Parliament, it is

For each K in the set of all coalitions, D, there is a set of points in the policy space, $W(K)$, such that for any point outside the set there is a point in the set that is preferred by all members of K, and no point in $W(K)$ is unanimously preferred to any other point in $W(K)$ by all members of K. $W(K)$ is commonly referred to as the compromise set (or Pareto set) of K. If we assume that deputies have circular (simple Euclidean) preferences, this is the area in W bounded by straight lines joining the ideal points of the blocs in the coalition. Each coalition defines a different compromise set.

Essential to Schofield's model is the concept of a *core*. Several authors have discussed the mathematical derivation and properties of the core (Cox 1987b, McKelvey and Schofield 1986, 1987), and I do not repeat them here. For my purposes, we define the core as the intersection of all compromise sets for all possible minimal winning coalitions. Call this set Core(D). If Core(D) is nonempty, then no coalition can propose an alternative policy point that is preferred by every member of some winning coalition. In general, if a core exists, it will be at the ideal point of one party – the core party (Schofield 1993, p. 6). Thus, a nonempty core implies legislative stability, because outcomes should reflect the ideal point of the core party.

According to Schofield (1993, p. 6), "a necessary and sufficient condition for a point x to be in Core(D) is that x is in the compromise set of every *minimal winning coalition* [italics added]." In one dimension, Core(D) is never empty because, as we know from the median voter theorem (Black 1958, Enelow and Hinich 1984), the median voter must be a member of every winning coalition; therefore, the position of the median voter is always in Core(D). However, in two or more dimensions, it is possible for there to be no point that is in all of the minimal winning coalitions; therefore, in two or more dimensions, Core(D) may be empty.

In two or more dimensions, if Core(D) is empty, then another set, a cycle set or Cycle(D), exists and is nonempty. A nonempty cycle set implies that outcomes within this set will cycle.

The basis of my empirical evidence for cycling is an operationalization of Schofield's model of a cycle set. Essentially, this test involves two

certainly a stretch to characterize any of the partisan groups (either factions or coalitions of factions) by means of a single ideological location. For one thing, there was more voter defection in the Russian Parliament than in most European parliaments. It is therefore important to stress that a cycle set is a model; thus, it will never be realized empirically in a precise way. I use this model only as tool with which to test for cycling systematically.

steps: (1) to determine whether or not a cycle set was present in any of the sessions of the Russian Parliament and (2) to determine whether or not the cycle set is nonempty.

Following Schofield, I assume that each partisan group in the Russian Parliament has an ideal point in a two-dimensional policy space. Schofield uses party manifestoes to determine the ideal points of political parties. I summarize the programmatic statements of factions in Chapter 5, but as I explain earlier, the information available on the political platforms of either the factions or the blocs is limited. Furthermore, neither the factions nor the larger coalitions of factions (either the two grand coalitions before the collapse or the three blocs afterwards) were political parties in any traditional sense; they were coalitions of like-minded deputies that existed within the parliament for legislative purposes.[3] As deputies' responses to the political and economic issues of reform changed, alliances also changed, as evidenced by the fact that two grand coalitions of factions existed before the collapse and three smaller coalitions (or blocs) of factions formed after the collapse. In this context the only sensible way to measure deputy preferences is based on how they voted. Therefore, I define the ideal point of a partisan group as the coordinate in a two-dimensional plane that corresponds to the median first principal component and the median second principal component for the members of that group (see Chapter 6 for a full discussion).

In Chapter 6, I present the median ideal points for factions. There are several reasons why in this chapter I use bloc ideal points to operationalize Schofield's model. In the first place, it is extremely impractical to try and discover the presence or absence of cycle sets given 14 fairly evenly sized political groups. No majority coalition can include fewer than seven factions, and the number of possible majority coalitions is very large, making the analysis extremely complex. In the second place, the relative location of bloc ideal points is analogous to the relative location of the faction ideal points, except that the bloc ideal points span a smaller subset of the issue space. Therefore, analyzing bloc ideal points ought to make it harder to identify cycle sets. Furthermore, the blocs were formed by the factions in order to better represent the key

---

[3] In my use of the model, I think of coalitions as informal. During most of the three-year period in which the Russian Parliament existed, Russia could best be characterized as a presidential system in which the President formed his own government, subject to limited parliamentary approval. Because no bloc had a majority of seats, coalitions were essential to legislative decision making, but there were no formal coalitions of blocs.

partisan groupings in the parliament and to enable these partisan alliances to more effectively influence policy. Therefore, I believe that the blocs are a better analogy to political parties than are the factions.

There is one final problem in applying the Schofield model to the Russian case: the large number of unaffiliated deputies. Following Schofield, I assume that each bloc controls a proportion of the parliamentary seats, which equals the proportion of the total membership that belongs to that bloc. However, an examination of the graphs of deputy ideal points presented in Chapter 6 shows that the ideal points of the unaffiliated deputies were distributed all over the issue space. To incorporate the unaffiliated deputies into my analysis, I assume that one-third vote with Russian Unity, one-third with Constructive Forces, and one-third with Coalition for Reform. However, I do not alter the location of the bloc ideal points to take into account these deputies. To do so would mean that I add particular deputies to particular blocs based on their voting record, which would bias the median bloc ideal point away from 0. Therefore, I continue to define the blocs the way they were defined by the deputies themselves and to identify the median ideal points of the blocs based only on the deputies who identified themselves as members of that bloc.

Examples

I illustrate the concept of a Core(D) and Cycle(D) graphically in Figures 7.1 and 7.2. In each figure, I represent the two-dimensional ideal points of three political groups in a legislature. These groups are modeled on the blocs that existed in the Russian Parliament starting in April 1992. The total number of deputies is 251, so that a winning coalition must have at least 126 members. I provide this example to illustrate the Schofield model, nevertheless, the example illustrates the importance of both the relative position and relative strength of the blocs.

In Figure 7.1, the three blocs are accorded membership such that Coalition for Reform, Russian Unity, and Constructive Forces each has approximately the same number of members. In this situation, there are three minimal winning coalitions – that is, coalitions with 126 or more members where the defection of one member causes the total to be less than 126. Of the three minimal winning coalitions, one is comprised of Constructive Forces and Russian Unity, one of Coalition for Reform and Constructive Forces, and one of Coalition for Reform and Russian Unity.

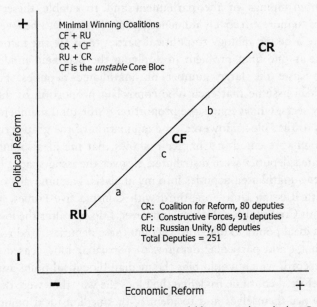

Figure 7.1. Configuration of bloc ideal points and bloc strength such that Constructive Forces is a core bloc. Constructive Forces is an *unstable* core bloc because its location at the core depends on the position of the other two blocs. If the ideal points of either Russian Unity or Coalition for Reform were to change, Constructive Forces would no longer be at the core.

In Figure 7.1, the three blocs are located such that the ideal point of Constructive Forces lies exactly along the compromise set of the coalition consisting of Russian Unity and Coalition for Reform. Therefore, because of its location, Constructive Forces would always participate in the coalition of Russian Unity and Coalition for Reform. In addition, Constructive Forces is a member of the other two minimal winning coalitions (Constructive Forces plus Russian Unity and Constructive Forces plus Coalition for Reform). In this graph, the issue space is one-dimensional and Core(*D*) consists of the median voter. Because I assume that all party members vote alike, there are in effect only three voters, the three blocs, and Constructive Forces is the median voter. It is a member of all minimal winning coalitions.

To see this, imagine a point in the compromise set of Russian Unity and Coalition for Reform (the line connecting Russian Unity and the Coalition for Reform's ideal points), depicted in the graph as point *a*. It is easy to see that the minimal winning coalition comprised of the Coalition for Reform and Constructive Forces prefers point *b*, which is

in the compromise set of Coalition for Reform and Constructive Forces
and is closer to Constructive Forces' ideal point than point *a*. However, the minimal winning coalition consisting of Russian Unity and
Constructive Forces prefers *c* to *b*, because *c* is closer to each member's
ideal point than is *b*. This exercise can be repeated until it is obvious
that only the point at Constructive Forces' ideal point is not preferred
by some other winning coalition. This is because Constructive Forces is
a member of every minimal winning coalition. Thus, the necessary and
sufficient condition for a core to exist is met; the point corresponding to
Constructive Forces' ideal point is in every minimal winning coalition.
Furthermore, because in this configuration of blocs Constructive Forces
is a core bloc, there is no point that can defeat Constructive Forces'
ideal point. This result is analogous to the median voter result in a one-
dimensional issue space. Because the three blocs line up along one dimension, Constructive Forces is the median bloc (or voter).

Thus, Constructive Forces is a core bloc, equivalent to a core party
in Schofield's model. However, Constructive Forces is not a *stable* core
bloc because if the location of the bloc's ideal point changes, it will
no longer be a member of every minimal winning coalition. This
configuration of bloc ideal points and bloc membership is analogous to
the situation that existed before the collapse of the Soviet Union; in
effect, only a single dimension is relevant in this configuration, and the
position of the median voter or group determines the legislative outcome.
So long as the issue space remains one-dimensional, the situation is
stable.

In Figure 7.2, membership among the blocs remains the same, but the
ideal points of the blocs have shifted. In this situation, there are again
three minimal winning coalitions, Russian Unity and Constructive Forces,
Constructive Forces and Coalition for Reform, and Russian Unity and
Coalition for Reform. However, no bloc is a member of all three coalitions.
Lines connecting each of the three pairs of coalition partners correspond
to the compromise sets of the three minimal winning coalitions. Clearly,
there is no point that lies along each of these three lines, and there is
no group that is a member of each of these three minimal winning
coalitions; therefore, there is no core and no core group in this configuration. Core(*D*) is empty, and "[w]hen the core is empty... then the
McKelvey (1976) and Schofield (1978) chaos theorems show that it is
possible for an endless sequence of coalitions to form, collapse, and
reform. In short, theory suggests that anything can happen" (Schofield
1993, p. 10).

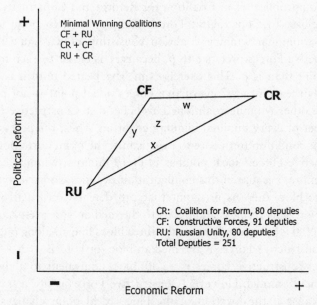

Figure 7.2. Configuration of bloc ideal points and bloc strength such that there is no core bloc. As in Figure 7.1, there are three minimal winning coalitions, Russian Unity and Constructive Forces, Constructive Forces and Coalition for Reform, and Russian Unity and Coalition for Reform. However, no bloc is a member of all three coalitions; therefore, no core exists. Also, when no core exists, a cycle set exists. The lines connecting each of the three blocs traces the cycle set, which supports cycles in the following way. For any point z in the set, there are three other points (w, x, y) close to z, such that each of the three points is preferred to z by one of the three bounding minimal winning coalitions.

In earlier work, Schofield (1991) has found that the area in which anything can happen is restricted to a region that he calls a cycle set, or Cycle(D). Furthermore, Schofield has shown that either Core(D) is nonempty or Cycle(D) is nonempty. In other words, if a core does not exist, then a cycle set does exist. Notice the set of points bounded by the three minimal winning coalitions; this set, Cycle(D), is shown in Figure 7.2. The set Cycle(D) supports cycles in the following way. For any point z in the set, there are three other points (w, x, y) close to z, such that each of the three points is preferred to z by one of the three bounding minimal winning coalitions. The coalition consisting of Constructive Forces and Coalition for Reform prefers w to z, the coalition consisting of Russian Unity and Coalition for Reform prefers x to z, and the coalition consisting of Russian Unity and Constructive Forces prefers *y* to *z*. Thus, around *z* there is a cycle. Hence, the set of points bounded by the three minimal winning coalitions is called a *cycle set*. Furthermore, for any point outside of Cycle(*D*), there is some point closer to Cycle(*D*) or within Cycle(*D*) that is preferred by a winning coalition. Therefore, as is the case when Core(*D*) is nonempty, when Cycle(*D*) is nonempty we expect that outcomes will be located within or near to this set. An important implication of Schofield's model is that although cycles may occur in certain legislative settings, they will be limited in scope to a subset of the alternative space. Thus, as we find in the Russian Parliament, cycling affected certain kinds of legislation, but it did not affect all legislation.

I use the concepts of Cycle(*D*) and Core(*D*) to test rigorously whether or not cycling was possible within the Russian Parliament.

The first step I follow in operationalizing Schofield's model is to use the median positions of the deputy blocs to determine whether or not cycle sets existed in the Russian Parliament at any time in its three-year existence. Next, I introduce two related methods to determine whether or not votes cycled; the point of this exercise is to determine whether or not I can detect a pattern of shifting coalitions, which result in a cycle of outcomes. In the first method, I identify those series of votes in which successful amendments were proposed by each coalition relevant to the cycle set. In the second, I perform an analysis on the transformed matrix of roll call votes for Sessions 4 and 5. This analysis uncovers the two-dimensional equivalent of ideal points for the votes. Using the two-dimensional location of the cycle sets and the two-dimensional location of the votes, I further investigate whether votes within a series are supported by all coalitions relevant to the cycle set.

Finally, I examine the content of amendments that were supported by cyclical majority coalitions and find that votes on the issue of human rights appear to have "cycled" during the first few months immediately after the collapse. I cannot detect this type of cycle in any of the other sessions.

Nonempty Core in Sessions 2, 3, and 6

In this section, I invoke evidence presented in Chapter 6 to show that cycle sets could not have existed in Sessions 2 and 3. Recall Figures 6.4a and 6.4b, in which the ideal points of the factions are depicted. Evidence is quite strong that before the collapse of the Soviet Union, the factions could be located along a single dimension. (I refer here to the factions because the blocs were not formed until Session 4.) During Session 2, most factions are located in a clump to the right of the origin, which means that, on balance, most factions were in favor of reform. This conclusion is supported by the mappings of individual deputy ideal points presented in Figure 6.1. Throughout much of Session 2, the position of the median voter was located within a loose majority coalition of deputies who generally supported reform.

During Session 3, each of the factions can be located at a distinct point along a single dimension (see Figure 6.4b). During Session 3 it is possible to identify the median faction, or core, which in this case is the group of independent (or unaffiliated) deputies. If one takes into account the membership in each of the factions, one finds that more than one-half of the deputies are either independents or members of one of the factions located to the right of the group of independent deputies; and, more than one-half of the deputies are either independents or members of one of the factions located at and to the left of the group of independent deputies. By extension, the individual deputy whose ideal point corresponds to the median position is always located within the group of independent deputies. That the independent deputies, located in the "marsh" between the conservatives and reformers, occupied the median position was widely acknowledged in the Russian media before the collapse of the Soviet Union and by the deputies themselves.

Given that the issue space was one-dimensional in Sessions 2 and 3 (the period of time before the collapse of the Soviet Union) and that, therefore, a core can be easily identified, a cycle set could not have existed in either of these two sessions. Therefore, I restrict my search for a cycle set to the period following the collapse of the Soviet Union. In addition, evidence presented in Chapter 6 suggests that while there may have been more than one issue dimension during Session 6, the number of roll call votes was so small (due to control by the chairman) that analysis is suspect. Analysis of the roll call votes shows that the factions were clumped in the center of the issue space in Session 6.[4] Therefore, I restrict my search for cycle sets to Sessions 4 and 5.

----

[4] For different reasons than were present in Session 2 and 3, the issue space appears to have been one-dimensional during Session 6 as well. In Session 6, the set of roll call votes was severely restricted by the chairman, limiting debate to one dimension: confrontation with the President of Russia. I discuss this further in Chapter 8.

Nonempty Cycle Set in Sessions 4 and 5

Recall that there were three deputy blocs – Coalition for Reform, Constructive Forces, and Russian Unity – each of which was officially registered in April 1992 (in the middle of Session 4). As I discussed earlier, the effect of the great diversity of preferences within each deputy bloc is to bias the median ideal point toward zero. In testing for the presence of a cycle set, this has the effect of decreasing the overall size of the area encompassed by the set. However, it ought not affect the shape of the cycle set, because each bloc was equally plagued by misfit members. In other words, the bloc Coalition for Reform had members with ideal points identical to those of the most extreme supporters of Russian Unity, and Russian Unity had approximately the same percentage of members with ideal points identical to those of the most extreme supporters of Coalition for Reform.

Using the membership and ideal points of the blocs, I determine whether or not a cycle set existed in either Session 4 or 5. The numbers of members in each bloc along with the median first and second principal component scores for the blocs are shown in Table 7.1.

There were three possible minimal winning coalitions among the deputy blocs in Session 4: Coalition for Reform plus Russian Unity, Coalition for Reform plus Constructive Forces, and Russian Unity plus Constructive Forces. The location of bloc ideal points for Sessions 4 and 5 are presented in Figure 7.3.

In Figure 7.3a, the line connecting the ideal points of Coalition for Reform and Russian Unity is the compromise set of the minimal winning coalition comprised of these two blocs; the line connecting the ideal points of Coalition for Reform and Constructive Forces is the compromise set of the minimal winning coalition comprised of these two

Table 7.1. *Membership and Ideal Points for Deputy Blocs in Sessions 4 and 5*

	Session 4			Session 5		
	Members	pc1	pc2	Members	pc1	pc2
Coalition for Reform	81	2.02	0.98	75	2.74	0.83
Constructive Forces	71	−0.43	0.47	72	−1.28	0.26
Russian Unity	74	−1.28	−0.57	74	−2.41	−0.83
Total deputies	226			221		

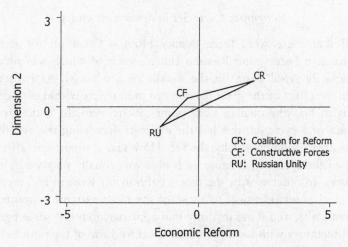

Figure 7.3a. Cycle set in Session 4. The cycle set falls within the triangle traced by lines connecting the median ideal points of the three blocs.

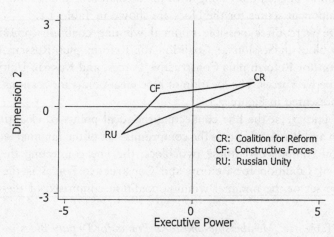

Figure 7.3b. Cycle set in Session 5.

blocs; and, the line connecting the ideal points of Russian Unity and Constructive Forces is the compromise set of the minimal winning coalition comprised of these two blocs. These three compromise sets do not intersect; therefore, no point is simultaneously in all three of the compromise sets. Hence, there is no core and no core bloc in this graph. Therefore, in Session 4, Core(D) is empty. Also, by definition, Cycle(D)

is nonempty; it is the area bounded by each of the three compromise sets of the minimal winning coalitions.

In Session 5, there were also three possible minimal winning coalitions (see Figure 7.3b): Coalition for Reform plus Russian Unity, Coalition for Reform plus Constructive Forces, and Russian Unity plus Constructive Forces, the same three that were present in Session 4. Again, there is no point that is in the compromise set of each of the three minimal winning coalitions; hence, there is again no core and no core bloc. Cycle(D) is nonempty and is located in the area bounded by the compromise sets of the three minimal winning coalitions. Thus, a cycle set existed in Sessions 4 and 5.

Cycle Sets and Agenda Control

According to Schofield, either Core(D) is empty or Cycle(D) is empty, and he further implies that outcomes (legislation) will tend to be located in or near whichever of these sets is present for a given configuration of parties and party strengths. Implicit in this model is the understanding that parties set the legislative agenda. In a parliamentary system in which a coalition of parties forms a government, parties almost surely do set the legislative agenda. When there exists a core party, the core party will likely dominate the agenda. When no core party exists, control over the agenda might shift from minimal winning coalition to minimal winning coalition; hence, outcomes would fall within the cycle set.

Early in the short history of the Russian Parliament, when, according to my analysis, the core was located within a loose coalition of deputies who supported reform, the leader of this core coalition (or group), Boris Yeltsin, was elected chairman of the parliament. Thus, while Yeltsin was chairman, a leader of one of the key deputy groups had the power to set the legislative agenda, which implies that before the collapse of the Soviet Union, parties (in this case one quasi-party) set the agenda. However, Yeltsin's successor, Ruslan Khasbulatov, was the leader of no group, so that after the collapse of the Soviet Union, in the absence of a core quasi-party, deputy groups within the parliament had little influence over the agenda. Indeed, one of the reasons that Khasbulatov was elected chairman of the parliament was that no group within the parliament had enough votes to elect its own leader.[5] Khasbulatov was just the

---

[5] Russian Unity and Coalition for Reform both offered alternative candidates, none of whom could get the requisite number of votes.

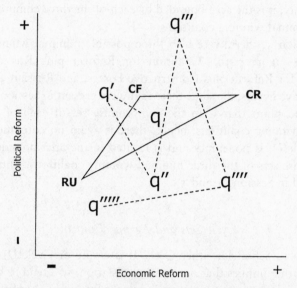

Figure 7.4. Illustration of cycling. If members of the minimal winning coalitions do not control the agenda, but rather a nonpartisan controls the agenda, outcomes not in the cycle set can be achieved. Starting with q, an agenda setter could offer a sequence of outcomes in an attempt to wind up with majority support for q''''. The median ideal points of the three blocs are indicated by RU for Russian Unity, CR for Coalition for Reform, and CF for Constructive Forces.

kind of compromise candidate one might expect in the absence of a core party.

In the presence of a cycle set, if a nonpartisan actor has the power to set the agenda, outcomes will not necessarily fall within or even near to the cycle set. Such an agenda setter could order alternatives so that he obtained an outcome well outside of the cycle set; thus, if a nonpartisan leader controls the legislative agenda, outcomes will not necessarily be restricted to a subset of the alternative space. In Figure 7.4, I show how a nonpartisan chairman intent on discrediting and challenging the government's policies on economic reform could propose a sequence of alternatives in order to achieve q'''', the most anti-government stance possible. In this representation, the agenda setter has control over the content as well as the order of the agenda; these powers correspond to the powers of the chairman of the Russian Parliament.[6]

---

[6] It is important to note that under these circumstances, the chairman can achieve q'''' only if deputies vote sincerely. Shepsle and Weingast (1984b) give a character-

Why would a partisan agenda setter be less likely to achieve outcomes outside of the cycle set? If a partisan leader controls the agenda, it is unlikely that he would propose alternatives very far from his party's ideal point. Presumably, if he was elected based on his party's support, he could just as easily be replaced by a more loyal figure. In fact, according to the rules of procedure, the chairman of the parliament could have been replaced at any time by a majority of the deputies. However, because there was never a core group within the post-Soviet parliament, and Khasbulatov was a compromise candidate, no group could credibly threaten to replace him; hence, Khasbulatov did not respond to partisan demands. Furthermore, his agenda-setting powers stemmed not from a position as party or group leader, but from budgetary prerogatives that he received as chairman of the Presidium (see Chapter 4). Using his power over the agenda, Chairman Khasbulatov had the potential to prevent certain issues from ever coming to the floor. Therefore, when an agenda setter exists, he can prevent outcomes from falling within the cycle set. Indeed, as soon as an agenda setter has manipulated outcomes sufficiently to reach a location close to his own ideal point, he will continue to control the agenda such that outcomes will remain near his ideal point. Under these circumstances, although the potential for cycling still exists (the cycle set still exists), cycling will no longer occur.

Based on my analysis of events, I expect to find cycling in Session 4. In addition, I expect to find the potential for cycling in Session 5, because the ideal points and membership of the deputy blocs did not change much from Session 4 to Session 5. However, because of Khasbulatov's control over the agenda, I do not expect to observe cycling in Session 5. In the following section, I present evidence that cycling occurred, but only for a short period in Session 4.

SYSTEMATIC DETECTION OF CYCLING

Cycling exists when deputies must make up their minds along more than one dimension at once and when they are presented with numerous related alternatives, each of which weights the dimensions differently. Thus, one way to detect cycling would be to examine sets of votes on *similar issues* to (1) see if the votes are located within the cycle set and

---

ization of the chair's power when deputies vote strategically. However, given the general lack of coordinated activity on the part of the Russian deputies throughout this study, I assume that deputies vote sincerely.

(2) see if they form a cyclical set of outcomes. The procedure by which the Russian Parliament considered amendments to draft laws provides an ideal framework in which to test whether or not cycling occurred. Because all votes concern the same piece of legislation, we can make the necessary and not unrealistic assumption that the underlying structure of the issue space is the same for each vote in the series.

First, we must define the area designated as a cycle set. Figures 7.3a and 7.3b show that in both Sessions 4 and 5 the cycle set is that area bounded by the three minimal winning coalitions in each session. Recall that outcomes "cycle" within a cycle set because there is no point within the set that cannot be defeated by another point within the set that is supported by one of the bounding minimal winning coalitions. Evidence of cycling ought to consist of a series of successful amendments, each of which is supported by at least one of the minimal winning coalitions that bounds the cycle set. In addition, all bounding coalitions must support at least one amendment. In cases where the above conditions are met, outcomes ought to form a cycle, such that some proposal *b* defeats *a*, some other proposal *c* defeats *b*, and some original proposal *a* defeats *c*.

In the Russian Parliament, most roll call votes were held on draft legislation in its second (and usually final) reading, because these were the most important votes brought before the legislature. As I discuss in detail in Chapter 4, passing a piece of legislation involved a series of votes on the draft law, including a series of amendments (sometimes numbering over a hundred), and a final vote on the amended draft. Thus, the first vote is on whether or not to pass the draft as a basis. In effect, this is a vote on whether or not to change the status quo. Then a series of amendments to the draft legislation are brought before the parliament one by one, each of which is voted up or down. Thus, each amendment is pitted against the amended status quo, which consists of the draft legislation complete with those amendments that have already passed. Finally, the draft law, including all amendments that have passed, is put to a final vote "as a whole." In effect, the draft is once again put to a vote against the original status quo. Note that the order in which amendments are considered is quite important in this process, providing an agenda-setter ample opportunity for manipulation (Riker 1986).

A deputy's right to submit amendments is well-supported in the Rules of Procedure, and the relevant committee's ability to dismiss a nongermane or inconsistent amendment is limited. For example, when deputies debated the Draft Law on Privatization in June 1992, they voted on an amendment that would have gutted the law completely.[7]

I look for evidence of cycling within each series of votes on particular pieces of legislation. In this way, I make sure that I am looking at sets of votes on similar issues. It is interesting to note that there were many more votes on amendments to legislation than on legislation as a whole. In Session 4, out of 194 roll call votes, there were only 31 separate laws or resolutions that were decided. In Session 5, out of 215 roll call votes, there were only 13 separate laws or resolutions that were decided. Thus, deputy groups achieved much of their impact through the amendment process.

In Session 4, roll call voting on a series of amendments preceded a final vote for only five draft pieces of legislation: (1) The Resolution on the Extraordinary Situation in the Checheno-Ingushskaia Republic of the RSFSR,[8] debated on November 11, 1991; (2) Chapter 2, The Basic Rights, Freedoms and Responsibilities of the Citizen, of the draft Russian Constitution,[9] debated on March 26, 1992; (3) Chapter 3, Citizen's Society, of the draft Russian Constitution, debated on March 27, 1992; (4) the Law on Privatization, debated on June 5, 1992; and (5) the Resolution on the Rehabilitation of the Cossacks, debated on July 11 and 15, 1992.[10]

In Session 5, roll call voting on a series of amendments by specific deputies or deputy groups preceded the final vote for only three draft pieces of legislation: (1) the Law on the Government, debated on October 7, November 6, November 11, and December 22, 1992; (2) Chapter 5, Guarantee of Rights and Freedoms, of the draft Russian Constitution, debated on November 19, 1992; and (3) Chapter 6, of the draft Russian Constitution, also debated on November 19, 1992.

I look only at successful amendments – that is, amendments that were actively supported by a winning coalition. Within each series of amendments, I determine whether or not each of the three bounding coalitions supported at least one of the successful amendments in each series and whether each successful amendment in a series was supported by one of

---

[7] The Committee on Industry and Energy made the amendment.
[8] The name of the former Russian Republic was not changed to the Russian Federation until December 25, 1991.
[9] This is the draft proposed by Oleg Rumiantsev's parliamentary Constitutional Commission.
[10] The Resolution was passed as a basis on July 11, and a series of amendments were put to vote on July 15.

the three coalitions that bounds the cycle set. If votes fell within the cycle set, both of these conditions should have been met.

To determine which coalition supported each of these amendments, I must rely on a rule of thumb. Because voting discipline within the blocs was so weak, I conclude that a bloc supported an amendment if more than half its members voted for the amendment; conversely, I conclude that a bloc opposed an amendment if more than half of its members voted against the amendment.

The fact that so many members of the blocs had ideal points that were opposite to those of the majority as well as the leadership of their bloc means that it is difficult to judge in close or unanimous votes whether or not a coalition actively supported a particular amendment. In all cases where an amendment passed, some members from each of the blocs voted in favor of the amendment. It is not the case, however, that all amendments appealed equally to all blocs, even when a majority of the members of each bloc supported an amendment.

For this reason, I also identify the two blocs that were most support-ive of each amendment. If we look at the graphical representation of the relationship between the location of the votes and the location of the ideal points of the four blocs (which I present later in Figures 7.5 and 7.6), we see that there was great diversity in the location of the votes. Some votes supported by majorities from each bloc are centrally located relative to the deputy blocs, implying that these votes were unanimously supported. Some votes supported by majorities from each bloc are not centrally located but instead are associated with one minimal winning coalition more closely than with another, which implies that these votes were actively supported by a subset of the blocs. If the location of a successful amendment is closer to blocs associated with one minimal winning coalition than to blocs associated with another minimal winning coalition, I conclude that the amendment was supported by the coalition to which it is closer.

First, I look at each series of votes in both Sessions 4 and 5 to see which minimal winning coalitions supported successful amendments. This evidence is presented in tabular form. Second, I map the loca-tion of each series of votes as well as the four blocs for Sessions 4 and 5 to show the relationship between the votes and the deputy blocs.

Taken together, evidence based on coalition support and on the relationship between votes and coalitions provides a means to determine whether votes fell within the cycle set in both Sessions 4 and 5. After examining Sessions 4 and 5 for evidence that the cycle set was nonempty, I discuss whether outcomes within the set formed a cycle.

VOTES IN THE CYCLE SET: EVIDENCE BASED ON COALITION SUPPORT

Cycle Set in Session 4: Tabular Evidence

In this section, I discuss the possibility that each of the five series of votes was located within the cycle set in Session 4. The first series of votes that I examine occurred in November 1991 and concerned the breakaway Checheno-Ingushskaia Russian Republic. (This was the beginning of the conflict between Russia and Chechnya.) The parliament was considering a resolution in support of actions taken by President Yeltsin to maintain the integrity of the boundaries of the Russian Federation. While the parliament asserted that all such means must be diplomatic rather than military, it did support the President's right to intercede in the crisis.

In Table 7.2, I summarize the voting behavior of each bloc for each amendment to the Resolution. For each successful (or "winning") amendment, I indicate in parentheses which bloc, if any, proposed the amendment: CR stands for Coalition for Reform, RU stands for Russian Unity, and CF stands for Constructive Forces.

For each bloc, I present the proportion of members that supported the amendment. Notice that in all cases, some proportion of votes from

Table 7.2. *Coalitions in Support of Amendments to the Resolution on the Checheno-Ingushskaia Russian Republic*

	Coalition for Reform	Constructive Forces	Russian Unity	Unaffiliated Deputies
Amendment 1	.48	.56	.62	.49
Amendment 2 (CR)	.83	.75	.75	.75
Amendment 3 (RU)	.72	.59	.75	.65
Amendment 4	.75	.66	.71	.69
Amendment 5 (CF)	.55	.59	.66	.55
Amendment 6 (CR)	.77	.61	.62	.57
Amendment 7 (CR)	.75	.53	.55	.65
Amendment 8 (CR)	.74	.54	.53	.69
Final vote	.86	.59	.68	.73

each of the three blocs is necessary to pass an amendment; this reflects the large numbers of misfit deputies in each bloc. I am most interested in blocs in which a majority or more of the members supported an amendment. If majorities from all three blocs support an amendment, I conclude that it was supported by a supermajority. If majorities from two blocs supported an amendment, I conclude it was supported by a minimal winning coalition. Obviously, actual voting behavior among bloc members is not as clean as I would like; nevertheless, there are important differences in the variety of minimal winning coalitions that support amendments in Sessions 4 and 5.

The overwhelming majority of the amendments as well as the Resolution itself enjoyed widespread support within the parliament. Of the eight successful amendments to the Resolution, seven were supported by majorities from each bloc; and, one, Amendment 1, was supported by a minimal winning coalition consisting of Constructive Forces and Russian Unity. Constructive Forces and Russian Unity were also the two strongest supporters of Amendment 5. For four of the amendments (Amendments 3, 4, 6, and 7), the two strongest supporters were Coalition for Reform and Russian Unity. Coalition for Reform and Constructive Forces were the two strongest supporters of Amendment 8 and of the final vote. All three blocs were strong supporters of Amendment 2.

From this information it is impossible to determine whether or not all three minimal winning coalitions supported amendments to this Resolution, because in seven of the eight cases the winning coalition may have consisted of a supermajority involving all three blocs. The Resolution appears to have enjoyed unanimous support, and an examination of the outcomes reveals that cycling did not occur in the debate and passage of the Resolution on Checheno-Ingushskaia.

The second series of votes that I examine concerned the draft of a new Russian Constitution, the same debate I discuss in detail in Chapter 2.

On March 26, 1992, deputies in the Russian Parliament debated the second chapter of the new draft constitution. In all, deputies passed nine amendments to Chapter 2 of the draft constitution. I summarize the voting behavior of the four blocs in Table 7.3.

Of the nine successful amendments, seven were passed by majorities from each of the blocs (Amendments 2, 3, 4, 5, 6, 7, and 8). Amendments 1 and 9 were passed by the minimal winning coalition of Constructive Forces and Russian Unity. Because of the large number of defectors from each bloc, the fact that only 51% of the members of

Table 7.3. *Coalitions in Support of Amendments to Chapter 2 of the Draft Russian Constitution*

	Coalition for Reform	Constructive Forces	Russian Unity	Unaffiliated Deputies
Amendment 1 (CR)	.43	.59	.57	.67
Amendment 2 (RU)	.72	.64	.62	.71
Amendment 3 (RU)	.65	.68	.74	.74
Amendment 4 (CR)	.62	.54	.51	.59
Amendment 5 (CR)	.71	.68	.75	.71
Amendment 6 (CF)	.62	.68	.66	.76
Amendment 7 (CF)	.54	.66	.70	.73
Amendment 8 (CF)	.51	.73	.60	.61
Amendment 9 (RU)	.42	.61	.64	.65
First final vote	.72	.59	.19	.63
Second final vote	.74	.58	.19	.53
Third final vote	.74	.56	.17	.59

Coalition for Reform supported Amendment 8 suggests that it, too, was supported by the minimal winning coalition of Constructive Forces and Russian Unity. By the same reasoning, I tentatively conclude that Amendment 4 was supported by the coalition of Coalition for Reform and Constructive Forces. In all three final votes, the constitution as a whole was supported by the minimal winning coalition of Coalition for Reform and Constructive Forces. Thus, two of the coalitions that bound the cycle set in Session 4 supported either successful amendments or the final version of the draft Chapter 2.

Of course, most amendments were supported by majorities from all three blocs; however, if we identify the two principal supporters of each of the amendments, we see that Constructive Forces and Russian Unity are the top supporters of six amendments, Coalition for Reform and Constructive Forces are the top supporters of two amendments, and Russian Unity and Coalition for Reform are the top supporters of one amendment. Thus, we cannot reject the possibility that all three minimal winning coalitions were decisive in their support of amendments to Chapter 2. Based on the analysis of voting results, we know that outcomes cycled in the debate on Chapter 2 of the draft constitution.

The third series of amendments that I examine occurred on March 27, 1992, and concerned the third chapter of the draft constitution. Only

Table 7.4. *Coalitions in Support of Amendments to Chapter 3 of the Draft Russian Constitution*

	Coalition for Reform	Constructive Forces	Russian Unity	Unaffiliated Deputies
Amendment 1	.57	.71	.43	.61
Amendment 2	.57	.64	.47	.61
Amendment 3	.43	.59	.60	.59
Amendment 4	.52	.69	.51	.59
Amendment 5 (CF)	.58	.69	.62	.63
Final vote	.66	.58	.26	.59

five amendments to the chapter passed. I summarize the voting behavior of the four blocs in Table 7.4.

Of the five successful amendments, majorities from Coalition for Reform and Constructive Forces joined in supporting two (Amendments 1 and 2), majorities from Russian Unity and Constructive Forces joined in supporting one (Amendment 3), and majorities from all blocs joined in supporting two (Amendments 4 and 5). The final vote was supported by a coalition of Constructive Forces and Coalition for Reform. Thus, two of the three minimal winning coalitions that bound the cycle set supported successful amendments to Chapter 3 of the draft constitution. Also, although only a bare majority of the members of Russian Unity supported Amendment 4, I cannot discount the possibility that the third minimal wining coalition, Russian Unity and Coalition for Reform, were jointly active in supporting Amendment 5. Furthermore, we know from an examination of voting results that outcomes cycled in the debate on Chapter 3 of the draft constitution.

The fourth series of votes that I examine occurred on June 5, 1992 and concerned the Law on Privatization. A draft of the law had been introduced on May 29 and had been returned for further work. In effect, members of the parliament with strong ties to the old Soviet-era economic bureaucracy felt that the first version of the Law on Privatization was not favorable enough to enterprise managers. The revised draft was submitted on June 5. Of the three successful amendments offered by a deputy group or representative of a group, one was offered by a leader of Russian Unity, one was offered by the Committee on Economic Reform, which was dominated by representatives of the Coalition for Reform, and one was offered by the Committee on Industry and Energy,

Table 7.5. *Coalitions in Support of Amendments to the Draft Law on Privatization*

	Coalition for Reform	Constructive Forces	Russian Unity	Unaffiliated Deputies
Amendment 1 (RU)	.83	.85	.68	.71
Amendment 2 (CR)	.75	.80	.68	.65
Amendment 3 (CR)	.82	.58	.45	.63
Amendment 4 (CR)	.82	.76	.47	.76
Amendment 5	.85	.86	.74	.78
Amendment 6	.86	.80	.64	.69
Amendment 7	.69	.75	.57	.65
Final vote	.88	.58	.43	.67

which was dominated by representatives of Constructive Forces. I summarize the voting behavior of the four blocs in Table 7.5.

Of the seven successful amendments, two (Amendments 3 and 4) were supported by the minimal winning coalition of Coalition for Reform and Constructive Forces. In addition, it was majorities from these two blocs that supported the final version of the bill. If we examine the top two supporters of the other five amendments, we see that in each case, the two strongest supporters were Coalition for Reform and Constructive Forces. In the case of the Law on Privatization, I conclude that the three minimal winning coalitions that bound the cycle set did *not* each propose a successful amendment. It is not surprising, therefore, that outcomes on this law did not cycle.

The final series of votes that I examine in Session 4 concerned the draft Resolution on the Rehabilitation of the Cossacks. Seven successful amendments were made to this resolution, all of which were proposed by the Committee on Human Rights, which was dominated by members of the Coalition for Reform. I summarize the voting behavior of the four blocs in Table 7.6.

Of the seven successful amendments to the draft resolution on the rehabilitation of the Cossacks, all amendments were made by the Committee on Human Rights, which was dominated by members of the Coalition for Reform. Of these seven, only one was not supported by a majority of each of the four blocs. Amendment 2 was supported by a coalition consisting of Coalition for Reform and Constructive Forces. However, because only 51% of the Coalition for Reform supported Amendment 3, I tentatively conclude that this amendment was supported

Table 7.6. *Coalitions in Support of Amendments to the Draft Resolution on the Rehabilitation of the Cossacks*

	Coalition for Reform	Constructive Forces	Russian Unity	Unaffiliated Deputies
Amendment 1 (CR)	.66	.54	.62	.45
Amendment 2 (CR)	.62	.53	.49	.51
Amendment 3 (CR)	.51	.56	.64	.53
Amendment 4 (CR)	.66	.68	.68	.53
Amendment 5 (CR)	.71	.66	.58	.63
Amendment 6 (CR)	.65	.63	.64	.63
Amendment 7 (CR)	.58	.58	.64	.57
Final vote	.32	.34	.55	.43

by a coalition consisting of Russian Unity and Constructive Forces. Thus, two of the three minimal winning coalitions supported amendments to this draft resolution.

If we examine the top two supporters of the other five amendments, we find that Coalition for Reform and Russian Unity supported Amendments 1 and 6, Coalition for Reform and Constructive Forces supported Amendment 5, Constructive Forces and Russian Unity supported Amendment 4, and all three blocs supported Amendment 7. Therefore, it is possible in at least two cases that the minimal winning coalition of Russian Unity and Coalition for Reform was decisive. If this was, indeed, true, we would expect to find that outcomes on this resolution cycled, which, in fact, they did.

Summary of Coalition Support in Session 4

The evidence presented in Tables 7.2 through 7.6 supports the conclusion that in each of the votes summarized above, except for the Resolution on the Checheno-Ingushskaia Russian Republic and the Law on Privatization, clearly two of the three coalitions that bound the cycle set in Session 4 supported successful amendments. Also, in each of these three series of votes, majorities from each of the blocs supported at least one additional amendment. Furthermore, if we look at the top two supporters of amendments in each of these three series, we see that in two of the three cases all three minimal winning coalitions was a "top supporter." Therefore, it is possible that all three minimal winning coalitions that bound the cycle set in Session 4 supported successful amendments in these series. Therefore, I conclude that all three of these vote series was located within the cycle set. I believe it is significant that all three votes concerned the issue of human rights. In the post-Soviet context, new definitions of human rights concerned changes in legal rights, property rights, and political rights; hence, the "issue" of human rights was multidimensional.

Because sizable majorities supported six out of the seven amendments to the Resolution on the Checheno-Ingushshkaia Russian Republic, we cannot know with any certainty if all three minimal winning coalitions were decisive on a particular amendment. However, if we look only at the top two supporters of each amendment, we see that each of the three minimal winning coalitions was a top supporter on at least one amendment. Therefore, I tentatively conclude that this vote series was also located within the cycle set even though votes in this series did not cycle.

In debating the Law on Privatization, only one minimal winning coalition (Coalition for Reform and Constructive Forces) supported two of the seven amendments as well as the final vote. Furthermore, if we identify the top two supporters of the remaining amendments, they are Coalition for Reform and Constructive Forces. Therefore, I conclude that the Law on Privatization was not located within the cycle set.

Before presenting graphical evidence to support my conclusions regarding the location of votes, I present a similar discussion of coalition support for successful amendments in Session 5.

Cycle Sets in Session 5: Tabular Evidence

In this section, I discuss the possibility that each of the three series of votes that occurred in Session 5 was located within the cycle set. From Figure 7.3b, we see that in Session 5 the cycle set is bounded by three minimal winning coalitions: Coalition for Reform plus Russian Unity, Coalition for Reform plus Constructive Forces, and Russian Unity plus Constructive Forces. To determine whether or not votes were located within the cycle set, I follow the same logic I applied to the analysis of Session 4. Thus, in Session 5, we are looking for a series of amendments in which at least one amendment is supported by each of the three minimal winning coalitions that bounds the cycle set.

The most important and time-consuming piece of legislation that deputies considered in Session 5 was the Law on the Government. It is no coincidence that the parliament demanded such a law one year after it had granted Yeltsin a one-year opportunity to carry out economic

When Majorities Fail

Table 7.7. *Coalitions in Support of Amendments to the Draft Law on the Government*

	Coalition for Reform	Constructive Forces	Russian Unity	Unaffiliated Deputies
Amendment 1 (CF)	.50	.69	.72	.69
Amendment 2 (CF)	.48	.62	.74	.56
Amendment 3 (RU)	.39	.69	.74	.50
Amendment 4 (CR)	.60	.74	.60	.52
Amendment 5 (RU)	.40	.53	.66	.63
Amendment 6 (RU)	.45	.62	.77	.60
Amendment 7 (CF)	.29	.69	.64	.58
Amendment 8 (CF)	.50	.69	.64	.73
Amendment 9 (CF)	.34	.57	.70	.63
Amendment 10 (CR)	.35	.62	.64	.71
Amendment 11 (CR)	.52	.62	.74	.69
Amendment 12 (President/CR)	.55	.57	.62	.71
Amendment 13 (CF)	.32	.60	.75	.63
Amendment 14 (CF)	.53	.62	.45	.60
Amendment 15	.58	.78	.75	.81
Amendment 16 (CF)	.39	.67	.72	.65
Amendment 17 (CF)	.32	.59	.75	.58
Amendment 18	.58	.72	.68	.73
Amendment 19	.77	.50	.47	.56
Amendment 20 (President/CR)	.89	.60	.42	.65
Final vote	.63	.72	.77	.71

reform by decree. After one year of rule by executive decree (at least to a certain extent and in certain areas), a majority of the parliamentary deputies wanted to return certain powers to the legislature. Conservative deputies wanted the power to slow economic reform, and most democratic deputies were critical of the superstrong Yeltsin presidency, because it seemed to them to be undemocratic. I summarize the voting behavior of the three blocs in Table 7.7.

Of the twenty successful amendments to the Law on the Government, eight were supported by a majority of the members of each bloc. Majorities from Russian Unity and Constructive Forces supported ten of the twelve amendments that were not supported by majorities from each bloc. Majorities from Coalition for Reform and Constructive Forces supported two amendments. Therefore, I conclude that two of the three minimal winning coalitions supported successful amendments to the Law on the Government.

An inspection of the eight amendments in which a majority from each bloc was supportive reveals that for seven of the eight amendments, the top two supporters were Russian Unity and Constructive Forces. Only in the case of Amendment 4 is it difficult to judge which of the three minimal winning coalitions might have been decisive. However, because the strongest supporter was Constructive Forces, with Coalition for Reform and Russian Unity being tied with 60% support each, it seems unlikely that the coalition of Russian Unity and Coalition for Reform was decisive. Therefore, I conclude that in the case of the Law on the Government, only two of the three minimal winning coalitions offered successful amendments. Therefore, this series of votes was not located within the cycle set. Graphical evidence presented later supports this conclusion that the series of votes on the Law on the Government did not fall within the cycle set in Session 5. As an examination of voting results reveals, outcomes did not cycle on this law.

There were two other series of votes in Session 5, each of which concerned the draft Russian Constitution. In debating Chapter 5 of the draft constitution on November 19, 1992, two amendments were proposed, neither of which passed. In debating Chapter 6, also on November 19, five amendments were proposed, none of which passed. Therefore, in neither of these cases were votes located within the cycle set.

Summary of Coalition Support in Session 5

We see from the somewhat tedious evidence presented above that in both Sessions 4 and 5 the minimal winning coalitions that bound the cycle set were relevant and active in both sessions. However, whereas all three minimal winning coalitions proposed successful amendments in Session 4, only two did so in Session 5. Evidence suggests that the minimal winning coalition consisting of Coalition for Reform and Russian Unity did not support successful amendments in Session 5. Furthermore, in debating Chapters 5 and 6 of the draft constitution, no successful amendments were supported by any minimal winning coalition. This suggests that the original drafts of the two chapters enjoyed unanimous support in the parliament.

Evidence presented so far suggests that in Session 4, some series of votes fell within the cycle set. However, in Session 5, votes did not appear to fall within the cycle set. In the next section, I present graphical representations of the relative location of votes and bloc ideal points. These visual representations support the tentative conclusions I have so far drawn.

MAPPING VOTES IN TWO DIMENSIONS

To further clarify the location of amendments in the eight votes discussed above, in the following two sections, I present graphs in which both the deputy blocs as well as the votes are mapped for Sessions 4 and 5. By graphing vote locations and bloc ideal points, I can investigate visually the relationship between the votes and blocs.

Mapping votes in two dimensions requires the introduction of a new technique that is related to principal components analysis. A biplot is a point–vector plot, in which one set of points is projected onto the other. To interpret a biplot, one projects the points perpendicularly onto the vectors in order to determine the relationship between the points and vectors. The vectors indicate direction from the origin; hence, they are indicated by arrows. With point–vector plots, it is not possible to interpret the distance between each set of points. Instead, to interpret the relationship among the blocs and votes, one projects the points perpendicularly onto each vector. It is the distance between the votes and the vector that reflect the proximity of the votes to the deputy blocs. In Appendix 7A, I present a technical discussion of the technique involved in this presentation.

Recall that the locations, or ideal points, of the deputies are based on how they voted on various issues. Deputies that are located close to each other are deputies that voted similarly. The locations of votes, analogous to ideal points, are based on which deputies voted for them. Thus, votes that are close together are votes that were supported by a similar set of deputies.

In Figures 7.5a–e, I plot the ideal points of the four blocs as well as the locations of all successful and unsuccessful votes (including amendments, votes on particular sections, and final votes) for the five pieces of legislation in Session 4. The three pieces of legislation from Session 5 are plotted in Figures 7.6a–c.

In each graph, a "+" corresponds to a vote that passed, and a "−" corresponds to a vote that failed. CR stands for the Coalition for Reform, CF stands for Constructive Forces, and RU stands for Russian Unity. In each of these figures, deputy blocs are represented by vectors and the votes by points.

Votes in Session 4

In the series of votes on the Resolution on the Checheno-Ingushskaia Republic and on Chapters 2 and 3 of the draft constitution, successful votes can be easily identified as being located in quadrants defined by two minimal winning coalitions, Coalition for Reform and Constructive Forces, and Constructive Forces and Russian Unity. Evidence that the coalition consisting of Coalition for Reform and Russian Unity supported particular votes is more difficult to detect, because such votes would be fairly centrally located. In the case of the Resolution on Checheno-Ingushskaia, one successful vote, located close to the vector for Russian Unity and close to the origin, appears to have been supported by the third minimal winning coalition, Coalition for Reform and Russian Unity. For votes on Chapters 2 and 3 of the draft constitution, the fact that the votes are widely dispersed among the quadrants supports the conclusion that different majorities supported successful amendments and that some of the centrally located amendments were supported by Coalition for Reform and Russian Unity.

In contrast, votes on the Law on Privatization are polarized along a single dimension (Figure 7.5d). All successful votes are located in the

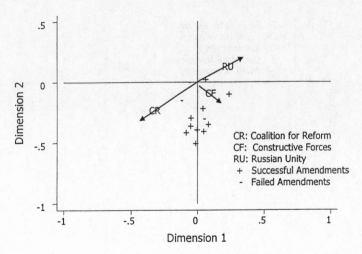

Figure 7.5a. Votes in Session 4 on the Resolution on the Checheno-Ingushskaia Russian Republic. In this series of votes, successful amendments are located within the quadrant defined by the vectors representing Coalition for Reform and Constructive Forces, Constructive Forces and Russian Unity, and Coalition for Reform and Russian Unity. Thus, the votes span the issue space defined by the three blocs and the three minimal winning coalitions, indicating that cycling was possible.

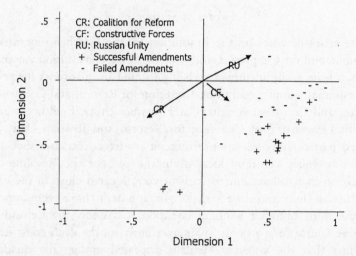

Figure 7.5b. Votes in Session 4 on Chapter 2 of the draft Russian Constitution. As in the vote on the Checheno-Ingushskaia Russian Republic, successful amendments are located within the quadrant defined by the vectors representing all three minimal winning coalitions. Again, the votes span the issue space defined by the three blocs and the three minimal winning coalitions, indicating that cycling was possible.

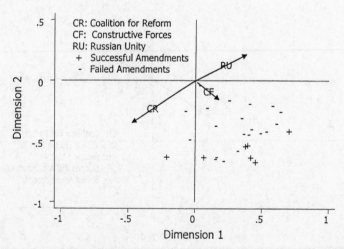

Figure 7.5c. Votes in Session 4 on Chapter 3 of the draft Russian Constitution. As in the other two cases, the votes span the issue space defined by the three blocs and the three minimal winning coalitions, indicating that cycling was possible.

quadrant defined by vectors corresponding to Constructive Forces and Coalition for Reform. Taken in conjunction with the tabular evidence presented above, the graphical representations suggest that votes on the Law on Privatization were identified with only one of the three minimal winning coalitions, Coalition for Reform and Constructive Forces. Despite the multiparty dynamic of the post-Soviet Russian Parliament, economic reform seems to have continued to be a one-dimensional issue even after the collapse of the Soviet Union.

As in the tabular evidence presented earlier, graphical representation of bloc ideal points and votes on the Resolution on the Rehabilitation of the Cossacks is difficult to interpret. All successful votes are located in the quadrant corresponding to the minimal winning coalition of Constructive Forces and Coalition for Reform or are centrally located. We know that in this series of votes, outcomes cycled; therefore, the central location of several of the successful votes suggests that these votes corresponded to either of the remaining two minimal winning coalitions.

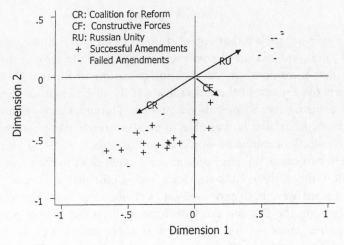

Figure 7.5d. Votes in Session 4 on the Law on Privatization. In this series of votes, successful votes are all located within the quadrant defined by the vectors representing Constructive Forces and Coalition for Reform. In this case, the votes do not span the issue space defined by the three blocs and the three minimal winning coalitions; therefore, cycling did not occur.

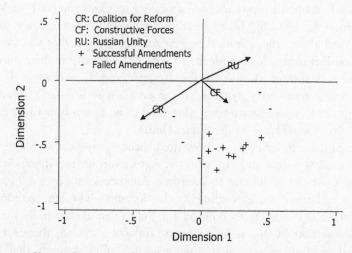

Figure 7.5e. Votes in Session 4 on the Rehabilitation of the Cossacks. In this series of votes, the location of the successful amendments is difficult to interpret, since none of the successful votes is located close to any of the blocs or even clearly located within a particular quadrant.

Votes in Session 5

In Figure 7.6a, we see that votes on the Law on Government, even the failed votes, are located almost exclusively within the area of the issue space that corresponds to the coalition consisting of Russian Unity and Constructive Forces. I believe that this was the direct result of the chairman's control over the amendment process. Through his position on the Presidium, Khasbulatov was able to exert a great deal of control over exactly which amendments would be considered.

Only two successful amendments are located close to the vectors of a coalition other than Russian Unity and Constructive Forces. These amendments were both proposed on December 22, 1992, the final day of debate on the Law on the Government. President Yeltsin proposed one of these amendments, and both were supported by a coalition consisting of Coalition for Reform and Constructive Forces. Thus, two of the coalitions that bound the cycle set in Session 5 appear to have supported successful amendments. However, based on Figure 7.6a, it seems unlikely that any successful amendment was supported by a coalition consisting of Coalition for Reform and Russian Unity. The distribution of votes in Figure 7.6a suggests that the votes on the Law on the Government did not fall within the cycle set in Session 5.

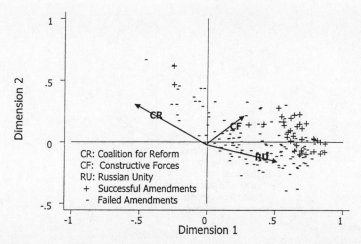

Figure 7.6a. Votes in Session 5 on the Law on the Government. In this series of votes, the majority of votes are located within the quadrant defined by the vectors representing Constructive Forces and Russian Unity. Two votes are located in the quadrant representing Coalition for Reform and Constructive Forces. No votes are centrally located. In this case, the votes appear to span the issue space defined by only two of the three minimal winning coalitions; therefore, cycling would not be expected.

The votes on Chapters 5 and 6 of the draft constitution are located such that they appealed to all blocs; thus, they passed unanimously. Knowing that each of these chapters was unanimously supported within the parliament, I conclude that such a configuration represents unanimity.

Cyclical Outcomes: Session 4

For the series of votes on Chapters 2 and 3 of the draft constitution and the Resolution on the Rehabilitation of the Cossacks, *cycles can be identified*. On March 25 both the second and third chapters of the constitution were passed as a basis, along with the entire draft. On March 26, ten amendments were passed successively. Finally, the deputies were asked to vote on the chapter as a whole. In effect, they were asked to pass officially that which they had already passed piece by piece. This final vote failed. Thus, on March 25, deputies were faced with a vote on the status quo (no new constitution) versus a change to the status quo (a new constitution). A majority of the members (not just a majority of those attending) supported changing the status quo. On March 26, for

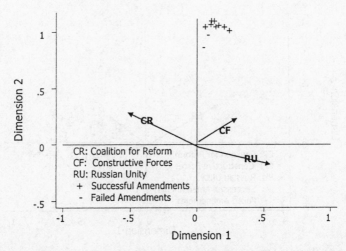

Figure 7.6b. Votes in Session 5 on Chapter 5 of the draft constitution. All votes in the series of votes on Chapter 5 of the draft constitution are located in close proximity to each other, but far from the vectors corresponding to the three blocs. It seems unlikely that cycling was possible.

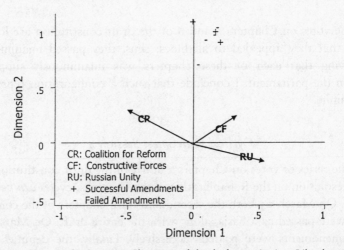

Figure 7.6c. Votes in Session 5 on Chapter 6 of the draft constitution. Like the votes on Chapter 5 of the draft constitution, all votes in the series of votes on Chapter 6 of the draft constitution are located in close proximity to each other, but far from the vectors corresponding to the three blocs.

each of the ten amendments, deputies were asked to choose between the current status quo (the amended version of Chapter 2) versus a new version of Chapter 2 (the current status quo plus a change), and in each case a majority chose the amended version of the status quo. Finally, the deputies were again asked to make a choice between the current status quo (in this case the amended version of Chapter 2) and the original status quo (no new constitution, or at least no Chapter 2). The deputies failed to pass the amended constitution as a whole and thus voted for the original status quo, which a majority had defeated only the day before.

The exact same thing happened on March 27 with the debate on Chapter 3. And, although a majority of deputies passed the draft constitution as a basis on March 25 and although other draft chapters were passed as a whole in Session 5, on March 27 the parliament voted to return to a previously defeated status quo.

On July 15 the parliament again considered an issue having to do with human rights, a resolution on the rehabilitation of the Cossacks. The resolution was passed as a basis for discussion on July 10; amendments to the resolution were discussed on July 15. The Committee on Human Rights, a committee dominated by members of the Coalition for Reform, proposed seven successful amendments. After the seven amendments had passed, the resolution failed to pass as a whole. Once again, on an issue of human rights, we detect a cycle of outcomes of the sort that occurred on March 26 and March 27 during the debate on sections of the constitution dealing with the same basic issue – human rights.

Noncyclical Outcomes: Session 4

The resolution on the situation in the Checheno-Ingushskaia Republic was passed first as a basis; the successful amendments passed easily by clear majorities (there were no close votes); the unsuccessful amendments (of which there were two) failed by huge majorities; and, finally, the project easily passed as a whole. In this case, outcomes did not cycle.

Three different blocs – Russian Unity, Coalition for Reform and Constructive Forces – offered the three successful amendments to the Law on Privatization. This suggests that the three amendments might have been inconsistent. However, in this case, leaders both in the parliament and outside of the parliament proved crucial. The Law on Privatization was prepared by the Ministry of Privatization, which was headed by Anatoly Chubais, a close associate of Yeltsin. Chubais had presented a first draft of the law on May 29, which was summarily rejected by the parliament. Thus, on June 5, Chubais and the relevant parliamentary committee, the Committee on Economic Reform, which was chaired by a strong democratic reformer, Krasavchenko, headed off possible criticisms of the revised draft. The most striking example of this concerned the first amendment listed in Table 7.5, which was proposed by the leader of Russian Unity. Krasavchenko had already met with Isakov and worked out a deal whereby the amendment would be put up for a vote, but the exact wording specifying the impact of Isakov's amendment would be worked out later by the Committee on Economic Reform.

No cycle occurred within the series of amendments to the draft Law on Privatization, and the Law on Privatization passed without a hitch on June 5.

Outcomes cycled in three of the five series of amendments that I examined. Each of these cycles was made up of votes on the issue of human rights. In fact, votes having to do with human rights are highly correlated with both the first and second dimensions estimated in Chapter 4; thus, votes on human rights tapped into more than one relevant dimension. Outcomes did not cycle in the series of votes on the Law on Privatization or in the series of votes on the situation in the Checheno-Ingushskaia Republic.

Noncyclical Outcomes: Session 5

Outcomes did not cycle in any of the three series of votes from Session 5. In the series of votes on the Law on the Government, almost all amendments were supported by the coalition of Russian Unity and Constructive Forces. These amendments helped to further increase the power of the legislature vis-à-vis the President. All amendments by the president in which he tried to reestablish certain presidential prerogatives failed; only two of the president's amendments passed, one of which was a compromise amendment and which was supported by majorities from all blocs. Amendments by the Committee on Legislation concerned technicalities and were also supported unanimously. Thus, although the coalition consisting of Russian Unity and Constructive Forces successfully passed several amendments that restricted the powers of the president, especially regarding his right to appoint the prime minister and other members of government, no successful amendment passed that reversed the distribution of power laid out in the amended law. The president and parliament reached a compromise of sorts, but there was never any question that the parliament had successfully attacked and reduced the powers of the president.

In contrast to the debate on the draft constitution that occurred in Session 4, the debate in Session 5 proceeded in a straightforward manner. Each chapter was passed as a basis; no amendments were passed; and, finally, each chapter passed as a whole. Like the vote on the Checheno-Ingushskaia Republic in Session 4, these two draft chapters seemed to enjoy majority support in Session 5 even though the wider debate on a new constitution remained stalled. In Chapter 8, I explore the reasons why votes on human rights did not cycle in Session 5.

CONCLUSIONS

In this chapter, I have empirically identified cycling in a transitional, poorly structured legislature. The methods that I present represent a first attempt to provide a means to verify systematically the presence of cycling and, hence, to identify the votes involved in the cycle(s). I conclude that cycling occurred in Session 4 but did not occur in Session 5.

In Session 4, cycling manifested itself in votes on human rights – in particular, on the votes on a new constitution, which tapped into several dimensions simultaneously. The lack of an appropriate constitution in which the powers of the legislative and executive branches of government were clearly and legally laid out was one of the most important causes of the destructive confrontation between president and parliament, a confrontation that all but paralyzed the legislature in 1993 and which ultimately resulted in armed confrontation between forces loyal to the president and the security forces employed by Chairman Khasbulatov. The analysis presented in this chapter suggests that the reason why deputies were unable to pass a draft constitution was because votes on the constitution cycled. Clearly, debate on the constitution was multidimensional, and the institutional design of the parliament was such that deputies were asked to vote on amendments that were themselves multidimensional.

Votes on privatization did not cycle for two reasons. In the first place, the law was probably the most important piece of legislation that the parliament debated during Session 4. Privatization was the cornerstone of the government's economic reform program, and the Minister of Privatization himself spent considerable effort in publicizing the law and in drumming up support within the parliament. It is not insignificant that he targeted the chairman of the parliament in this campaign. In addition, the Privatization Ministry was able to work with the relevant committee within the parliament, the Committee on Economic Reform.

In June 1992, when the debate on the Law on Privatization occurred, Chairman Khasbulatov, while exerting considerable influence over deputies from the floor and consolidating his control over the Presidium behind the scenes, did not yet dominate the agenda, especially on the issue of economic reform. Issues having to do with economic reform were placed on the parliament's agenda by actors outside of the parliament, namely, the president and his government. Thus, in the debate on the Law on Privatization, the Minister of Privatization, Anatoly Chubais, acted as the agenda setter for the parliament.

Chubais certainly could not dominate the parliament, as is clear from the fact that his first draft was voted down; but, by setting the agenda and defining the issue, Chubais effectively ensured that privatization was a single-dimension issue: He defined the issue in such a way that deputies voted either for continuing economic reform or for turning the clock back to communism.[11] In the end, Chubais was able to push the law through a parliament that was, in fact, fairly hostile to many aspects of privatization.

The story of the Law on Privatization shows that even in June 1992, when the confrontation between the Chairman of the Parliament and the President of Russia was already the subject of many newspaper stories, a well-organized and unified bloc of support could combat the powerful chairman and succeed. Thus, if a core bloc had existed during Session 5, the ability of the parliament's chairman to set the agenda would have been dramatically reduced. Not only would such a chairman have been beholden to a majority within the core bloc, the leaders of such a core could have launched successful campaigns for particular legislation.

In Chapter 8, I discuss the differences in the power of the Chairman of the Parliament before and after the collapse of the Soviet Union. In particular, I focus on the differences in what Chairman Yeltsin, a partisan chairman operating in a one-dimensional issue space, and Chairman Khasbulatov, a nonpartisan chairman operating in a multidimensional issue space, were able to achieve.

---

[11] This is exactly the strategy that Yeltsin had always used, both as Chairman of the Parliament and as President of the Russian Federation, to keep debate on economic reform confined to one dimension.

Appendix 7A

BIPLOTS OF VOTES AND BLOCS

Results of the principal components analysis that I presented in Chapter 4 were obtained by using the covariance matrix of roll call votes, where the votes were the variables and the deputies were the observations. Visually, think of a matrix in which each column corresponds to a vote and each row corresponds to a deputy. It is also possible to think of the data in the opposite configuration, in which each column corresponds to a deputy and each row corresponds to a vote. If we designate the variables as p and the observations as n, where $p < n$, a principal component analysis of the $p \times p$ covariance matrix is known as *R-analysis*, and the principal component analysis of the $n \times n$ covariance matrix is known as *Q-analysis*. So far, I have presented the results of only R-analysis. Before presenting the results of Q-analysis, I will discuss the relationship between the two methods. In this presentation, I follow Jackson (1991, pp. 189–193).

Principal component scores (sometimes called z *scores*) can be expressed as linear combinations of the data and the matrix of eigenvectors. Conversely, the original matrix of data can be expressed as a linear combination of the eigenvectors and the principal component scores. Let X represent the original data matrix of zeros and ones and let L be the diagonal matrix of eigenvalues. Let U represent the eigenvectors for the variables (*R-analysis*), and let U^* represent the eigenvectors for the observations (*Q-analysis*). In *R-analysis*, the eigenvectors for the variables, U, are used to obtain the principal component scores for the observations, the matrix Z. In *Q-analysis*, the eigenvectors for the observations, U^*, are used to obtain the principal component scores for the variables, the matrix Z^*. Thus, Z, the matrix of principal component scores can be expressed as[12]

---

[12] For ease of presentation, I use matrix notation throughout this section. The matrix Z consists of p (the number of variables) columns and n (the number of observations) rows. Each column corresponds to a principal component, and each row corresponds to the score for a particular observation. The matrix X consists of the mean deviations of the original matrix of 1's and 0's. The matrix U consists of p columns and p rows. The operations involved in multiplying X by U are equivalent to those depicted linearly in Chapter 4, equations (1)–(5). In equation (2), U' is the transpose of the matrix of eigenvectors, U.

$$Z = XU \tag{1}$$

Furthermore, if all principal components are used, the original matrix of data can be expressed in terms of the principal components and the eigenvectors,

$$X = ZU' \tag{2}$$

The matrix of principal components can be expressed not only in terms of the original variables and the eigenvectors, but also in terms of the eigenvectors and the diagonal matrix of the square roots of the eigenvalues. Hence, the principal components for the observations, Z, are expressed in terms of the eigenvectors for the observations, U^*, and $L^{1/2}$, the diagonal matrix of square roots of the eigenvalues; and, the principal components for the variables, Z^*, are expressed in terms of the eigenvectors for the variables, U, and $L^{1/2}$:

$$Z^* = UL^{1/2} \tag{3}$$

$$Z = U^*L^{1/2} \tag{4}$$

From equations (1), (3), and (4), it is clear that we can express the original data matrix in terms of the square roots of the eigenvalues and the eigenvectors for both *R*- and *Q-analysis*.

$$X = U^*L^{1/2}U' \tag{5}$$

Equation (5) is the fundamental identity defining *singular value decomposition*, or SVD.

From equation (5), we see that it is possible to derive the eigenvectors and principal components for both the standard data matrix, where the columns corresponds to the variables, and the matrix used in *Q-analysis*, where the columns corresponds to the observations, *in the same operation*. From this it is possible to plot both the U and U^* on the same graph, a form of multidimensional scaling. Such plots, known as biplots, can take many forms, but all are based on the fundamental identify defining SVD, equation (5). Notice that it is possible to rewrite equation (5) as

$$X = AB' = U^*L^{c/2}L^{(1-c)/2}U' \tag{6}$$

where $0 \le c \le 1$, $A = U^*L^{c/2}$, and $B' = L^{(1-c)/2}U'$. If less than the full set of principal components is used, then equation (6) is only an estimate of X, $\hat{X}$. Let us assume that only two components are retained. In that case,

A, which in my example corresponds to the deputy ideal points, will be $n \times 2$; and **B**, which corresponds to the vote locations, will be $p \times 2$.

Any value from 0 to 1 may be chosen for c. For diagnostic purposes, a value of .5 is appropriate, because both **A** and **B** will be weighted equally. Therefore, in the examples presented in Chapter 7, $c = .5$.

8

The Dynamics of Agenda Control in the Russian Parliament

In Chapters 5 and 6, I present empirical evidence to show that there were important differences in the structure of deputy preferences before and after the collapse of the Soviet Union. In Chapter 7, I present evidence to show how differences in the structure of deputy preferences led to differences in the nature of majority rule after the collapse of the Soviet Union. In the one-dimensional world that existed before the collapse, majority rule was well behaved; that is, outcomes did not cycle, and the chairman was constrained by the existence of a stable majority. In the multidimensional world that existed after the collapse, majority rule was not well-behaved; that is, either outcomes cycled (as they did in Session 4) or unstable majorities were susceptible to manipulation by the chairman.

In this chapter, I complete my empirical case by investigating how the nature of majority rule affected the behavior of the two chairmen. I hypothesize that before the collapse of the Soviet Union, when the issue space was one-dimensional, the presence of a stable majority limited what Yeltsin could achieve. After the collapse, when the issue space was multidimensional, the absence of a stable majority provided Khasbulatov with the opportunity to achieve his most desirable outcome.

Using two models of agenda setting, Romer and Rosenthal's (1978) model of the powers of an agenda-setter in a one-dimensional legislative framework and McKelvey's model of the powers of an agenda-setter in a multidimensional legislative framework, I test two propositions: (1) Chairman Yeltsin was limited in his ability to dominate the legislature by the presence of a stable majority, and (2) Chairman Khasbulatov manipulated shifting majorities to obtain his own most-preferred outcome. In carrying out these tests, I provide empirical evidence that Chairman Yeltsin obtained outcomes consistent with the Romer and

Rosenthal "setter" model and that Chairman Khasbulatov obtained outcomes consistent with McKelvey's predictions.

IMPLICATIONS OF AGENDA CONTROL IN
ONE DIMENSION

Before the collapse of the Soviet Union, the issue space was one-dimensional and Boris Yeltsin was Chairman of the Russian Parliament and Presidium. In this section, I discuss Yeltsin's powers and accomplishments as the parliament's agenda setter.

Assumptions of the Setter Model

In their classic paper, Romer and Rosenthal (1978; also see Rosenthal 1990) model the powers of an agenda setter in a one-dimensional setting. They show that contrary to expectations, an agenda setter can sometimes do better for himself than merely obtaining the outcome that corresponds to the position of the median voter.

The restrictive assumptions made by Romer and Rosenthal in their original model correspond remarkably well to conditions in the former Russian Parliament. Whereas in many legislative settings, it is unrealistic to endow any one individual or group with monopoly power over the agenda, in the Russian Parliament such an assumption is realistic. Because partisan groups were only weakly organized in the Russian Parliament and committees were weak, institutional avenues for agenda control that are present in the U.S. Congress did not exist in the Russian Parliament. Institutionally, the only body that was endowed with control over the agenda in the Russian national legislature was the Presidium. In this case, as joint chair of the parliament and the Presidium, a single individual, the chairman, had more power over the agenda than is typical in democratic legislatures.

Thus, it makes sense to use the Romer and Rosenthal setter model to understand the power of the agenda setter in the Russian Parliament. Indeed, two scholars have adapted this model in an analysis of the peculiar set of voting rules of the Congress of People's Deputies, the parent body of the Russian Parliament (Myagkov and Kiewiet 1994). It is important to note, however, that the model can only be applied to the Russian case if we make the necessary assumption that the issue space is *one-dimensional*. As I have shown, the issue space was one-dimensional before the collapse of the Soviet Union, and it is during this period that the setter model is applicable. After the collapse of the Soviet Union, the issue space was clearly not one-dimensional; hence, an application of the setter model after the collapse of the Soviet Union is inappropriate.

To apply the Romer and Rosenthal model to the period prior to the collapse of the Soviet Union, one must make several simplifying assumptions. First, as I do throughout the book, I assume that preferences are single-peaked. (For a discussion of single-peaked preferences and their importance see Chapter 3.) Second, I assume that deputies choose sincerely; that is, they vote according to their true preferences. Third, I assume that the agenda setter has full information about the preferences of the deputies. To apply the Romer and Rosenthal model to the Russian context, I must also specify the preferences of the agenda setter as well as the institutional rules of the game. Taking these in reverse order, I first review the rules of parliamentary decision making (a full discussion is presented in Chapter 4); next I describe the preferences of the agenda setter, which in this case is the first chairman of the parliament, Boris Yeltsin. Finally, I provide some justification for making the three simplifying assumptions noted above – that is, that preferences are single-peaked, deputies vote sincerely, and the chairman has full information on deputy preferences.

Institutional Rules of the Game

As I discuss in Chapter 4, the chairman of the parliament (also chairman of the Presidium) was able to influence the parliament's agenda in several ways. First, he was able to influence the agenda generally by exerting his influence over the questions that the full parliament addressed and those that it did not address; for example, Yeltsin pushed the issue of Russian sovereignty, and Khasbulatov pushed the issue of parliamentary versus presidential control over the government. Second, he could influence the decision to assign a piece of legislation to a particular committee, thus he could influence the content of legislation. Khasbulatov used this power to assign legislation to committees that were supportive of him and his objectives.[1] Third, he was able to

---

[1] In interviews with me, Sergei Markov, Viacheslav Bragin, and Lev Ponomarev all discussed the fact that Khasbulatov assigned legislation strategically to loyal committees.

influence the order in which questions were addressed on a given day, although this could be changed by a majority vote of the deputies. Fourth, because the Presidium was responsible for submitting amendments to the appropriate committee, the chairman of the Presidium could influence the order in which amendments were debated and even influence whether or not a particular amendment was considered. Finally, the chairman controlled who had the floor; he had the right to recognize a deputy or to prevent a deputy from speaking.[2]

The manner in which voting on draft legislation took place in the Russian Parliament corresponds well with the setter model. In the process of considering draft legislation, the members of parliament were asked first to choose between two alternatives, to pass the draft "as a basis" or to reject the draft, thereby reverting to the status quo.[3] Thus, the initial vote on any piece of legislation was a vote in which the whole idea of a new law was set against the status quo – that is, no new law. In this situation, the status quo corresponds to the Romer and Rosenthal "reversion point." In their 1978 article, the authors describe votes on budgetary allocations. If a proposed budget does not pass, the reversion point is the budget that will automatically take effect in the absence of a newly approved allocation. In the context of the Russian Parliament, the reversion point is the status quo – the legal framework that will result if no new law is passed.

As described in Chapter 4, if the draft passed as a basis, subsequent votes involved pairs of alternatives, one that corresponded to the current version of the draft and one that corresponded to the current version plus an amendment. If an amendment passed, the amended version became the current version, which was then set against another amendment. In each case, the status quo corresponded to the current version of the draft law (amended or not amended), and the alternative corresponded to an amended version of the current draft. Finally, after all amendments had been considered, the final (usually amended) draft was voted on "as a whole." This means that the final version of the draft law was once again set against the initial reversion point, the status quo as it existed without the new law.

---

[2] In his interview with me, Lev Ponomarev describes how Khasbulatov kept democrats from speaking, simply by never calling on them.

[3] Laws were usually given two readings, and the first unamended draft was passed as a basis in either case. Most drafts that were decided by roll call vote were drafts placed before the parliament for a second reading; hence, the process I describe most accurately reflects the consideration of a draft in its second reading.

This voting procedure corresponds in essentials with Romer and Rosenthal's model. In all cases, only a pair of alternatives is considered at a time; and in each pair, one alternative corresponds to the status quo.

Yeltsin's Ideal Point

In addition to establishing the institutional rules of the game, in order to apply the setter model to voting behavior in the Russian Parliament, we must establish the preferences of the agenda setter. Let us assume, simply and plausibly, that Boris Yeltsin sought first and foremost to promote the career of Boris Yeltsin, with his ultimate goal being to usurp Mikhail Gorbachev's position as leader of the Soviet Union.[4]

In March 1989, Yeltsin was elected to the Congress of People's Deputies of the Soviet Union. As a member of the reformist "Interregional Group" within the Congress, Boris Yeltsin increased his national reputation and prestige, as he was seen by millions of Russians on television openly and courageously criticizing the Soviet leadership and even Gorbachev himself. When elections to a Russian Congress of People's Deputies were held in March 1990, it came as no surprise that Yeltsin was easily elected from his home district of Sverdlovsk.

Yeltsin was elected Chairman of the Russian Parliament in May 1990 during the first session of the Congress of People's Deputies of the Russian Republic. Yeltsin was the unchallenged leader of the loose coalition of democratic deputies dedicated to reforming the moribund command economy and continuing the country's progress toward an open and free society. Yeltsin was also unquestionably the most popular political figure in Russia at that time. As I show in Chapters 5 and 6, during the first few months of the Russian Parliament,[5] the location of deputy ideal points and the location of faction ideal points suggests that the median voter at that time was moderately in favor of reform. Therefore, it is not surprising that Yeltsin was elected chairman.

---

[4] There are many excellent accounts of the power struggle between Boris Yeltsin and Mikhail Gorbachev (Kiernon 1993, Hough 1994, Dunlop 1993). In each account, the authors agree that at some point Yeltsin's struggle to increase the pace of reforms became a struggle to steal the fire from Gorbachev himself.

[5] Roll call votes were not recorded until Session 2; therefore the closest proxy we have to deputy ideal points in Session 1 are ideal points in Session 2.

By 1990, it had become clear to Yeltsin that if he became the leader of Russia, and if Russia had sufficient political autonomy from the USSR, he would achieve the essence of his political ambitions (Dunlop 1993, Chapter 2). Thus, Yeltsin's best strategy was to promote Russian sovereignty and to push for the creation of the office of Russian President. Evidence from the legislative record suggests that this was precisely the strategy that Yeltsin adopted. Russian sovereignty was the most important and dominant issue on the parliamentary agenda throughout Yeltsin's term as chairman. Also, in Session 3, the parliament passed the necessary legislation to create the post of Russian President, a post that everyone in the parliament knew would be filled by Yeltsin.

As agenda setter, and as an extremely talented politician, Yeltsin helped characterize the status quo against which his initiatives were set. Thus, deputies were faced with choices between the "Soviet command economy" and a Russian market economy, between the Communist Party of the Soviet Union and Russian democracy.

According to Dunlop (1993, pp. 54–55), Yeltsin understood that Russia was the key to his successful challenge to Gorbachev. When, in the fall of 1990, Gorbachev failed to endorse a promising plan for economic reform, and, later, when he began to promote and endorse hard-line, anti-reform communists, Yeltsin made the quite logical case that reform was impossible at the level of the Soviet Union. Consequently, while Yeltsin was Chairman of the Russian Parliament, *the majority*[6] of Russian citizens as well as people's deputies accepted his characterization of the status quo.

Although many people (including myself) believe that Yeltsin was sincerely interested in promoting Russian democracy and in improving the living standards of Russia's citizens, there is no question that Yeltsin behaved strategically to discredit Gorbachev and the Soviet regime and to promote his own political ambitions. Yeltsin's attacks on Gorbachev, his attack on the privileges of Communist Party personnel, and especially his pursuit of both Russian sovereignty and the institutionalization of a Russian Presidency led inexorably to his own triumph over Gorbachev;

---

[6] There is no question that a majority of Russian citizens also endorsed Yeltsin's pro-Russia reform program. His easy victory in the June 1991 presidential election was a resounding endorsement of Russian democracy and economic reform. In addition, as evidence from this chapter shows, throughout his chairmanship, Yeltsin consistently obtained support for his initiatives in the parliament.

in effect, he led the parliament in creating a power base separate from the Soviet Union and in creating an office whereby he could be in charge of that power base. As Dunlop (1993, pp. 54–55), has described, Yeltsin played the "Russia Card" and won.

Based on the above assessment of Yeltsin's political ambitions, I define his ideal point as the desire to occupy the supreme leadership post in Russia.

Application of the Model

For the purposes of this chapter, a complete, technical discussion of the setter model is not appropriate. A full discussion of the Romer and Rosenthal model is presented in their 1978 article in *Public Choice*. In addition, Rosenthal provides a straightforward summary of the model in an article published in 1990. Following Rosenthal's example, I present a graphical summary of the main implications of the setter model.

For the purposes of the model and following the logic of the presentation in Chapter 7, I make the simplifying assumption that voting in the Russian Parliament before the collapse of the Soviet Union can be explained by group affiliation. As I show in earlier chapters, there were two grand coalitions as well as a number of independent deputies before the collapse of the Soviet Union. Thus, I model the parliament at that time as having three voters: a democrat (the median voter in the coalition of democratic deputies), a conservative (the median voter in the coalition of communist conservatives), and a centrist (the median voter in the group of unaffiliated deputies). As I do throughout this study, I assume that each of these three idealized voters has single-peaked preferences around their ideal points and that they vote sincerely. Finally, I assume that the chairman had complete information on the location of the ideal points of the three groups; this is the most realistic of the three assumptions, because the chairman was certainly aware of the voting record of the deputies as well as the political positions of each coalition.

In Figures 8.1a and 8.1b, I show the ideal points of the democratic and conservative coalitions as well as the ideal point of the group of unaffiliated deputies in Sessions 2 and 3, respectively. The peaks of the preference curves for each group correspond to the ideal points of the median voter in each group, and the end points of the tails of the curves correspond to the ideal points of the extreme members of each group. In drawing the curves, I constrained each to have the same height; however, the curves were not drawn to represent area, and thus

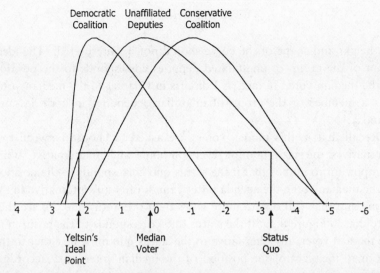

Figure 8.1a. Yeltsin's agenda-setting potential in Session 2. The range of outcomes that Yeltsin could have achieved is located between his ideal point and the status quo. This range is large and is defined by the location of the median ideal points of the democratic coalition, conservative coalition, and unaffiliated deputies as well as by Yeltsin's own ideal point. Because his own ideal point is located within this range, Yeltsin should have been able to achieve his own most-preferred outcome in Session 2.

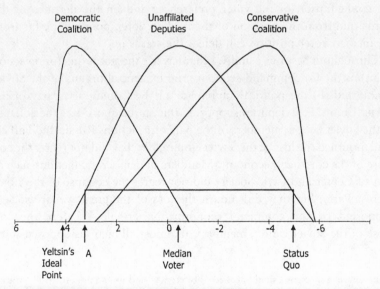

Figure 8.1b. Yeltsin's agenda-setting potential in Session 3. The range of outcomes that Yeltsin could have achieved is somewhat smaller than that in Session 2, and it is located between the status quo and the point identified as A. The point A corresponds to the best that the agenda setter can achieve, given this configuration of preferences.

the height and shape of the curve should not be interpreted.[7] The ideal point of the group of unaffiliated deputies corresponds to the position of the median voter. In fact, as I discuss in Chapter 6, the median voter was a member of the group of unaffiliated deputies in both Sessions 2 and 3.

Recall that in this model, voters are asked to choose between two alternatives, the status quo (or reversion point) and an alternative. What is important to note is that if the status quo corresponds to the position of the median voter, the agenda setter cannot offer any alternative to the status quo that will obtain more votes than the status quo. To see this, note that in Figure 8.1a, if the status quo corresponds to the position of the median voter, any alternative to the status quo must lie either to the left or to the right of the position of the median voter; and, according to the median voter theorem, the number of voters to the left or right of the median voter is always less than the number of voters on the opposite side and including the median voter. Thus, any alternative to the median voter position will be defeated.

However, if the status quo corresponds to some point that is *not* the position of the median voter, there exist points other than the position of the median voter that can defeat the status quo. In fact, depending on the configuration of the voter preferences and on the distance of the status quo from the position of the median voter, points quite far from the median voter position can defeat the status quo.

Throughout Sessions 2 and 3, I characterize the status quo (or reversion point) as the (a) command economy run by central organs of the Soviet Union and (b) the political supremacy of the Communist Party of the Soviet Union. Few deputies supported this status quo. After the collapse of the Soviet Union, members of the patriotic factions Russia and Fatherland mourned the loss of the Soviet empire, but they did not regret the collapse of the command economy. Members of democratic factions such as Left of Center and Civic Society did not regret the collapse of the Communist Party, but they did mourn the loss of the great welfare society supported by the command economy. Nevertheless, before the collapse of the Soviet Union, members of almost all factions opposed some

[7] The curves represent "single-peaked" preferences and are analogous to illustrative diagrams presented by Rosenthal (1990). The median and extreme ideal points of group members serve to anchor the preference curves and are important when figuring out the pivotal voter for particular reversion points.

aspect of the "Soviet" status quo. The only exception was the faction Communists of Russia. Members of this faction uniformly supported the supremacy of the Communist Party as well as the command economic system. Therefore, I use the median ideal point of this faction as a proxy for the status quo in Figures 8.1a and 8.1b.

Although Yeltsin was not an official member of any faction, he was undeniably the leader of the democratic coalition of deputies. Throughout the three years of the parliament's existence, members of Democratic Russia were the most loyal of Yeltsin's supporters. When other democratic groups faltered in support of economic reform, members of Democratic Russia remained committed to Yeltsin's policies. Later in his career, after assuming the office of President, Yeltsin appointed several key democratic parliamentary leaders, including members of Democratic Russia, to serve in his administration, and Yeltsin continued to fill administrative posts with former members of the democratic factions, especially Democratic Russia. Such appointments demonstrate not only that Yeltsin rewarded loyal supporters, but also that the preferences of members of Democratic Russia were close to his own. Certainly, the platform of the faction Democratic Russia was the most strongly supportive of both the transition to a market economy and the creation of a Russian presidency of all democratic platforms. Therefore, in applying the Romer and Rosenthal model, I use the median ideal point of the faction Democratic Russia as a proxy for Yeltsin's ideal point.

Based on the preference curves depicted in Figure 8.1a, we see that in Session 2, if the status quo corresponds to the ideal point of the faction Communists of Russia, the point at which a majority of the three voters is indifferent between it and the status quo (reversion point) corresponds to Yeltsin's ideal point. All points bounded by the status quo and Yeltsin's ideal point are closer to the ideal points of two of the three voters than is the status quo. Therefore, in Session 2, the chairman ought to have been able to achieve outcomes very close to his ideal point.

Based on the preference curves depicted in Figure 8.1b, we see that in Session 3 the point at which a majority of the voters is indifferent between it and the status quo is denoted A. All points bounded by the status quo and A are closer to the ideal points of two of the three voters than is the status quo. Therefore, in Session 3, the agenda setter could not achieve his ideal point, but he could achieve outcomes far more supportive of reform than that supported by the median voter; that is, he could achieve outcomes close to A.

The logic of the model is such that unless the status quo corresponds to the position of the median voter, the agenda setter can achieve outcomes closer to his ideal point than would be predicted by the median voter result. If the setter's ideal point is quite far from that of the median voter, and if he seeks to alter the status quo, his power to do so is considerable. So long as his ideal point lies within the position of the median voter and A, he can achieve his ideal point. If his ideal point lies beyond A, he can only get as close to his ideal point as A. If his ideal point lies between the position of the median voter and the status quo, the setter will also be able to achieve his ideal point.

Predictions of the Romer and Rosenthal Setter Model

Using the techniques described in Chapter 7, I produce biplots of the votes and ideal points of the factions.

The setter model predicts that the more extreme the status quo (the farther from the position of the median voter), the more the agenda setter may achieve. In the context of the Russian Parliament, this means that the farther the status quo was from the ideal point of the unaffiliated deputies, the more Yeltsin could achieve. On issues of economic reform, the status quo corresponded to the old command economy, a point far from the position even of the unaffiliated deputies (in this case the median voter), and thus one would predict that on such issues Yeltsin would have been able to achieve much in the way of economic reform legislation. On issues of political reform, the status quo corresponded to maintaining the Communist Party's monopoly on state power, a point far from the ideal point of most deputies, including the unaffiliated deputies, and thus on this issue one would expect that Yeltsin would have been able to achieve much in the way of lessening the Communist Party's hold on political power. An examination of the evidence suggests that due to a low reversion point, in these two areas Yeltsin achieved results far more radical that would be predicted based on the position of the median voter.

In Figures 8.2a and 8.2b, I show biplots of the location of faction ideal points as well as the locations of all roll call votes that represent a change to the status quo (indicated by "+") for Sessions 2 and 3. Recall that I use the ideal point for the Communists of Russia faction as a proxy for the status quo. In both Sessions 2 and 3, the position of the median voter corresponds to the median ideal point for the group of unaffiliated deputies.

In Session 2 (Figure 8.2a), all successful attempts to change the status quo (positive votes) are located to the right of the median voter (the reformist end of Dimension 1). In Session 3 (Figure 8.2b), most of the successful attempts to change the status quo are located to the right of the median voter.

As shown in Figures 8.1a and 8.1b, the agenda setter ought to have been able to achieve an outcome closer to his ideal point in Session 2 than in Session 3, although in both sessions, because the status quo was distinct and more conservative than the position of the median voter, he ought to have been able to achieve outcomes much more reformist than was desired by the median voter. Therefore, the results shown in Figures 8.2a and 8.2b are consistent with the predictions of the Romer and Rosenthal model. That is, in Session 2, all successful votes are located to the right of the unaffiliated deputies, and all but six successful votes

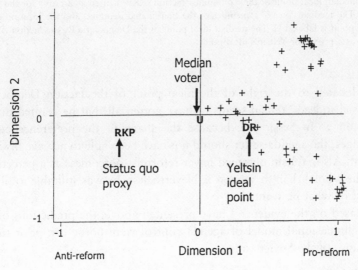

Figure 8.2a. Yeltsin gets everything he wants in Session 2. This graph shows the location of votes to change the status quo (indicated by "+") in relation to Yeltsin's ideal point, the status quo, and the ideal point of the median voter. As shown, all votes are located to the right of the median voter and either close to Yeltsin's ideal point or even more reformist than Yeltsin's ideal point. The median ideal point of the Communist faction (RKP) is used as a proxy for the status quo. The median voter is a member of the unaffiliated deputies, and the location of his ideal point is labeled U. The median ideal point of the Democratic Russia faction (DR) is used as a proxy for Yeltsin's ideal point.

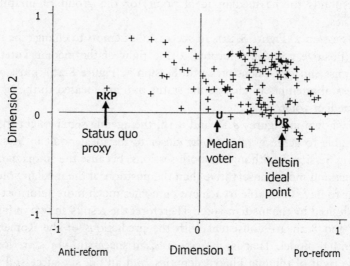

Figure 8.2b. Yeltsin gets most of what he wants in Session 3. Most of the changes to the status quo (indicated by "+") are located to the right of the median voter, but unlike in Session 2 a sizable number are located closer to the status quo than to Yeltsin's ideal point. The median ideal point of the Communist faction (RKP) is used as a proxy for the status quo. The median voter is a member of the unaffiliated deputies, and the location of his ideal point is labeled U. The median ideal point of the Democratic Russia faction (DR) is used as a proxy for Yeltsin's ideal point.

are located to the right of the ideal point of the faction Democratic Russia; indeed, Yeltsin seems to have gotten all that he wanted during Session 2. In Session 3, because the shape of the preference curves changes, the agenda setter should not have been able to achieve his ideal point. Also, Yeltsin obtained fewer reformist outcomes (as a percentage of the whole) than in Session 2. Nevertheless, he was still able to obtain most of what he wanted.

Based on the evidence I have presented above, the predictions of the one-dimensional model of agenda control were borne out prior to the collapse of the Soviet Union.

IMPLICATIONS OF AGENDA CONTROL IN TWO OR MORE DIMENSIONS

After the collapse of the Soviet Union, the issue space was multidimensional and Ruslan Khasbulatov was chairman of the parliament and

Presidium. In this section, I discuss Khasbulatov's powers and accomplishments as the parliament's agenda setter.

Assumptions of the Cycling Model

I describe McKelvey's model of cycling in a legislative setting in detail in Chapter 3 and thus do not repeat that full discussion here. However, it would be useful to recall that McKelvey's model predicts that if cycling occurs in a majority rule legislature, it is possible for an agenda setter to manipulate the order in which particular issues come up to vote and so achieve his own most-preferred outcome. Unlike the Romer and Rosenthal model, there are no constraints on what the agenda setter may achieve.

As in the one-dimensional setter model, deputies are assumed to have single-peaked preferences and to vote sincerely. Also, the chairman is assumed to know the preferences of the deputies.

Institutional Rules

As in the setter model, McKelvey's model assumes that deputies are only asked to vote on two alternatives at once. As reviewed above, voting in the Russian Parliament corresponded to this requirement.

Khasbulatov's Ideal Point

As in the setter model, in order to determine how close an agenda setter is able to come to obtaining his ideal point, it is necessary to establish what that ideal point is. In applying the cycling model to the period after the collapse of the Soviet Union, we must provide a reasonable assessment of Khasbulatov's ideal point.

For some months after Yeltsin had left the parliament to assume his office as Russia's President, the office of chairman remained empty. Ruslan Khasbulatov had been Yeltsin's first deputy chairman, and Yeltsin had strongly supported Khasbulatov to succeed him; however, neither the democrats nor the conservatives trusted Khasbulatov. As Yeltsin's choice, Khasbulatov alienated the conservatives, but, his credentials as a democrat were not sufficient to convince the majority of democratic deputies to vote for him. Finally, after Khasbulatov's pro-democracy stand during the August coup attempt, a sufficient number of democratic deputies were willing to vote for him, and he was elected chairman on October 28, 1991.

Despite the fact that Khasbulatov was most indebted to democratic support for his election to the chairmanship, he was not affiliated with any faction within the parliament, and thus he was beholden to no deputy group for his office.[8] The fact that no core quasi-party existed after the collapse of the Soviet Union further freed Khasbulatov from any obligation to a particular deputy group, because no single faction or bloc had the power to remove him from office.

On the other hand, no single deputy group, whether faction or bloc, had enough votes to pass anything alone. To achieve his objectives, Khasbulatov could not rely on a political alliance with one of the blocs. Instead, Khasbulatov had to rely on other means to create a winning coalition to support his initiatives.

In a one-dimensional setting, although an agenda setter may be able to achieve his ideal point or close to his ideal point, he can only do so as long as his ideal point falls within an area determined by the relative positions of the median voter and reversion point. In other words, what an agenda setter can achieve is limited. Furthermore, the tactics by which he achieves an outcome as close to his ideal point as possible are quite different from those that an agenda setter would use in a multidimensional setting.

In a one-dimensional setting, the agenda setter will try and characterize the status quo in such a way that it is as far from the ideal point of the pivotal voter as possible. In addition, he will try and move the ideal point of the pivotal voter as far from that of the status quo and as close to his own ideal point as possible. The manner in which the agenda setter frames the issues and the extent to which the agenda setter himself is able to frame the issues is very important in this context.

In a multidimensional setting in which no core deputy group exists, an agenda setter is not concerned with the location of deputy ideal points. If he can manipulate the agenda such that deputies are offered a succession of alternatives, each of which appeals to a different minimal winning coalition, the agenda setter can ultimately achieve an outcome equal to his ideal point. His best strategy, therefore, is to offer alternatives that appeal to the appropriate minimal winning coalition. In

---

[8] Yeltsin was never officially the member of any faction, yet he was clearly a democrat closely allied with Democratic Russia.

addition, if he is able, a chairman in such a position will attempt to make it worthwhile for minimal winning coalitions to support successive proposals. An agenda setter in such a situation will change alliances easily, until finally he reaches his ideal point, at which point in time outcomes and alliances will be stable.

Former deputies characterize Khasbulatov as a man who, indeed, changed alliances easily. From a strong supporter of Yeltsin before the collapse of the Soviet Union, Khasbulatov became one of Yeltsin's loudest critics. During Session 4, although he joined communist conservatives in criticizing Yeltsin's economic reform program, Khasbulatov joined with the Coalition for Reform and other centrist deputies to pass the Law on Privatization. As I show in Chapter 7, legislative outcomes cycled during Session 4. The variation in Khasbulatov's political alliances during Session 4 is the natural result of a multidimensional legislative setting in which no core deputy group exists and in which the chairman has not yet consolidated his control over the agenda. By the beginning of Session 5, even though a core deputy group still did not exist, Khasbulatov had amassed considerable control over the parliamentary agenda.

Starting in the fall of 1992, according to leaders both of Democratic Russia and the nationalist faction Russia, Khasbulatov began to be especially solicitous of the leaders of Change-New Policy, the key faction in the bloc Constructive Forces. Indeed, he formed a close working relationship with this faction.[9] As was mentioned in Chapter 5, the leaders of Change-New Policy were responsible for almost all successful amendments to the Law on the Government. Considering that Change-New Policy, the key member of the bloc Constructive Forces, was a member of no minimal winning coalition and hence should not have played a pivotal role in the parliament, it is very significant that Change-New Policy was responsible for a disproportionate number of the total number of amendments that were considered in Session 5.

The bloc Russian Unity offered other successful amendments. Sergei Baburin explained how his bloc was able to work with Khasbulatov, given that they were not political allies, as he made quite clear. The goals

---

[9] Khasbulatov himself, in an interview with this author, singles out the members of Change-New Policy for praise. Lev Ponomarev accuses the leaders of Change-New Policy of accepting substantial favors from Khasbulatov, such as vacation homes and apartments in Moscow.

of Russian Unity, insofar as that bloc sought to halt economic reform, coincided with Khasbulatov's goals, because an attack on economic reform was also an attack on Yeltsin and his authority. Thus, the bloc Russian Unity put forward about half of the amendments to the Law on the Government.

During Session 5, Khasbulatov exerted his full agenda control only over the Law on the Government. It was only on this subject that the Presidium dramatically restricted the ability of the Coalition for Reform to submit amendments. When debating chapters in the draft constitution, for example, the deputies considered amendments from Coalition for Reform as well as from Russian Unity and Constructive Forces. From this I conclude that *Khasbulatov's main goal as chairman was not to impede the work of the parliament or even to stop economic reform; his goal was to reduce the power of President Yeltsin and increase the power of the parliament and of his own office.* The most extreme versions of the Law on the Government were designed to do just that. Even the final version that the deputies passed in December represented a victory for Khasbulatov, because as a result the parliament was able to replace the radical reformer Gaidar with Victor Chernomyrdin, a man favored by the bloc Constructive Forces.

Throughout Session 6, few roll call votes were held, and all involved a direct attack either on the democratic leaders remaining in the parliament or on Yeltsin's government. Deputies voted to disband the committees on Legislation and Economic Reform. Deputies also voted to replace the democratic leader of the Committee on Mass Media, Viacheslav Bragin, with a close ally of Khasbulatov, Vladimir Lisin. In addition, deputies voted to curtail freedom of the press for the newspaper *Izvestia*, which had been particularly critical of Khasbulatov after the April referendum.

It is telling that Khasbulatov also launched a successful attempt to disband the Legislation Committee. This committee was not a center for democratic opposition to Khasbulatov; however, it was the committee whose responsibility it was to ensure that the process by which the parliament considered legislation was carried out according to the Constitution and the parliamentary rules of procedure. Khasbulatov's misuse of parliament funds, his violation of procedural rules within the meetings of the Presidium, and his inappropriate restrictions on amendments by certain deputies, committees, or groups were gross violations both of the constitution and the parliamentary rules of procedure. In his effort to control the legislative process, Khasbulatov found the Committee on

Legislation to be highly inconvenient. The former chairman of the Committee on Legislation, Mikhail Mitiukov, believed that the motive for disbanding the Committee on Legislation was to increase confrontation with the executive. He noted that the liquidation of the parliament of the Soviet Union began with the reorganization of a similar committee.[10] The fact that a majority of parliamentary deputies voted in favor of disbanding the Committee on Legislation underscores the self-destructive behavior of the deputies, especially during the last session, Session 6, of the parliament.

Based on the above analysis of Khasbulatov's behavior as chairman, I conclude that his most-preferred legislative outcome was a reduction in the powers of the executive and an accompanying increase in the powers of the legislature.

Predictions of Cycling Model

In a multidimensional, multiparty setting in which no core deputy party (or group) exists, work by McKelvey (1976), Schofield (1978), and others suggests that there is no limit on what a person or group with the power to set the legislative agenda can achieve. Unlike in the one-dimensional setting in which what the agenda setter can achieve depends on the prior status quo (reversion point), in a multidimensional setting with cyclical majorities, the agenda setter can always achieve his own ideal point. In Chapter 2, I discuss fully McKelvey's theory and its implications, especially in regard to the power of the agenda setter, so I forego repeating the discussion here. I merely state that if cycling occurs, based on McKelvey's findings, one would expect that the agenda setter, if he exists, would achieve his ideal point.

Throughout Session 4, by means of his harsh and often personal attack on Yeltsin and his government, Khasbulatov revealed the extent of his personal ambition. However, during Session 4, Khasbulatov had not yet consolidated his power as agenda setter, and, because of the extraordinary powers that the parliament had granted the president in November 1991, Yeltsin continued to set the legislative agenda throughout the summer of 1992. Recall that some outcomes cycled in Session 4; however, legislation having to do with economic reform did not cycle because Yeltsin and his government were still able to dominate the legislative agenda on these issues. However, because Khasbulatov had not yet consolidated his

[10] Interview with ITAR-TASS correspondent Yuri Filippov, June 28, 1993.

control over the Presidium and thus over the agenda, and because Yeltsin's government did not actively interfere in the workings of the legislature on other issues, legislation concerning human rights cycled in Session 4. Therefore, during Session 4, one would not expect outcomes to reflect the ideal point of the chairman. Instead, one would expect to see votes on subjects other than economic reform, both successful and unsuccessful, distributed fairly evenly among all minimal winning coalitions.

In Figure 8.3a, I plot the location of votes and blocs for all roll call votes in Session 4. As predicted, votes in Session 4 are well-distributed throughout the areas corresponding to each of the blocs. This suggests that during Session 4, all blocs were able to submit amendments; therefore, the chairman did not restrict amendments, and there is no evidence of the harsh agenda control that would have been necessary for Khasbulatov to achieve his ideal point in Session 4.

As I discuss above, by September 1992, Khasbulatov had consolidated his power over the parliament's Presidium. If Khasbulatov had indeed consolidated his power over the parliamentary agenda, I would expect that in Session 5 more votes and amendments would have been offered by Khasbulatov's allies than by his opponents.

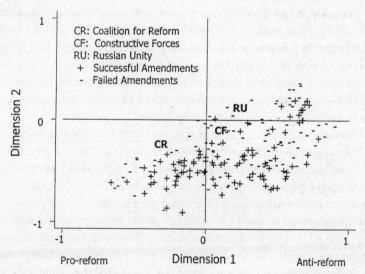

Figure 8.3a. Roll call votes and location of bloc ideal points in Session 4. Successful and unsuccessful votes are well-distributed throughout the issue space, indicating little manipulation of the agenda by the chairman.

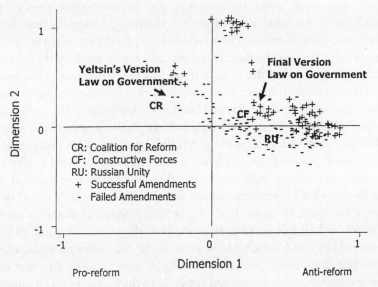

Figure 8.3b. Roll call votes and bloc ideal points in Session 5. Most votes are located in the area corresponding to the coalition of Russian Unity and Constructive Forces. Few votes and few successful votes are located near the Coalition for Reform. The distribution of votes provides evidence that the chairman manipulated the debate on the Law on the Government by using the Presidium's power to review and distribute amendments.

In Figure 8.3b, I plot the location of all roll call votes and blocs in Session 5. It is clear that in terms of offering amendments, either successful or unsuccessful, the Coalition for Reform was at a distinct disadvantage. Almost all votes are located in an area that corresponds to the coalition of Russian Unity and Constructive Forces.

Although scholars such as Remington et al. (1994) and Sobyanin (1994) argue that the preferences of the deputies shifted dramatically starting at the end of the summer 1992, this claim is not supported by evidence I present in this book. In Chapter 6, I show that the location of deputy ideal points hardly changes from Session 4 to Session 5, and the location of faction ideal points hardly changes as well. Thus, the dramatic change from Session 4 to Session 5 in the overall location of votes is not due to a change in the preferences of the deputies.

A comparison of Figures 8.3a and 8.3b shows that whereas alternatives covering the entire issue space were proposed during Session 4, in Session 5, whole areas in the two-dimensional issue space are empty.

Also, almost all votes in Session 5 are located in the conservative quadrant of the issue space. Figure 8.3b strongly suggests that during Session 5, someone or something was able to prevent amendments offered by the reformers and by the democratic center from reaching the floor. My account suggests that this agenda setter was the parliament's chairman.

The essential argument of this book is that because cycling occurred after the collapse of the Soviet Union, the chairman of the parliament, using his powers to set the legislative agenda, was able to achieve his ideal point. Indeed, evidence suggests that he achieved an outcome close to his ideal point as early as Session 5, at least with regard to the Law on the Government. In Figure 8.3b, I show the location of the final vote on the Law on Government along with President Yeltsin's initial draft. The final location of the Law on the Government is distant from the position of Yeltsin's initial draft along both dimensions one and two. As measured by the location of the Law on the Government, Khasbulatov achieved an outcome close to his ideal point, an outcome that restricted the president's ability to appoint the head of the Cabinet and an outcome that restricted the government's ability to continue its program of economic reform.

By Session 6, Khasbulatov's control over the parliament was an accepted fact. Many democratic deputies stopped attending, in effect

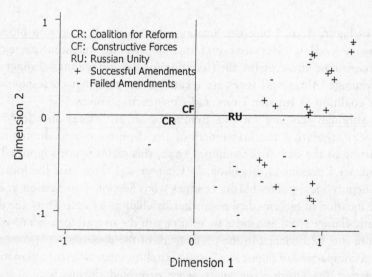

Figure 8.3c. Roll call votes and bloc ideal points in Session 6. All votes but one are located in the area closest to the minimal winning coalition of Russian Unity and Constructive Forces.

voting against all issues. In Figure 8.3c, I plot the location of all roll call votes and blocs in Session 6. Notice that all votes are located in the area corresponding to a minimal winning coalition of Russian Unity and Constructive Forces.

In describing Khasbulatov's power during Session 6, it is an understatement to say that he was able to achieve his ideal point. During the parliament's final year, the legislature fully supported Khasbulatov in his confrontation with President Yeltsin, a confrontation that intensified throughout the year and which eventually destroyed the parliament. The deputies, themselves, voted to disband the Committee on Legislation, a first step in the self-destruction of the parliament.

Reflections on Yeltsin and Khasbulatov

In comparing the styles of the two leaders, Ponomarev described Khasbulatov as rude and overbearing, whereas he described Yeltsin as respectful. Yeltsin listened respectfully to committee reports, whereas Khasbulatov was always impatient. Yeltsin encouraged debate during sessions of parliament; Khasbulatov actively discouraged debate, unless it was to support his own position. Yeltsin never used his power as chairman to turn off the microphone while a deputy was speaking; Khasbulatov frequently did so. While Yeltsin was chairman of the Presidium, decisions were taken by a vote of all those present, as dictated in the Rules of Procedure; however, after the first few months of Khasbulatov's chairmanship, voting by members of the Presidium stopped. Decisions were made by Khasbulatov alone and supported by obedient or mute committee chairmen.

The difference in the styles of the two chairmen can be understood if we focus on the incentives that each leader faced while he was chairman. As chairman, Boris Yeltsin was the leader of one of the two coalitions in the parliament, the coalition of democrats. As such, he was beholden to this group for his election. In addition, as Ponomarev and other democratic deputies explain, in the first few months after the parliament was elected, the democrats had only a slight majority in the parliament, and the numbers of centrist deputies increased somewhat during Session 3. Thus, if Yeltsin had ignored his democratic supporters or had alienated the centrist deputies, he would have been replaced as chairman by a coalition of conservative and centrist deputies. Furthermore, in order to maintain his unified support among democrats and centrists, Yeltsin had to "lead" the parliament. He had to make use of all of his considerable talents as a political leader to hold together his majority in parliament. For the first few months after the collapse of the Soviet Union and from his office as president, Yeltsin continued to play this role on certain issues – in particular, on issues of economic reform.

Khasbulatov, on the other hand, was neither the leader of a particular faction or bloc nor was he beholden to one faction or bloc for his office. Although in this sense Khasbulatov's office as chairman was secure, his ability to get things done was equally susceptible to the realities of cyclical majorities. Just as he was beholden to no group in parliament, no group in parliament had a stake in the positions that he supported. Thus, if Khasbulatov had not resorted to manipulating deputies' behavior behind the scenes, he could never have pursued a set of policy objectives with any success. Indeed, Khasbulatov did not achieve any particular set of policy objectives during Session 4 when evidence shows that outcomes did indeed cycle.

Given that a stable majority did not exist in the parliament, a strategic player acting in his own self-interest would certainly have sought to use his power as chairman of the Presidium to influence the parliament's agenda. Also, given the absence of a stable majority, he would have been able to do so.

Yeltsin the "leader" and Khasbulatov the "manipulator" were ambitious, talented men who acted according to the incentives determined by institutional variables beyond their control.

CONCLUSIONS

In a legislature in which institutional rules do not empower alternative sources of agenda control, especially committees, and in which preferences are such that the ability of political parties to control the agenda is also weak, the chairman has extraordinary powers – he is, in effect, the agenda setter. As Romer and Rosenthal have shown, even in a one-dimensional political setting, the powers of such an agenda setter are considerable. However, in a multidimensional political setting, the powers of the agenda setter may be absolute. If, as is likely when committees are weak and deputy preferences are heterogeneous, majorities cycle within the legislature, an agenda setter can dominate legislative outcomes.

The existence of cyclical majorities in and of itself is not devastating. Recall that during Session 4, which outcomes cycled, the parliament passed several important pieces of legislation, legislation that laid the foundations for the continuation of economic reform. The existence of cyclical majorities is devastating only when an agenda setter also exists. Thus it is a combination of poor institutional design along with the multidimensional political environment that resulted from the collapse of the Soviet Union that, at the most fundamental level, led to the failure of the first Russian Parliament.

9

Implications of Disequilibrium in Transitional Legislatures

When I began the project that led to this book, my primary motivation was to answer two seemingly unrelated questions: (1) Why did Russia's first competitively elected legislature become embroiled in a confrontation with the Russian president that led ultimately to its own demise? (2) Is cycling an empirical phenomenon that bears on transitional democracies?

As a student of Russian politics, I found the first question puzzling. Because the Russian legislature lost its confrontation with President Yeltsin – after all, the president disbanded the legislature on September 22, 1993, and all the legislative members lost their jobs – it is hard to make sense of the parliament's yearlong preoccupation with reducing executive power. During 1993, the country's economy continued to shrink, organized crime increased, and much of the military went unpaid. In short, there were many problems facing the new democracy, but the country's representative institution ignored these problems and did its best to prevent the president from attending to them as well. Even stranger, when given the opportunity to pass a new constitution that would have preserved their own jobs as well as strengthen the powers of the legislature vis-à-vis the executive branch, the parliament in conjunction with the Congress could not do so.

As a student of legislatures, I felt that the second question represented a gaping hole in the formal theory of legislatures. The phenomenon of cycling is of central theoretical importance to formal scholars of legislatures. Indeed, the assumption that cycling exists or could exist has inspired students of the U.S. Congress to identify the institutional mechanisms that prevent a breakdown in majority rule. However, if cycling is rare or even empirically nonexistent, how can the potential for cycling provide incentives for elites to design legislative institutions that prevent cycling? As a student interested in emerging democracies, it struck me that the moment of institutional transition is just that moment when the empirical importance of cycling will, if it exists, manifest itself.

In this book, I present the single, complex answer to both of these questions. Cycling is an important empirical phenomenon. It occurred in the Russian Parliament under just those conditions theory predicts; it prevented deputies from passing a new constitution; and, it provided a powerful and ambitious chairman with inordinate control over parliamentary outcomes. Because the chairman used his control of the parliament to engage in an unsuccessful confrontation with the president, cycling was one of the most important factors leading to the parliament's failure as a representative institution.

For formal scholars of legislative institutions, it should be a relief to learn that cycling does exist empirically. The evidence I present in this study takes cycling out of the realm of pure theory and shows that it does happen and that it can be studied like any other important empirical phenomenon.

For scholars interested in the Russian transition, it will not be a surprise to learn that Russia's first competitively elected legislature failed due to flaws in institutional design and in the weakness of partisan organizations. However, I hope it is surprising to learn just how complex was the story of legislative failure in the Russian parliament. In his recent book on the Russian legislature, Thomas Remington (2001) gives a fascinating account of the evolution of the rules governing Russia's national legislature, including today's Duma and Federation Council. Institutional choices are made by political elites and are influenced by historical legacy, political struggle, and current events. The ramifications of these choices are unpredictable and far-reaching.

For students of democratic transitions, I hope my study demonstrates that institutional change can be studied and that democracies in transition provide fertile ground in which to do so. I have shown that formal theories concerning the problematic aspects of majority rule derived through the study of a stable institution in only one country, namely the U.S. Congress, can be of use in explaining institutional change in a highly unstable, transitional environment. It may be that the appropriate setting in which to test the importance of those institutions that seem to make majority rule work is in a time of institutional transition, when the rules are as yet in flux. It is then that the empirical consequences of particular rules can best be observed. Hence, just as the world's emerging markets provide great opportunities to study how markets function, so too do the world's emerging democracies provide great opportunities to study how democracies function.

My study dovetails with recent work on legislative institutions. From a focus on committees and rules, formal students of legislatures have come more and more to emphasize the role that political parties play in stabilizing majority rule institutions. In the Russian Parliament committees were weak; the rules were such that nongermane amendments were always in order; hence, the committee system was never able to enforce an equilibrium structurally (Shepsle 1979). However, cycling occurred only when the number of parties was greater than two. Thus, the partisan organization of a legislature can be sufficient to prevent cycling, just as Aldrich (1995a) demonstrates. So long as the Russian Parliament was dominated by two relatively homogeneous coalitions, cycling did not occur. Once the number of partisan groups increased, which occurred in response to the increase in the number of relevant policy issues after the collapse of the Soviet Union, cycling became a problem. It was then that the weaknesses of the parliament's institutional design became apparent. Clearly, committees and rules affect how a legislature functions, but they do so within the broader context of party structure. Rules that work in a two-party environment may not work in a multiparty environment.

One of the major contributions of the recent work on the role of political parties in the U.S. Congress is to demonstrate that partisans control the agenda, and they do so mainly through committees. As many Congressional scholars have pointed out, the agenda-setting powers of the committee chairmen are considerable. Therefore, if parties control the assignment of members to committees, and especially if they control the assignment of chairmanships, parties have considerable control over the legislative agenda through the committee system. It appears from work on the U.S. Congress that parties do, indeed, impact a legislature through the rules, because it is through the rules that parties are able to affect the legislative agenda.

In the U.S. Congress, the power to set the agenda is divided among the Speaker and committee chairmen, each of whom is selected by the majority party. Hence, different people and different groups (committees and parties) have agenda setting power at different times and in different contexts. I believe that this is very important. Based on my study of the Russian Parliament, I suggest that the primary difference between a highly institutionalized (i.e., stable legislature) and an underinstitutionalized (i.e., unstable legislature) is the degree to which agenda setting power is *dispersed* rather than *concentrated*. In the U.S. Congress, while it is normal for a single party to set the legislative agenda, it is rare for a single individual to have the opportunity to set the agenda.

My study of the Russian Parliament demonstrates the importance of dispersed agenda-setting power; after all, I study the pathological effects of concentrated agenda-setting power. In the U.S. Congress, parties work through the committees to control the legislative agenda. This is a complex system of crosscutting agenda control. The majority party chooses the Speaker and committee chairmen. Committee chairmen serve both as party members and as heads of autonomous decision-making units within the legislature. Whether parties are strong or weak, agenda-setting power is dispersed.

In the Russian Parliament before the collapse of the Soviet Union, committee chairmen had an allegiance to one of the two grand coalitions. As I showed in an earlier chapter, the majority of committee chairmen were affiliated with the democratic coalition. During this period, the chairman (who was analogous to a Speaker in the U.S. House) was also a member of the majority coalition. Therefore, the majority coalition worked through the committee system (and through the Presidium) to achieve its policy agenda. So long as partisan glue united the parliament's chairman and a majority of the committee chairmen, the weakness of the committee system was hidden. Once the partisan structure dissolved, however, it became immediately clear that the parliament's institutions could not alone prevent cycling. Furthermore, absent a common party goal, the committee chairmen were found not to be agenda setters. When it became clear that no stable majority existed among committee chairmen (and hence no stable majority existed in the Presidium), it was also apparent that the parliament's chairman was the only actor in the Russian Parliament with the power to set the legislative agenda, because he could override the autonomy of the committee chairmen. Without the unity and strength of purpose that the presence of a majority party provides, agenda-setting power in the Russian Parliament was found to be concentrated in the hands of the chairman.

In this way, my study extends our understanding of the role of political parties in a legislature. Parties play a crucial role in ensuring that agenda-setting power is dispersed. In a two-party setting, when parties are strong (that is, the preferences of deputies within each party are homogeneous), party members have control over legislative leaders. Legislative leaders who are selected by a unified party can be removed by a unified party. The threat of removal is much more credible when the party rank and file share preferences. The leaders of parties in which members share homogeneous preferences will be more responsive to their parties and less able to pursue particularistic policy agendas. Even in the absence of a committee system, agenda control is dispersed because ultimate control over the legislative agenda rests with the party majority.

On the other hand, when parties are weak (that is, the preferences of deputies within each party are heterogeneous), party members have less control over legislative leaders. Under these circumstances, a two-party system begins to function more like a multiparty system. A group of representatives with heterogeneous preferences has a great deal of trouble controlling its leaders, and so it has less influence over legislative outcomes. Even in the presence of a strong committee system, legislative leaders (committee chairmen) are able to pursue particularistic policy agendas and ignore the broader goals of their party. But so long as there are many agenda setters and appropriate legislative rules – in particular, a strong committee system – the legislature will make coherent and consistent decisions and cycling will not occur. However, absent a strong committee system, either control over the agenda will cycle as different majorities form over different issues (again one would see cycling), or control over the agenda will become concentrated.

When preferences are heterogeneous, legislative leaders are no longer responsible to a unified majority for their positions. In this situation, if there is only one legislative leader – one person with agenda-setting power – and this leader is beholden to no particular party or coalition, he or she cannot be easily removed. Such a leader will quickly see that his best method of staying in power is to ally himself strategically first with one minimal winning coalition, then with another, and another, and another, *ad infinitum*. The same method the chairman uses to manipulate the agenda to achieve his own best outcome can be used to maintain his position as parliamentary leader.

In the Russian Parliament, had the committee system been strong or had there never been more than two parties, agenda control would have remained dispersed, and the legislature's history would have been quite different. Cycling, in and of itself, is not the primary problem that plagued the Russian Parliament. The primary problem was cycling (a) in the absence of a strong committee system and (b) in the presence of a chairman with agenda-setting powers.

Given the above, I draw the following conclusions. The most important goal in designing a legislature is to ensure that control over the agenda is dispersed. If a legislature has a truly two-party system, it will function well even absent a strong committee system. However, if a legislature lacks a two-party system, cycling cannot help but occur unless legislative design prevents it. A party system in which deputies' preferences are heterogeneous, absent a strong committee system, is likely to lead to a concentration of agenda-setting powers. Nature abhors a vacuum, and the absence of a unified majority provides an excellent opportunity for a political entrepreneur to concentrate power in his own hands. Given that there are almost no transitional democracies with only two (or even two major) political parties, the importance of institutional design looms ever larger.

Is the fact that cycling occurred in the Russian Parliament an anomalous event, or is this a more general problem in transitional legislatures? For several reasons, cycling ought to be a general problem during times of transition. During the early years of a democratic transition, the policy space is multidimensional. In addition, there are usually many political parties, none of which is able to obtain a majority of seats in the legislature. These two conditions are mutually reinforcing. Because no majority party exists, a stable majority must include a coalition of parties. However, because the issue space is multidimensional, coalitions of parties cannot be stable. For example, parties that share ideal points on the issue of economic reform may not share ideal points on other important issues, such as the role of the church (in Poland), the rights of minorities (in the former Baltic Republics of the Soviet Union), federalism (in the former Czechoslovakia), or punishment of political crimes by former communists (East Germany). When parties debate legislation that taps into more than one issue, we expect to see shifting majority coalitions.

At the same time, we should expect cycling to be typically short-lived. It is important, perhaps as important as formal theory would have us believe, and the implications of cycling are significant. But, nature abhors a vacuum, and if the institutional rules are not in place to address instances of cycling, someone or some group will step in and take advantage of the possibilities that a breakdown in majority rule creates. The amount of time that will transpire between the manifestation of cycling and its resolution will, therefore, be short. In the Russian case, cycling was an important factor in explaining why the transition to democracy has been so difficult: Russian elites have again and again designed institutions to concentrate agenda control. During a time of transition, these may be precisely the opposite characteristics that the situation calls for.

Work by scholars who have studied the problem of stability in multi-party European parliamentary systems suggests that, from the point of view of formal theory, it is inescapable that cycling will sometimes be a problem (Laver and Schofield 1991, Laver and Shepsle 1996). What my study of the Russian Parliament suggests is that we need to be as interested in how institutions cope with cycling as we are with the incidence of cycling itself. So long as agenda control is dispersed, cycling does not have to lead to long-term legislative failure.

Cycling occurred in the Polish Sejm early on in its transition. In July 1992, the legislature debated an economic plan, prepared by the new government, which was designed to serve as the blueprint for a radical program of economic reform. On the day of debate, a majority of deputies first voted in favor of the government's plan, thus rejecting the status quo, which was a continuation of piecemeal reform of the command economy. During the course of debate, deputies voted to amend the plan several times. Finally, they were asked to approve the final, amended version of the economic plan. A majority rejected it (presumably this majority differed from the one that approved the plan earlier in the debate), an example of cycling analogous to that which occurred in the Russian Parliament.[1]

As in the Russian Parliament, the Polish Prime Minister was astonished when a majority of deputies rejected the new economic plan in favor of a return to the status quo – that is, no plan. In part as a result of this fiasco, the government fell. After a month of negotiations, a new governing coalition of seven parties took its place. That government lasted only nine months. In a parliament with 29 parties, none of which controlled more than 12% of the seats, stability was difficult to achieve. Ultimately, the Polish President was forced to dissolve the legislature and call for new elections. President Walesa's solution to the problem of cycling was superficially similar to that used by President Yeltsin (Yeltsin dissolved the Russian legislature in September 1993 and called for new elections); however, institutional differences between Poland and Russia meant that the fallout from the Polish President's actions was much different from the fallout from the Russian President's actions.

Poland has a parliamentary system of government; technically, it has a mixed presidential–parliamentary system similar to that of France

---

[1] See account in RFE/RL, July 1992.

today. This means that when the executive dissolves the legislature, it does not engender a constitutional crisis. The power to dissolve the legislature is a constitutional characteristic of parliamentary systems of government. In no pure presidential system does the president have the constitutional right to dissolve the legislature. Thus, the Polish President solved the problem of cycling constitutionally, whereas the Russian President was forced to do so extraconstitutionally.

Again, the institutional context in which cycling occurs is critical. When the Russian Parliament became incapable of making lasting decisions, the presence of an inherently nonpartisan Presidium and a chairman with agenda-setting powers became highly problematic. The democratic nature of the legislature was compromised. In the larger context of a presidential system, this led to open confrontation between the executive and legislative branches of government and an extraconstitutional solution. By contrast, the Polish mixed presidential–parliamentary system provided a constitutional solution to the problem. When cycling first manifested itself, Walesa first tried replacing the government in power. When that did not provide a long-term solution to the problem, he called for new elections. With these built-in solutions to stalemate or disfunctionality, parliamentary systems may be better designed to handle the problem of cycling than are presidential systems, especially presidential systems in times of transition. These insights into how presidential and parliamentary systems cope with problems of majority rule speak to the ongoing debate about the choice of executive/legislative design in emerging democracies (Lijphart 1992; Elster, Offe, and Preuss 1998).

Shugart and Carey (1992) have noted that although political scientists advocate parliamentary systems, practical politicians, when given the choice, usually choose presidential systems. Especially in a time of crisis, a strong executive would seem to be more efficient, better able to deal with crises (less constrained, able to act quickly) than the legislature, encumbered as it is by political parties and their inevitable differences. However, recent work on the newly independent countries of Eastern Europe and the former Soviet Union suggests that concentration of power in the hands of the president invites corruption and inefficiency (Hellman 1998, Triesman 1996).

In his empirical study of the former republics and client states of the Soviet Union, Joel Hellman finds that countries that adopted a presidential system of government had a significantly worse record on economic stabilization than those countries that adopted parliamentary or mixed parliamentary/presidential systems of government.[2] It is important to note that presidential systems in the former Soviet Union look much like presidential systems in Latin America; they are highly unbalanced systems in which most laws are issued by presidential decree. According to Hellman's findings, countries in which a president is nonexistent or in which the president's powers are balanced by those of the national legislature are experiencing the most success in transforming their economies and polities in the wake of Soviet collapse. Is it not possible that it is precisely because agenda control is more dispersed in parliamentary than presidential systems that parliamentary systems are handling times of transition better?

In designing institutions for transitional countries, elites must consider the "fit" between institutions and the structure of preferences both in the legislature and in the population at large. Because preferences are unorganized during a transition, and given the presence of multiple political parties, the potential for outcomes to cycle exists. Under these circumstances, legislative institutions must provide institutional mechanisms either to prevent cycling or to solve the problem of cycling when it occurs. In legislatures of presidential systems, a strong committee system seems essential. However, creating a strong committee system in the absence of a strong two-party system may be difficult. The norms that govern committee assignments and the role of parties in the committees may very well have been designed by parties to serve their needs. This may help to explain why the American Congressional committee system is unique.

Another avenue of attack may be more appropriate in transitional democracies. Even though it is almost impossible to achieve a two-party system in emerging democracies, legislatures can be designed to encourage strong parliamentary majorities. In a parliamentary system, parties are strong, and the incentives to form a unified majority coalition are also strong. Even in the presence of several major parties, the rules of a parliamentary system help to form and maintain a stable majority. Also, if the majority proves unstable, parliamentary rules demand either a change in the majority coalition or new elections. From this perspective, parliamentary forms of government may be superior to presidential ones

---

[2] In a unpublished version of his 1998 *World Politics* article, Hellman presents results of a regression analysis in which he finds that the single most important predictor of successful economic reform in the postcommunist countries is whether or not they adopted a parliamentary or mixed parliamentary form of government (1997).

in containing the pathological consequences of cycling – that is, con-centration of agenda control.

Although it is not new to argue that parliamentary systems of gov-ernment are superior to presidential systems (Linz 1990), my argument – that the rules of parliamentary systems may be better able to handle the problem of cycling – is a new perspective on the relative strengths and weaknesses of parliamentary and mixed presidential/parliamentary versus presidential systems. If it is true that parliamentary systems are better able to cope with a breakdown in majority rule, then the choice of presidentialism may have serious consequences for the consolidation of democracy.

Possibly because of the failure of Stalinist communism and the extraordinary success of many market-based democracies, most of the countries that have emerged after the collapse of the Soviet Union are in the process of redesigning both their economies and their political systems based on the Western model of competitive democratic polities and competitive market economies. This turns out to be an extremely difficult task, especially when it occurs in a context of institutional col-lapse and when both the polity and economy must be reformed simul-taneously (Elster 1993). Indeed, conditions in the former Soviet Union and Eastern Europe after the collapse of the Soviet Union can be quite accurately described as chaotic. How do effective and useful institutions, rather than ineffective and harmful ones, emerge in this context? There is absolutely no guarantee that the collapse of harmful institutions will lead to the emergence of helpful institutions in the former Soviet Union.[3] On the contrary, new Russian institutions, such as the enormously pow-erful and ubiquitous criminal organizations or the dictatorial Russian presidency, may be no better than the institutions they replaced, namely, the Communist Party and its General Secretary.

---

[3] Douglass North makes a very similar kind of argument (North 1990, p. 25). In his view, "Institutions exist to reduce the uncertainties involved in human interaction." However, he goes on to add, "There is nothing in the above statement that implies that the institutions are efficient." Efficiency, in the language of economists, is good. Thus, North states explicitly that institutions are not necessarily good. Reducing uncertainty does not have to result in a situation that is better. For example, the Russian mafia reduces the uncertainty inherent in contracting in an institutionally poor environment, where the judicial system and/or the state is incapable of mon-itoring or enforcing contracts; however, the mafia is a far more costly and ineffi-cient monitor than a functioning judicial system. The mafia is inefficient, and judging by Russia's lack of economic growth, the mafia appears to be just as inef-ficient as was the Communist Party.

A collective truth that seems to emerge from studies of countries in transition is that very precise characteristics of institutions matter. While it is certainly true that to change a command economy to a market economy one must liberalize prices and free property rights, these changes alone are insufficient to ensure the emergence of a competitive, market economy. Indeed, work by social scientists who are both students of and active participants in the marketization of the former Soviet Union and Eastern Europe has shown that the institutional changes necessary to create a market economy are numerous, complex, and in many cases unpredictable (Barberis et al. 1996, Sachs 1996, Woodruff 1999, Frye 2000). These economists and political scientists have also come, at least implicitly, to the view that nature abhors a vacuum. Once the institutions of the command economy have been seriously undermined and before the complex set of institutions necessary to contain a market economy have emerged, opportunities exist for individuals with control over key economic resources to appropriate unclaimed property and to disrupt reform. Indeed, such individuals may have the opportunity to ensure that they benefit under the new institutions; hence, the process of institutional change itself creates opportunities for institutional entrepreneurs to control the rules so that they benefit. Widespread spontaneous privatization, theft, and bribery have accompanied changes in Russia's economic institutions (Frye and Shleifer 1997, Varese 1997).

I draw the same kinds of conclusions from my study of the Russian Parliament. Democratization demands that representative institutions be created. However, the specific rules governing the relationship of these institutions, the executive and legislative branches of government, are crucial to how the new democracy will function. There is absolutely no guarantee that elections will lead to democracy.

Obviously, many more factors than cycling in the Russian legislature are needed in order to understand the full story of Russia's ongoing transition to democracy. However, this study underscores just how important the representative institution and its ability to function is to democracies in transition and, by implication, to democracies period. A functioning legislature is crucial to a functioning democracy, but majority rule is treacherous. It requires careful attention to institutional details to design a legislature that can withstand the chaos of a transition to democracy.

References

Aldrich, John. 1995a. A Model of a Legislature with Two Parties and a Committee System, in *Positive Theories of Congressional Institutions*, Kenneth A. Shepsle and Barry R. Weingast, eds. Ann Arbor: University of Michigan Press.

——— 1995b. *Why Parties?* Chicago: University of Chicago Press.

Andrews, Josephine, and Alexandra Vacroux. 1994. Political Change in Leningrad: The Elections of 1990, in *Local Power and Post-Soviet Politics*, Jeffrey Hahn and Theodore Friedgut, eds. Armonk, NY: M. E. Sharpe.

Andrews, Josephine, and Kathryn Stoner-Weiss. 1995. Regionalism and Reform in Provincial Russia. *Post-Soviet Affairs* 11:295–304.

Ansolabehere, Steve, James M. Snyder, Jr., and Charles Stewart. 2001. The Effects of Party and Preferences on Congressional Roll-call Voting. *Legislative Studies Quarterly* 26:533–572.

Arrow, Kenneth. 1963. *Social Choice and Individual Values*, 2nd ed. New Haven, CT: Yale University Press.

Aslund, Anders. 1991. *Gorbachev's Struggle for Economic Reform*. Ithaca, NY: Cornell University Press.

——— 1995. *How Russia Became a Market Economy*. Washington, D.C.: The Brookings Institution.

Bach, Stanley, and Steven Smith. 1988. *Managing Uncertainty in the House of Representatives*. Washington, D.C.: The Brookings Institution.

Bahry, Donna, and Lucan Way. 1994. Citizen Activism in the Russian Transition. *Post-Soviet Affairs* 10:330–366.

Barberis, Nicholas, Maxim Boycko, Andrei Shleifer, and Natalia Tsukanova. 1996. How Does Privatization Work? Evidence from the Russian Shops. *The Journal of Political Economy* 104(4):764–790.

Baron, David, and John Ferejohn. 1989. Bargaining in Legislatures. *American Political Science Review* 83:1181–1206.

Baron, David P. 1998. Comparative Dynamics of Parliamentary Governments. *American Political Science Review* 92(3):593–610.

Black, Duncan. 1958. *The Theory of Committees and Elections*. London: Cambridge University Press.

References

Blasi, Joseph, Maya Kroumova, and Douglas Kruse. 1997. *Kremlin Capitalism: Privatizing the Russian Economy.* Ithaca, NY: ILR Press/Cornell.

Brown, Archie. 1993. The October Crisis of 1993: Context and Implications. *Post-Soviet Affairs* 9(3):183-195.

Budge, Ian. 1994. A New Spatial Theory of Party Competition: Uncertainty, Ideology and Policy Equilibria Viewed Comparatively and Temporally. *British Journal of Political Science* 24:443-467.

Budge, Ian, David Robertson, and Derek Hearl. 1987. *Ideology, Strategy, and Party Change: Spatial Analysis of Post-war Electoral Programmes in 19 Democracies.* Cambridge: Cambridge University Press.

Budge, Ian, Hans-Dieter Klingemann, Andrea Volkens, Judith Bara, and Eric Tanenbaum. 2001. *Mapping Policy Preferences: Estimates for Parties, Electors, and Governments 1945-1998.* Oxford: Oxford University Press.

Bunce, Valerie, and M. Csanadi. 1993. Uncertainty in the Transition – Post-communism in Hungary. *East European Politics and Societies* 7:240-275.

Burke, Edmund. 1774. "Mr. Edmund Burke's Speech to the Electors of Bristol." In *Select Works of Edmund Burke: Miscellaneous Writings*, 1999, pp. 3-13. Indianapolis, IN: Liberty Fund.

Coase, Ronald. 1994. *Essays on Economics and Economists.* Chicago: University of Chicago Press.

Colton, Timothy. 1986. *The Dilemma of Reform in the Soviet Union.* New York: Council on Foreign Relations.

1990. The Politics of Democratization: The Moscow Election of 1990. *Soviet Economy* 6:285-344.

1994. Professional Engagement and Role Definition Among Post-Soviet Legislators, in *Parliaments in Transition: The New Legislative Politics in the Former USSR and Eastern Europe*, Thomas F. Remington, ed. Boulder, CO: Westview Press.

1995. Superpresidentialism and Russia's Backward State. *Post-Soviet Affairs* 11:144-148.

2000. *Transitional Citizens: Voters and What Influences Them in the New Russia.* Cambridge, MA: Harvard University Press.

Cooper, Joseph, and David Brady. 1981. Institutional Context and Leadership Style: The House from Cannon to Rayburn. *American Political Science Review* 75:411-425.

Cox, Gary. 1987a. *The Efficient Secret: The Cabinet and the Development of Political Parties in Victorian England.* Cambridge: Cambridge University Press.

1987b. The Uncovered Set and the Core. *American Journal of Political Science* 31:408-423.

2000. On the Effects of Legislative Rules. *Legislative Studies Quarterly* 25:169-192.

Cox, Gary, and Mathew McCubbins. 1993. *Legislative Leviathan: Party Government in the House.* Berkeley: University of California Press.

Denzau, Arthur T., and Robert J. Mackay. 1981. Structure-Induced Equilibria and Perfect-Foresight Expectations. *American Journal of Political Science* 25:762-779.

References

Dobrokhotov, L. N., V. N. Kolodezhnyi, A. I. Kozhokina, and G. V. Lobantzova. 1994. *El'tsin–Khasbulatov: Edinstvo, Kompromiss, Bor'ba*. Moscow: Russian Independent Institute of Social and National Problems.

Downs, Anthony. 1957. *An Economic Theory of Democracy*. New York: Harper & Row.

Duch, Raymond. 1993. Tolerating Economic Reform: Popular Support for Transition to a Free Market in the Former Soviet Union. *American Politcal Science Review* 87:590–608.

Dunlop, John. 1993. *The Rise of Russia and the Fall of the Soviet Empire*. Princeton, NJ: Princeton University Press.

Elster, Jon. 1993. The Necessity and Impossibility of Simultaneous Economic and Political Reform, in *Constitutionalism and Democracy: Transitions in the Contemporary World*, Douglas Greenberg, Stanley N. Katz, Melanie Beth Oliviero, and Steven C. Wheatley, eds. Oxford: Oxford University Press.

Elster, Jon, Claus Offe, and Ulrick K. Preuss. 1998. *Institutional Design in Post-Communist Societies: Rebuilding the Ship at Sea*. Cambridge: Cambridge University Press.

Embree, George. 1991. RSFSR Election Results and Roll Call Votes. *Soviet Studies* 43:1065–1084.

Emmons, Terence. 1983. *The Formation of Political Parties and the First National Elections in Russia*. Cambridge, MA: Harvard University Press.

Enelow, James M. 1997. Cycling and Majority Rule, in *Perspectives on Public Choice: A Handbook*, Dennis C. Mueller, ed. Cambridge: Cambridge University Press.

Enelow, James M., and Melvin J. Hinich. 1984. *The Spatial Theory of Voting: An Introduction*. Cambridge: Cambridge University Press.

Fenno, Richard. 1973. *Congressmen in Committees*. Boston: Little Brown.

1978. *Home Style: House Members in Their Districts*. Boston: Little Brown.

Ferejohn, John. 1974. *Pork Barrel Politics*. Stanford: Stanford University Press.

Ferejohn, John, Morris Fiorina, and Richard McKelvey. 1987. Sophisticated Voting and Agenda Independence in the Distributive Politics Setting. *American Journal of Political Science* 31:169–194.

Fiorina, Morris P. 1977. *Congress: Keystone of the Washington Establishment*. New Haven, CT: Yale University Press.

1981. *Retrospective Voting in American National Elections*. New Haven, CT: Yale University Press.

Fish, Steven. 1995a. *Democracy from Scratch: Opposition and Regime in the New Russian Revolution*. Princeton, NJ: Princeton University Press.

1995b. The Advent of Multipartism in Russia, 1993–95. *Post-Soviet Affairs* 11(4):340–383.

Friedgut, Theodore. 1994. Perestroika in the Provinces: The Politics of Transition in Donetsk, in *Local Power and Post-Soviet Politics*, Theodore Friedgut and Jeffrey Hahn, eds. Armonk, NY: M. E. Sharpe.

Frydman, Roman, Andrzej Rapaczynski, and Joel Turkewitz. 1997. Transition to a Private Property Regime in the Czech Republic and Hungary, in *Economies in Transition: Comparing Asia and Eastern Europe*, Wing Thye Woo, Stephen Parker, and Jeffrey D. Sachs, eds. Cambridge, MA: The MIT Press.

References

Frye, Timothy. 2000. *Brokers and Bureaucrats: Building Market Institutions in Russia*. Ann Arbor: University of Michigan Press.

Frye, Timothy, and Andrei Shleifer. 1997. The Invisible Hand and the Grabbing Hand (in the Transition from Socialism). *The American Economic Review* 87(2):354–358.

Gamm, Gerald, and Kenneth Shepsle. 1989. Emergence of Legislative Institutions: Standing Committees in the House and Senate, 1810–1825. *Legislative Studies Quarterly* 14(1):39–66.

Geddes, Barbara. 1996. Initiation of New Democratic Institutions in Eastern Europe and Latin America, in *Institutional Design in New Democracies: Eastern Europe and Latin America*, Arend Lijphart and Carlos H. Waisman, eds. Boulder, CO: Westview Press.

Gibson, James, Raymond Duch, and Kent Tedin. 1992. Democratic Values and the Transformation of the Soviet Union. *Journal of Politics* 54:329–371.

Gilligan, Thomas W., and Keith Krehbiel. 1990. Organization of Informative Committees by a Rational Legislature. *American Journal of Political Science* 34:531–565.

Hahn, Jeffrey. 1993. Attitudes Toward Reform Among Provincial Russian Politicians. *Post-Soviet Affairs* 9:66–85.

Hall, Richard L. 1995. Empiricism and Progress in Positive Theories of Legislative Institutions. In *Positive Theories of Congressional Institutions*, Kenneth A. Shepsle and Barry R. Weingast, eds. Ann Arbor, MI: University of Michigan Press.

Heckman, James, and James Snyder. 1992. A Linear Latent Factor Model of Voting. Unpublished manuscript.

1996. Linear Probability Models of the Demand for Attributes with an Empirical Application to Estimating the Preferences of Legislators. National Bureau of Economic Research, working paper series. Presented at the 1996 meetings of the American Political Science Association, San Francisco.

Heckman, James J., and James M. Snyder, Jr. 1997. Linear probability models of the demand for attributes with an empirical application to estimating the preferences of legislators. *Rand Journal of Economics* 28(S1): S142–S189.

Helf, Gavin, and Jeffrey Hahn. 1992. Old Dogs and New Tricks: Party Elites in the Russian Regional Elections of 1990. *Slavic Review* 51:511–530.

Heller, William B. 2001. Making Policy Stick: Why the Government Gets What it Wants in Multiparty Parliaments. *American Journal of Political Science* 45:780–798.

Hellman, Joel. 1997. Competitive Advantage: The Politics of Stabilization in Postcommunist Transitions. Paper presented at the 1996 meetings of the American Association for the Advancement of Slavic Studies, Boston.

Hellman, Joel S. 1998. Winners Take All: The Politics of Partial Reform in Postcommunist Transitions. *World Politics* 50:203–234.

Hough, Jerry, and Merle Fainsod. 1979. *How the Soviet Union is Governed*. Cambridge, MA: Harvard University Press.

Hough, Jerry. 1994. The Russian Election of 1993: Public Attitudes Toward Economic Reform and Democratization. *Post-Soviet Affairs* 10:1–37.

References

Huber, John. 1996. The Vote of Confidence in Parliamentary Democracies. *American Political Science Review* 90:269–282.

Jackson, J. Edward. 1991. *A User's Guide to Principal Components*. New York: John Wiley & Sons.

Joliffe, I. T. 1986. *Principal Components Analysis*. New York: Springer-Verlag.

Kato, Junko. 1996. Review Article: Institutions and Rationality in Politics – Three Varieties of Neo-Institutionalists. *British Journal of Political Science* 25:553–582.

Kiernan, Brendon. 1993. *The End of Soviet Politics*. Boulder, CO: Westview Press.

Kiernan, Brendon, and Joseph Aistrup. 1991. The 1989 Elections to the Congress of People's Deputies in Moscow. *Soviet Studies* 43:1049–1064.

Kiewiet, Roderick, and Mathew McCubbins. 1991. *The Logic of Delegation: Congressional Parties and the Appropriations Process*. Chicago: University of Chicago Press.

King, Gary, James E. Alt, Nancy Elizabeth Burns, and Michael Laver. 1990. A Unified Model of Cabinet Dissolution in Parliamentary Democracies. *American Journal of Political Science* 34:846–871.

Kitschelt, Herbert, Zdenka Mansfeldova Radoslaw Markowski, and Gabor Toka. 1999. *Post-Communist Party Systems: Competition, Representation, and Inter-party Cooperation*. Cambridge, NY: Cambridge University Press.

Kline, Paul. 1994. *An Easy Guide to Factor Analysis*. New York: Routledge.

Koford, Kenneth. 1989. Dimensions in Congressional Voting. *American Political Science Review* 83:949–962.

1990. Dimensions, Transaction Costs and Coalitions in Legislative Voting. *Economics and Politics* 2:59–82.

Krehbiel, Keith. 1988. Spatial Models of Legislative Choice. *Legislative Studies Quarterly* 13(3):259–319.

1991. *Information and Legislative Organization*. Ann Arbor, MI: University of Michigan Press.

Laver, Michael and Kenneth A. Shepsle. 1996. *Making and Breaking Governments: Cabinets and Legislatures in Parliamentary Democracies*. Cambridge: Cambridge University Press.

Laver, Michael, and Norman Schofield. 1991. *Multiparty Government: The Politics of Coalition in Europe*. Oxford, England: Oxford University Press.

Lijphart, Arend. 1992. Democratization and Constitutional Choices in Czecho-Slovakia, Hungary and Poland, 1989–91. *Journal of Theoretical Politics* 4(2):207–223.

Linz, Juan J. 1990. Perils of Presidentialism. *Journal of Democracy* 1:51–69.

Londregan, John, and James Snyder. 1994. Comparing Committee and Floor Preferences. *Legislative Studies Quarterly* 19:233–266.

Mayhew, David. 1974. *Congress: The Electoral Connection*. New Haven, CT: Yale University Press.

McConachie, Lauros G. 1989. *Congressional Committees*. New York: Crowell.

McFaul, Michael, and Sergei Markov. 1993. *The Troubled Birth of Russian Democracy: Parties, Personalities and Programs*. Stanford, CA: Hoover Institution Press.

References

McFaul, Michael. 2001. Explaining Party Formation and Nonformation in Russia: Actors, Institutions, and Chance. *Comparative Political Studies* 34: 1159–1187.

McKelvey, Richard. 1976. Intransitivities in Multidimensional Voting Models and Some Implications for Agenda Control. *Journal of Economic Theory* 12:472–482.

McKelvey, Richard, and Norman Schofield. 1986. Structural Instability of the Core. *Journal of Mathematical Economics* 15:179–198.

1987. Generalized Symmetry Conditions at a Core Point. *Econometrica* 55: 923–933.

McLean, Iain, and Arnold B. Urken. 1995. *Classics of Social Choice*. Ann Arbor, MI: University of Michigan Press.

Montinola, Gabriella R. 1999. Politicians, Parties, and the Persistence of Weak States: Lessons from the Philippines. *Development and Change* 30: 739–774.

Moser, Robert. 1993. The impact of the electoral system on post-communist party development: The case of the 1993 Russian parliamentary elections. *Electoral Studies* 14:377–398.

Myagkov, Mikhail, and D. Roderick Kiewiet. 1996. Czar Rule in the Russian Congress of People's Deputies. *Legislative Studies Quarterly* 21:5–40.

North, Douglass. 1990. *Institutions, Institutional Change and Economic Performance*. Cambridge, UK: Cambridge University Press.

Ordeshook, Peter C., and Thomas Schwartz. 1987. Agendas and the Control of Political Outcomes. *American Political Science Review* 81:179–199.

Ostrow Joel. 1996. Institutional Design and Legislative Conflict: The Russian Supreme Soviet – A Well-Oiled Machine, Out of Control. *Communist and Post-Communist Studies* 29:413–433.

Plott, Charles. 1967. A Notion of Equilibrium and Its Possibility Under Majority Rule. *American Economic Review* 57:787–806.

Polsby, Nelson. 1968. The Institutionalization of the U.S. House of Representatives. *American Political Science Review* 62:148–168.

Poole, Keith, and Howard Rosenthal. 1985. A Spatial Model for Legislative Roll Call Analysis. *American Journal of Political Science* 29:357–384.

1987. Analysis of Congressional Coalition Patterns: A Unidimensional Spatial Model. *Legislative Studies Quarterly* 12:55–75.

1991. Patterns of Congressional Voting. *American Journal of Political Science* 35:228–278.

Prokop, Jane. 1996. *Industrial Policy and Marketization in Russia's Regions, 1990–1994*. Dissertation, Harvard University Department of Government.

Przeworski, Adam. 1991. *Democracy and the Market: Political and Economic Reforms in Eastern Europe and Latin America*. Cambridge: Cambridge University Press.

Radkey, Oliver. 1950. *The Election of the Russian Constituent Assembly of 1917*. Cambridge, MA: Harvard University Press.

Remington, Thomas F. 2001. *The Russian Parliament: Institutional Evolution in a Transitional Regime, 1989–1999*. New Haven, CT: Yale University Press.

References

Remington, Thomas, and Steven Smith. 1995. The Development of Parliamentary Parties in Russia. *Legislative Studies Quarterly* 20(4):457–489.

1997. Theories of Legislative Institutions and the Organization of the Russian Duma. *American Journal of Political Science* 42:545–572.

Remington, Thomas, Steven Smith, D. Roderick Kiewiet, and Moshe Haspel. 1994. Transitional Institutions and Parliamentary Alignments in Russia, 1990–1993, in *Parliaments in Transition: The New Legislative Politics of the Former USSR and Eastern Europe*, Thomas Remington, ed. Boulder, CO: Westview Press.

Remnick, David. 1993. *Lenin's Tomb: The Last Days of the Soviet Empire*. New York: Random House.

Rhode, David. 1991. *Parties and Leaders in the Postreform House*. Chicago: University of Chicago Press.

1995. Parties and Committees in the House: Member Motivations, Issues, and Institutional Arrangements in *Positive Theories of Congressional Institutions*, Kenneth Shepsle and Barry Weingast, eds. Ann Arbor, MI: University of Michigan Press.

Riker, William. 1980. Implications from the Disequilibrium of Majority Rule for the Study of Institutions. *American Political Science Review* 74:432–446.

1982. *Liberalism Against Populism*. Prospect Heights, IL: Waveland Press.

1986. *The Art of Political Manipulation*. New Haven, CT: Yale University Press.

Romer, Thomas, and Howard Rosenthal. 1978. Political resource allocation, controlled agendas, and the status quo. *Public Choice* 33:27–43.

Rosenthal, Howard. 1990. The Setter Model, in *Advances in the Spatial Theory of Voting*, James M. Enelow and Melvin J. Hinich, eds. New York: Cambridge University Press.

Sachs, Jeffrey. 1996. The Transition at Mid Decade. *The American Economic Review* 86(2):128–133.

Sakwa, Richard. 1993. *Russian Politics and Society*. London: Routledge.

Schofield, Norman. 1978. Instability of Simple Dynamic Games. *Review of Economic Studies* 45:575–594.

1993. Political Competition and Multiparty Coalition Governments. *European Journal of Political Research* 23:1–33.

Shane, Scott. 1994. *Dismantling Utopia: How Information Ended the Soviet Union*. Chicago: Ivan R. Dee.

Sharlet, Robert. 1993. Russian Constitutional Crisis: Law and Politics Under Yeltsin. *Post-Soviet Affairs* 9(4):314–336.

Shepsle, Kenneth A. 1979. Institutional Arrangements and Equilibrium in Multidimensional Voting Models. *American Journal of Political Science* 23:27–60.

1986. Institutional Equilibrium and Equilibrium Institutions, in *Political Science: The Science of Politics*, Herbert Weisberg, ed. New York: Agathon.

Shepsle, Kenneth A., and Barry Weingast. 1984a. When Do Rules of Procedure Matter? *Journal of Politics* 46:206–221.

1984b. Uncovered Sets and Sophisticated Voting Outcomes with Implications for Agenda Control. *American Journal of Political Science* 28:49–74.

References

1987. The Institutional Foundations of Committee Power. *American Political Science Review* 81:85–104.

1995. *Positive Theories of Congressional Institutions.* Ann Arbor, MI: University of Michigan Press.

Schickler, Eric, and Andrew Rich. 1997. Controlling the Floor: Parties as Procedural Coalitions in the House. *American Journal of Political Science* 41(4):1340–1375.

Shugart, Matthew S., and John M. Carey. 1992. *Presidents and Assemblies.* Cambridge: Cambridge University Press.

Sinclair, Barbara. 1995. House Special Rules and the Institutional Design Controversy, in *Positive Theories of Congressional Institutions,* Kenneth Shepsle and Barry Weingast, eds. Ann Arbor, MI: University of Michigan Press.

Smith, Steven S., and Thomas F. Remington. 2001. *The Politics of Institutional Choice: The Formation of the Russian State Duma.* Princeton: Princeton University Press.

Snyder, James M., Jr. 1992. Committee Power, Structure-Induced Equilibria, and Roll Call Votes. *American Journal of Political Science* 36:1–30.

Sobyanin, Alexander. 1994. Political Cleavages Among the Russian Deputies, in *Parliaments in Transition: The New Legislative Politics of the Former USSR and Eastern Europe,* Thomas Remington, ed. Boulder, CO: Westview Press.

Sobyanin, Alexander, and D. Yur'ev. 1991. *S'ezd narodnykh deputatov RSFSR v zerkale poimennykh golosovanii: rasstanovka sil i dinamika razvitiia politicheskogo protivostoianiia.* Moscow.

Solnick, Steven. 1998. *Stealing the State: Control and Collapse in Soviet Institutions.* Cambridge, MA: Harvard University Press.

Stoner-Weiss, Kathryn. 1997. *Local Heroes: The Political Economy of Russian Regional Government Performance.* Princeton, NJ: Princeton University Press.

Strom, Kaare. 1990. A Behavioral Theory of Competitive Political Parties. *American Journal of Political Science* 34:565–598.

Triesman, Daniel. 1996. The Politics of Intergovernmental Transfers in Post-Soviet Russia. *British Journal of Political Science* 26:299–335.

Tsebelis, George, and Jeannette Money. 1998. *Bicameralism.* Cambridge: Cambridge University Press.

Tullock, Gordon. 1981. Why So Much Stability? *Public Choice* 37(2):189–202.

Urban, Michael. 1990. *More Power to the Soviets: The Democratic Revolution in the USSR.* Brookfield, VT: E. Elgar.

1997. *The Rebirth of Politics in Russia.* Cambridge: Cambridge University Press.

Varese, Federico. 1997. The Transition to the Market and Corruption in Post-Socialist Russia. *Political Studies* XLV:579–596.

Warwick, Paul. 1979. The Durability of Coalition Governments in Parliamentary Democracies. *Comparative Political Studies* 11:465–498.

Weingast, Barry R. 1979. A Rational Choice Perspective on Congressional Norms. *American Journal of Political Science* 23:245–262.

References

1989. Floor Behavior in the U.S. Congress: Committee Power Under the Open Rule. *The American Political Science Review* 83(3):795–815.

Weingast, Barry R. and William J. Marshall. 1988. The Industrial Organization of Congress; or, Why Legislatures, Like Firms, Are Not Organized as Markets. *Journal of Political Economy* 96:132–163.

White, Stephen, Richard Rose, and Ian McAllister. 1997. *How Russia Votes*. Chatham, NJ: Chatham House Publishers.

Whitefield, Stephen and Geoffrey Evans. 1998. The emerging structure of partisan divisions in Russian politics. In *Elections and Voters in Post-Communist Russia* Matthew Wyman, Stephen White, and Sarah Oates, eds. Glasgow: Edward Elgar.

Woodruff, David. 1999. *Money Unmade: Barter and the Fate of Russian Capitalism*. Ithaca, NY: Cornell University Press.

Index

debate and vote on in Session 4,
164, 165t., 207, 242
inconsistency of Parliament
regarding, 8
individual rights, 32
issue dimensions and partisan
positions on, 116, 124f.5.5,
125, 207

ideology, 106, 107–8
impeachment proceedings, 120
independents
post-Soviet collapse, 136t.5A.1
pre-Soviet collapse, 111.
See also Non-party deputies (NP)
indifference
indifference curves, 127
voter indifference, 23
individual rights, 32
industrialists, 118
Industrial Union (Ind)
ideal points for, 152f., 153f.,
153
political positions, 118, 137t.5A.1
Industry and Energy Committee,
204–5
institutional collapse, 157, 173
August 1991 coup attempt, 7, 30,
60, 100, 142, 238
collapse of the Soviet Union, 25,
28–31
disbanding of the Parliament, 15,
69, 219
storming of the Parliament
building, 15–16, 69, 219.
See also constitutional crisis
institutional design
cycling mitigated or prevented by,
4, 6, 9, 80–5, 253–6
distributive, 246, 250–1, 252–3
legislative design, 20, 86, 103–5,
249, 253
majority rule and (*See also*
majority rule), 87, 96–7, 98
procedural rules (*See also* Rules of
Procedure), 240, 249
of the Russian Parliament, 6, 9,
21, 89–91
and transitional democracies (*See
also* transitional democracies),
256n.2, 256–7, 258

transitional institutions and,
103n.32, 104
underinstitutionalization, 4, 5,
9–16, 250
of the U.S. Congress, 84, 87, 248,
250–1.
See also committee system;
equilibria; political parties
institutionalism, neo, 4n.2, 19–20
"intelligentsia," 115, 116
Isakov, Vladimir, 42, 43n.25, 218
issue space. *See* policy space
Izvestia
Khasbulatov's attack on, 13,
14n.13, 166t., 166, 240

Jackson, J. Edward, 177n.25, 221
Joliffe, I. T., 177n.25
judicial system, 10

Kato, Junko, 4n.2
Khasbulatov, Ruslan
as the Chair of Parliament, 14–15,
18, 142, 238, 239
as the Chair of the Presidium, 11,
12, 21, 56, 90n.4, 226–7
efforts to remove him from office,
12n.7, 13–14, 101, 120, 157
his abandonment of a new
constitution, 61, 62n.4, 62,
63–6, 67
his confrontation with President
Yeltsin, 62–6, 132, 140, 220,
241, 245
his role in debate of the Law on
the Government, 13n.11
his role in the draft constitution
debate, 25, 38–9, 40–1, 42, 48,
49, 52
leadership style of compared with
Yeltsin's, 22, 99, 102, 140,
238, 244, 245–6
limitation of executive power his
primary focus, 26–7, 59, 61,
67, 68–9, 130, 240, 241
not affiliated with any faction,
12n.7, 12, 197, 238, 246
political goals and preferences
of, 228–9, 230, 237–8,
239
shifting policy positions, 13